THE BILLIONAIRE MURDERS

ALSO BY KEVIN DONOVAN

Secret Life: The Jian Ghomeshi Investigation
The Dead Times
Crime Story, The Hunt for the Body Parts Killer
(co-author Nicholas Pron)

THE
BILLIONAIRE
MURDERS

THE MYSTERIOUS DEATHS OF
BARRY AND HONEY SHERMAN

KEVIN DONOVAN

VIKING

VIKING

an imprint of Penguin Canada, a division of Penguin Random House Canada Limited

Canada • USA • UK • Ireland • Australia • New Zealand • India • South Africa • China

First published 2019

www.penguinrandomhouse.ca

LIBRARY AND ARCHIVES CANADA CATALOGUING IN PUBLICATION

Title: The billionaire murders / Kevin Donovan.
Names: Donovan, Kevin, 1962- author.
Identifiers: Canadiana (print) 20189054212 | Canadiana (ebook) 20189054220 | ISBN 9780735237032 (softcover) | ISBN 9780735237049 (HTML)
Subjects: LCSH: Sherman, Barry, 1942-2017. | LCSH: Sherman, Barry, 1942-2017—Death and burial. | LCSH: Sherman, Honey, 1948-2017. | LCSH: Sherman, Honey, 1948-2017—Death and burial. | LCSH: Murder—Investigation—Ontario—Toronto. | LCSH: Philanthropists—Ontario—Toronto—Biography. | LCSH: Businesspeople—Ontario—Toronto—Biography. | LCSH: Pharmaceutical industry—Ontario—Toronto. | LCSH: Murder victims—Ontario—Toronto—Biography.
Classification: LCC HV6535.C33 T67 2019 | DDC 364.152/309713541—dc23

Cover and book design by Leah Springate
Cover images: (houses) Rick Madonik/Contributor/Getty Images; (sky) Markus Gjengarr/Unsplash

Printed and bound in Canada

10 9 8 7 6 5 4 3 2 1

Penguin
Random House
VIKING CANADA

*To Michael Cooke and John Honderich for giving me
the assignment, and to Bert Bruser for making sure it was done right.
And to my wife, Kelly Smith, for laser focus and
tough questions every step of the way.*

To Michael Cooke and John Honderich for giving me the assignment, and to Bert Bruser for making sure it was done right. And to my wife, Kelly Smith, for laser focus and tough questions every step of the way.

CONTENTS

CONTENTS

PROLOGUE

IN THE YEAR LEADING UP TO HIS DEATH, Barry Sherman was consumed by one thought. What if he did not have enough time? Enough time to do everything he wanted to do in life. At seventy-five, he had already accomplished a great deal. He had built a generic drug empire, faced countless critics, and won more battles than he'd lost. He'd amassed a personal fortune approaching $5 billion. Still, he drove an older car, spent more hours at work than he needed to, and was perpetually unsettled. There was no God, of that he was certain, no afterlife. Consciousness ended with the grave. And so, every day, he did the one thing that was sure to make him happy. He worked.

It had always been that way. Outsiders, even friends who knew him well, were perplexed by Barry Sherman. For most people, if you earned that kind of money, you were entitled to spend it on items that made life more fun. But that was not something Barry Sherman did well. His contemporaries in the pharmaceutical world made their millions and accumulated—deservedly, most would say—the trappings of wealth: fine cars, first-class travel, a mansion in the city, and a cottage on a lake. Jack Kay, Sherman's longtime second-in-command, drove an X-class Mercedes-Benz. At their offices at the Toronto headquarters of Apotex, immediately to the right of the front door, were two named parking spots, Barry Sherman's and Jack Kay's. Barry's rusting convertible was a stark contrast to Kay's gleaming Benz.

"Jack, don't you worry about what our employees will think?" Sherman asked his friend on many occasions. "They work so hard, and while they're well paid, they don't make what it would take to afford that kind of car. I worry about what they would think."

Kay would just shake his head.

What Sherman did do with many of his millions was give it away to causes he or his wife, Honey, deemed worthy. He made the money; Honey ensured it went to the right places, where the impact would be the greatest. Both were tireless fundraisers. Their four children, cousins, extended family, and close friends were also the beneficiaries of the Sherman family wealth, though it became a sore point at times when the children and other family members asked for too much. And their house was not a happy home—one parent harsh and critical, the other soft and patient.

This is a book about the murders of Honey and Barry Sherman and the twists and turns of the police and private investigations. But it is also a book about their lives, stretching back to grade school and through the successes and failures of growing an empire and raising a family. Creating a full portrait has been hampered by the secrecy surrounding the investigations into their deaths, and even more so by the belief of their family and some friends that the Sherman laundry, dirty or clean, should remain unaired. Another factor that played in the minds of many was their personal safety. With the killer or killers at large, there was real fear among family, friends, and business associates that they would strike again. Being linked to the Shermans when they were alive was something to which many aspired. In death, there was a risk.

The bizarre circumstances of their deaths would make headlines around the world. Plausible theories and wild speculations circulated in print and online, as police, private detectives, and forensic experts conducted their investigations. Was it a business deal gone wrong? International assassins, who flew in and out of Toronto after staging a macabre scene to buy time? Or was it a simpler, more commonplace killing, involving someone they knew?

ONE

WRONG TURN

ON THE MORNING OF FRIDAY, December 15, 2017, family, friends, and colleagues of Barry and Honey Sherman woke, shook off sleep, and set about their normal routines. But for some, a nagging thought persisted. Something was amiss. An email not returned, an empty desk in the executive office, a vacant seat at a charity boardroom table. At 50 Old Colony Road, in Toronto's suburban North York, snow was softly dusting the ground, melting quickly on the heated driveway and obscuring any footprints that may have been made on the front lawn or unheated steps over the previous two days. It had been cold, ten degrees below freezing, and as the sun rose behind clouds, it promised to be another grey, wintry day in Canada's biggest city. Many of the people who owned homes on the street had already flown south to escape the cold weather, so it was not unusual at this time of year for a house in the neighbourhood to be quiet. At the rear of the house was an outdoor pool, long closed for the season, a tennis court surrounded by a fence, and two patios. In a basement underneath the tennis court, stretching north on the property, was a lap pool rarely used by the homeowners. In front of the house, one vehicle was parked on the circular driveway, a light gold Lexus SUV that was ten years old. Judging by the snow lining its fenders and windows, it had been there at least overnight. Beside it, on the left, was a long bed of snowball hydrangeas, their withered brown flower heads perked up by little hats of fresh snow. A ramp to the right of the Lexus led down to a closed garage door that opened into a six-car underground garage nestled in the basement of the house with utility and recreation rooms on the ends closest to the road, and the lap pool at the far north end.

At 8:30 A.M., two people arrived on a clockwork schedule: a cleaning lady on her regular Friday visit, and a woman who came twice a week to water the plants in the home. The cleaning lady parked in the centre of the circular drive. The woman who came to water the plants trudged along the street, passing the large For Sale sign at the curb. The house had been on the market three weeks with an asking price of $6.9 million. Just the day before, a Toronto magazine had revealed publicly for the first time that the property was for sale: "Pharma Titan Barry Sherman is selling his modern North York mansion." Inside 50 Old Colony, the woman watering the orchids and other plants filled her can and went from room to room. The cleaning lady got busy as well. Hanukkah had begun the previous Tuesday evening and included in her assigned duties today was helping Honey prepare potato latkes, which she would cook later that day at the home of one of the Sherman children. The main floor was 3,600 square feet, anchored by a grand entrance topped with a chandelier and a curved staircase heading up to the second floor. The six-bedroom house, including the expansive lower level, was well over 12,000 square feet in total.

Both women began their chores on the main floor. While they were working, a phone rang. The cleaning lady followed the sound into a powder room, where she found an iPhone lying on the tiled floor. By the time she picked up the phone it had stopped ringing. When she moved upstairs, she noticed that the bed in the master bedroom had not been slept in and that the room was unusually tidy. Normally, on cleaning day, the bed was unmade and clothes from the night before were casually strewn on the bed or a chair. The cleaning lady busied herself dusting surfaces and picture frames.

Around 10 A.M., Elise Stern arrived. Dark-haired, with a thin, angular face, Stern was a twenty-year veteran real estate agent who shared the listing for the house with Judi Gottlieb, who was the senior realtor on the file. Just the other day, Gottlieb had shown the house to two men who struck her as odd ducks. But in her business you met all kinds. Gottlieb and her husband were now in Florida on vacation, and in her place Stern was showing the house today. Gottlieb was a longtime friend of the Shermans and had travelled with Honey internationally, including an unforgettable visit to India. Elise Stern was involved because she was close friends with Honey Sherman's sister, Mary Shechtman, who helped her wealthy older sister with all of her real estate transactions. There was some confusion over whether it was okay to have a showing today. Both Stern and Shechtman had tried to reach the Shermans that morning to make sure it was all right, but they'd had no luck. A couple, a man and woman, were interested in the property, and Stern decided she would take a chance on bringing them to the house. She ushered them in the front door along with their agent.

The Old Colony Road property was purchased as a building lot by Barry and Honey Sherman in 1985, and they set about constructing what in its day was a spectacular home that soon had its own story to tell. The story involved a protracted trip through the courts—something not uncommon for the Shermans—with the Shermans alleging poor building practices on the part of the contractors and emerging as winners, recouping most of the money they had spent to build the house. Now, after many years, the Shermans were moving to an even nicer address, closer to growing grandchildren, on a large pie-shaped lot in Forest Hill, one of Toronto's most exclusive neighbourhoods, and a house—complete with a retractable roof over one portion—that would easily cost $30 million or more to build, decorate and furnish.

A short online item in *Toronto Life* magazine announcing that the Sherman home on Old Colony was on the market described the thirty-year-old property as a "poured-concrete colossus" and noted the extensive use of opaque glass block throughout, a popular building material in the 1980s that let light into private spaces. Still lovely, and immaculately kept, it was nevertheless dated. With the modern penchant of knocking down houses and building new ones, the agents knew they would need just the right purchaser. Then again, the lot was large enough and well located and a builder might want to tear the home down and start from scratch. The area, inhabited predominantly by Jewish families for decades, was now home to a growing number of Chinese and Russian families.

As the snow continued to fall, the agents and clients toured the upper two floors, with Elise Stern pointing out the features: the expansive master bedroom with a section dedicated to gym equipment and a large sitting area with couches, television, and fireplace; the spiral staircase that allowed residents to go from the master bedroom and sitting area on the second floor to the basement; the marble bathrooms and Jacuzzi tubs; the five other bedrooms; the many nooks and crannies for a family to enjoy. The owners raised four children in the house, and Stern showed off all the room for spreading out.

The tour continued back on the main floor: a large kitchen that could certainly use updating but had been ground zero for many an event; the spacious dining room, where a future prime minister had dined not too long before; bathrooms big and small. Then Stern led them down to the lower level using the spiral staircase. At the bottom, they passed a sheet metal art installation depicting a life-sized woman leading a sheep by a rope around its neck. Stern walked ahead of the agent and his clients. The lower floor was much bigger than the other levels, its footprint extending under the tennis court out back. Stern led the way down a wide hallway lined by glass block, the garage to their right, and storage, bathroom, and a large cedar sauna to their left. She stooped to pick up some stapled-together pages from the tiled floor. That was odd, she thought. It was a home inspection report for 50 Old Colony. Someone must have dropped it coming in from the garage. Stern continued to a locked glass door at the end of the hallway, pressed a red safety button at shoulder height to release a magnetic lock, and walked in, outlining as she did so the features of the lap pool they were about to see.

Stern stopped abruptly, not letting the clients advance. "Oh, I am so sorry," she said, then turned suddenly and pushed the small group back. "They are doing . . . yoga. We'll come back." In an instant, Stern's eyes had swept the rectangular room. She had taken in the strange tableau and reacted.

In one of the rooms upstairs, the Shermans had another art installation, this one of two life-sized human figures, male and female. Both Stern and Gottlieb had found it unusual, but just as clients viewing a home could sometimes be different, so too could the homeowners. Real estate agents, successful ones, learned not to judge. In Stern's quick look into the pool room, it seemed like there was a similar art installation positioned by the pool. Then her brain caught up, adrenalin surged, and her heart beat faster. She apologized and said they could all view the pool room at a later date if there was interest. Still, as she related to the Sherman children later, at that moment she wondered if the Sherman couple were performing some sort of odd meditation.

Trying not to appear overly rushed, Stern escorted the clients and their agent upstairs. They were upset at being told to leave so quickly. The agent in particular was angry. He would later tell a Canadian Broadcasting Corporation reporter that he initially thought what he saw in his brief glance into the room was something left over from Halloween and that his clients, from mainland China, were superstitious and considered the experience a "bad omen." Stern calmed the agent and his clients down, chatted with them for a few minutes, made sure they had a copy of the listing, shook hands, and said goodbye. She then called to the cleaning lady and the woman watering the plants. The cleaning lady, who occasionally helped Honey Sherman in the kitchen, was getting the flour, potatoes and other supplies ready to assist Honey with their Friday morning cooking plan. Something was off, Stern told the two women, the image of what she had glimpsed so briefly now coalescing in her mind. Not an art installation, she thought. Not a Halloween display. Not meditation.

Stern asked the cleaning lady to go down and look into the pool room. She came back a few minutes later, shaken. She had difficulty speaking. "Call the police," she stammered, and she described what she had seen. Stern did not immediately call the police. Instead, she called Mary Shechtman in Florida, who told Stern to call the police. Then Shechtman hung up and started dialing numbers for the Sherman children, getting through first to Jonathon Sherman, Barry and Honey's son. Finally, after a delay of almost ninety minutes from the discovery of the bodies, a call was made to the Toronto Police 911 system from the house on Old Colony Road. Police records show it coming in at 11:43 A.M. Within one minute, police were en route, along with two paramedic crews and firefighters. Two officers and the paramedics entered the front door, passed under the chandelier, and quickly tramped down to the pool area. As first responders, their job was to save lives, and no care was taken to preserve the scene.

Barry Sherman, multi-billionaire founder of Apotex and well-known philanthropist, was in a seated position, legs outstretched, the right leg crossed neatly over the left, his back to the lap pool. He was wearing his glasses, perched undisturbed on his nose. His bomber-style jacket was pulled slightly off his shoulders and down, which held his arms at his sides. Beside him, Honey, his wife of forty-seven years, known as the "queen" of Toronto's Jewish community, was in a similar position, the light coat she wore also pulled off her shoulders, holding her hands at her sides. They were both VSA, paramedic and police code for "vital signs absent." A quick estimate by the paramedics suggested the couple had been dead for at least a day if not more. Rigor mortis, the condition where the muscles stiffen after death, had passed, and the limbs were relaxed and limp. The reason they were still in a sitting position and had not slumped over or tipped back into the pool was that each of the Shermans had a man's leather belt around their neck that was tied above their head to the three-foot-high stainless steel railing around the end of the lap pool. Both were fully dressed, their coats over top of clothes they had worn that day. Barry's face was untouched; Honey's was damaged, but by what was unclear.

"I've got bad news."

Joel Ulster, Barry Sherman's oldest friend, was in the empty guest bedroom of his new Manhattan apartment, where he was meeting with contractors. He and his husband, Michael, had just purchased a new spot along the Hudson River, and there was a good deal of work to be done before move-in day. Joel and Barry had met in high school when they were sixteen. They had been business partners, friends, and confidants, and over the years Barry had provided generous advice and support to Joel's four children from his first marriage and to Joel and Michael's two adopted children.

"Barry and Honey were murdered at home," came the words over the cell phone from Toronto. "They found their bodies."

Ulster stepped away from the contractors. He could hear voices in the background at the caller's end. It sounded like there were several people in the room all talking at once. He heard "murdered" again. A moment ago, he'd been thinking about renovations, where to put their mountain bikes in the apartment, what Broadway or off-Broadway play he and Michael would see next. Now, on the line from Toronto, was Mark Steiner. Mark's father, Fred, was an old friend of Joel and Barry's. The three of them had been business partners back when they were all just starting out in the early 1970s and they had remained close friends.

"What are you saying . . . ?" Ulster said, his voice trailing off. When he first heard Mark stammer he had bad news, he had feared that Fred had died.

"They have been murdered. They are dead," Mark repeated.

Joel and Michael were to fly to Toronto that weekend for a dinner get-together with Barry and Honey. One of Joel's sons had planned to treat the Shermans to thank them for their generosity in giving him advice and some financial support on his first foray into business. Two days later, when Joel was in Toronto with the grieving Sherman family and the restaurant called to ask if they were keeping the reservation for a large table, he could barely manage a reply. He still couldn't believe he was in Toronto for a funeral and wasn't about to sit down to dinner with his friend of fifty years.

Yellow police tape went up around the entire Sherman property a few hours after the bodies were discovered. One end of it was tied to the large For Sale sign near the curb. On the street immediately to the north, a cruiser pulled into the driveway of the home that backed onto the Shermans' house and officers got out to check the grounds of that property. On Old Colony, more uniformed officers arrived in marked cruisers, then detectives in suits driving unmarked cars, and finally forensic teams in white CSI-style overalls. Coroner Dr. David Giddens had been notified, and he arrived at the house. So too did a forensic pathologist, Dr. Michael Pickup. Police took statements from those present, including a man, a personal trainer, who had a regular Friday afternoon appointment with Honey. He showed up at the yellow police tape and started sobbing when a bystander told him the news. A woman who lived across the street approached the police. Her home had two security cameras trained on her own property, but they picked up the Sherman home in the background. She and her husband had looked at the tape and seen something they thought police needed to have a look at. "We'll send someone over, ma'am," an officer said. Two days later, the helpful couple was still waiting, concerned that the seven-day loop on their system would be overwritten by the next week's footage before police arrived. The Sherman home, like many on the street, lacked outdoor security cameras. There was a security video camera in the pool room, where the bodies were discovered, but it had never been set up.

In an industrial area to the northwest—at a location referred to, in an admiring way by employees and a scoffing way by rivals, as "the corner of Barry and Sherman"—news of the founder's demise reached the headquarters of Apotex, the generic drug firm that employed six thousand people in Canada. Sherman had built Apotex into a billion-dollar empire starting in the early 1970s with the help of Jack Kay. At her desk, Joanne Mauro was crying. Barry Sherman had hired her as a "girl Friday" for a summer forty-two years before, when she was in Grade 11. That job had become permanent when she graduated high school, and for all those years Mauro had been Sherman's executive assistant. Honey Sherman's sister, Mary, who had been looking for the Shermans that morning to arrange the showing of the house, had called Mauro at 9 A.M. She wasn't overly concerned that she couldn't track down Honey or Barry, just curious. A little over an hour later, Shechtman called back, her voice shaking. "Joanne, something's happened. Something's happened to them."

The Sherman family, including Barry and Honey's four adult children, were informed over the next few hours. One of their children was away in Mexico; one had just returned from a trip to Japan; another had just had a baby; and the fourth was planning a wedding with Honey's help. Barry's sister, Sandra, who was with her husband in Palm Desert, California, received a call telling her that her brother was dead.

Friends in the couple's business and social circles began hearing whispers that something terrible had happened. Jack Kay, Barry Sherman's second in command at Apotex for more than three decades, was in New York City with his wife and had just returned to his hotel from a shopping trip on Fifth Avenue when he got the news from Barry and Honey's daughter Alex. Bryna Steiner, Honey Sherman's oldest friend, received a call from the wife of Barry Sherman's main lawyer, Harry Radomski. Bryna called her husband, Fred, at the office and said, "I have terrible news. I am coming over to tell you. Just sit tight." The Steiners and Shermans had been the best of friends since a chance meeting in Florida in 1970 brought them together. After Bryna delivered the news to her husband, they both had the same thought. Had anybody told Joel Ulster, Barry's oldest friend? The Steiners asked their son Mark, who was in the adjacent office, to make the call. Unlike the Sherman children, Mark had followed his father into the family business. In another part of Toronto, two women Honey counted among her closest of confidants learned the news. Honey and the two women—they jokingly called themselves Thelma, Thelma, and Louise—had just returned from an epic golf trip to South Carolina. Despite hip and shoulder replacements, arthritis, and other infirmities, Honey had driven most of the way, as she always insisted on doing, in her decade-old gold Lexus SUV.

Like a dark cloud, the news travelled through the inner circles of the Sherman family and friends, but for a few hours it was kept from the public. Then, just before 4 P.M., the story broke in the Toronto media that two bodies had been found inside the home of Apotex founder Barry Sherman. A few minutes later, a tweet went out on social media from Dr. Eric Hoskins, Ontario's health minister, who had dealt with the Shermans both professionally and as a friend. Television crews, reporters, and photographers rushed to Old Colony Road.

Hoskins, who had heard the information earlier but waited until it became public, confirmed the identity of the bodies found in the Sherman home. He wrote on Twitter, "I am beyond words right now. My dear friends Barry and Honey Sherman have been found dead. Wonderful human beings, incredible philanthropists, great leaders in health care. A very, very sad day. Barry, Honey, rest in peace."

News travelled across the country and internationally. People who knew the Shermans stopped whatever they were doing and listened, then went online to search for information.

Frank D'Angelo, movie producer, soft-drink maker, restaurateur, and the most unlikeliest of Barry Sherman's friends, was driving north with his partner, Gemma, to spend a couple of days relaxing in Collingwood when Gemma, who had been idly looking at her phone, began crying in the passenger seat. She told him the news and D'Angelo almost drove into a ditch.

Judi Gottlieb, the agent with the listing for the Shermans' house and their friend for thirty years, was just walking into the Saks Fifth Avenue store in Miami when she heard. In the midst of her shock, her mind turned to the dozens of prospective buyers and the curious who had traipsed through the house.

Kerry Winter and his siblings, who were Barry Sherman's cousins, had been locked in a bitter and very public legal fight seeking 20 percent of Sherman's fortune. Winter made a phone call to another relative and raised the possibility that one of his brothers had "done it."

For the Sherman children, struggling with the enormity of what had happened, there was suddenly a void. As son Jonathon would say at the funeral service the following week, in the first two days after learning their parents were dead, the four siblings kept expecting them to walk through the door and say, "Everything will be fine."

"If ever a crisis would strike, we always had two people to call for help," Jonathon Sherman would recall. "One would provide calmness, level-headedness, and perspective. And the other would instantly take charge of the situation."

The Sherman heirs' thoughts turned to their own safety and the safety of people at Apotex. A private security company was retained to watch over the Sherman children and their families, as well as key Apotex employees.

The snow continued to fall at Old Colony Road. Early in the evening, television cameras rolled as medical technicians with the coroner's office wheeled two stretchers with body bags out of the residence, loaded them into black coroner's wagons, and drove off.

The bodies gone, two police officers got in front of the cameras to give statements to the media waiting outside the house. Reporters who had been working their sources had the belief, unconfirmed, that a double murder had been committed. The first officer to speak was Constable David Hopkinson, a uniformed officer in the public relations department of the Toronto Police Service.

"The circumstances of their death appear suspicious, and we are treating it that way," said Hopkinson, standing outside the home with a heavy police winter coat over his uniform and protective vest. He said police were inside "taking apart the scene right now," and he invited anyone with information to contact the Toronto Police.

A few hours later, Brandon Price, a detective from the Toronto Police homicide squad, emerged from the Sherman house to provide a second statement. It was dark, past the dinner hour. Price told reporters that detectives had found no sign of forced entry and were not currently looking for any suspects. His comments raised eyebrows among the reporters. Why would they not be looking for suspects? "I just wanted to alleviate some concerns in the neighbourhood," Price said.

Questioned further by reporters, the detective made the same point in a slightly different way. "At this point, indications are that we have no outstanding suspect to be going after."

The comments provoked more questions: With the house for sale, were the police looking into who had viewed the property? When were the Shermans last seen alive? How did they die? All Price would do, no matter the question, was repeat what he had already said. No suspects were being sought.

The reporters were a mix of veterans and interns. The veterans grumbled at how, in the "old days," police gave out a lot more information. The interns and a few of the veterans went door to door on the street, asking homeowners what, if anything, they knew. As deadlines approached, the reporters left to file their accounts of the mysterious deaths. On Saturday morning, one newspaper's headline sent a second shock wave through the community and far beyond, to New York, London, Mumbai, Sydney, Hong Kong, and other major cities where the Shermans and Apotex had a connection.

"Murder-Suicide Suspected in Deaths of Toronto Billionaire and Wife" was the bold headline in the print edition of the *Toronto Sun* tabloid. As the day wore on, the *Toronto Star*, *The Globe and Mail*, and all other media—television, radio, and online—had different takes on the same theme. Barry Sherman had strangled his wife and taken his own life, according to police sources.

Having just landed in Toronto, his head in a fog, Joel Ulster took a call from his son Mark, who was at home looking at the *Toronto Sun* newspaper. "It's not good, Dad," Mark said. "What the newspaper is saying is not good. Are you sure you want to know?"

TWO

BEING BARRY

"HEY, BUTTERBALL!"

Bernard Sherman slouched low in his desk in the classroom at Forest Hill Collegiate, his black-framed glasses riding low on his nose. The teacher at the blackboard wanted his attention. The unflattering nickname had stuck; teachers and students alike used it. Doughy, round of face and body, with few friends and always tired, that was Sherman, a sixteen-year-old who seemed out of place in the boisterous class. "Sluggish" was another label applied to him by teachers. Sherman answered as briefly as possible and went back to looking down at his desk.

The high school was located in the affluent Toronto neighbourhood of Forest Hill, north of Toronto's downtown core. Forest Hill took its name from the summer home in the mid-1800s of a wealthy businessman, before urban sprawl took over, and the area surrounding the school was heavily treed, with winding streets that seemed in some parts to have their own mind and purpose. The houses were big by the standards of the

day, with neatly kept gardens and lawns. In 1958, Bernard
Sherman was one of about five hundred students in the relatively new, twenty-four-classroom school, built just after the
Second World War and boasting a "new electrical sound system"
and internal telephones so that teachers could speak to the
office from the classrooms. The majority of the students were
Jewish, sons and daughters of upwardly mobile parents, reflecting an influx of immigrants to Canada's largest city and this particular part of Toronto. The school's motto translated from
Latin was "Not for ourselves alone," and though there is no evidence that Bernard took notice of it during his five years at
Forest Hill, many of the remarks Sherman would make about
his philanthropy in the future would reflect that thought.

In those days, Bernard Charles Sherman was only just starting to be called Barry. His mother liked the name but urged him
in certain circumstances to use Bernard, because it sounded
more distinguished and would serve him better as an adult. In
later years, Honey would call him Chuck. Barry was born in
Toronto on February 25, 1942, the son of Herbert and Sara
Sherman. Sara was a Winter. Her younger brother, Lou, would,
for a short time, figure prominently in Barry's life, and Lou's
offspring would haunt him in and out of courts for the rest of
his days. Herbert and Sara were themselves born in Canada,
just after the turn of the century, when their own parents had
separately fled anti-Semitism in Russia and Poland.

In a reflective and never-finished memoir called "A Legacy of
Thoughts," penned by Sherman while on a vacation with his
own family years later in Africa, he recalled how his "first ten
years were unremarkable." They had a good life but not an
exciting life, he and his older sister, Sandra—who Sherman
called Sandi—in their modest home in Forest Hill. Father
Herbert was the president of the American Trimming Company,

a small firm that made zippers. One Saturday morning, when Sherman was ten, his father took him to work, an unusual experience for the lad. Sherman asked his father what he could do. His father sat him at a table with a pile of zippers and told him they had to be counted into boxes of twenty.

"In order to please him, I worked quickly," Sherman recalled. So quickly that when his father checked some time later, he was surprised that many more zippers were boxed than could be done by his own paid staff in that amount of time. Herbert Sherman opened a few boxes to check the count, which offended Barry. The counts were all accurate.

A few weeks later, Herbert went to work and did not come home. He had a massive heart attack in his office and died immediately. The Shermans learned that he'd had a congenital heart defect, which he had elected not to tell his family about. In his later musings, Sherman decided that his father had not informed his mother because he did not want to "burden" her with the concern. "Obviously, he should have told her," Sherman wrote. Herbert had a small ownership interest in the zipper company but not enough to support two children when the interest was sold. Sara returned to work as an occupational therapist to support her family, a job she had given up when her children were born.

The perpetual tiredness Barry felt at school would dog him his entire life, and no firm diagnosis to explain his lethargy was ever given. An early nickname coined by a Grade 5 teacher was Grandpa, followed by Butterball in high school. None of these taunts seemed to bother him. At both levels of school, Barry was often yelled at for letting his mind wander instead of focusing on the lesson on the board or in the books. For his entire life, he was plagued by insomnia. His close friends in later years said it was because his mind never shut off; he would lie in bed for hours, thinking, dreaming, and scheming. When sleep finally came, it was deep, and as a child he often had a hard time waking for school.

One day, his homeroom teacher took his side and suggested to another teacher that perhaps they should go a bit easier on the boy. Sherman described the incident in his unfinished memoir. "I do not recall feeling any great sense of loss upon my father's death. However, some weeks later, I was at school in a class being taught by a specialty teacher, and the teacher began to scold me for daydreaming and being inattentive. Coincidentally, at that moment, my homeroom teacher entered the room, and on hearing what was happening, said aloud to the specialty teacher that I had suffered 'a recent family tragedy' and should be excused for inattentiveness." Sherman was surprised that his teacher even knew his father had died, but he did wonder if there was a correlation between losing his father and how he behaved in class. And a germ of a thought grew. "Although I do not know to what extent, if any, I was affected by my father's death, a psychologist would likely suggest that the drive to achieve which I later exhibited was caused, at least in part, by a resulting insecurity."

At Forest Hill Collegiate, Barry Sherman did not take part in athletics of any sort. He was a middling student at best until his senior years. There were no girlfriends. He had a regular gig babysitting a next door neighbour's child in the afternoon and evenings, and that was how he spent his time, watching Western movies on television whenever he got the chance. By his senior years, two things happened. First, Sherman began to manifest a belief that would stay with him his whole life: that he was right about everything. Second, he met Joel Ulster.

It was a contest in the *Toronto Daily Star* in the late 1950s that drew Sherman and Ulster together. The newspaper ran a series of brainteasers every few days and invited readers to figure them out and mail their answers to the paper. Memories dimmed over the years, and it's not clear who spotted the contest first in the pages of the *Star*, but Ulster recalls that Sherman, once aware of it, was convinced that the two would win. They got busy, clipping out the puzzles, answering the questions, and sending their answers off by post to the old Toronto Star Building on King Street, east of Toronto's financial district. They made it to the tiebreaker and lost, though Sherman was convinced that they were in fact the winners. This was the same student who, on more than a few occasions in Grade 13, challenged a teacher about a statement in a textbook, and was right. Newspaper contest over, they became fast friends.

Ulster was no dummy; he had a better than average memory and was adept with language. "But Barry was smart. Really smart. Nobody else saw it at that time, but I did," Ulster recalls. "He was the smartest person I ever met in my life. He could go through layers and layers of information and stay focused on it. He had a different kind of intelligence."

In his final year of high school, Sherman discovered his aptitude for math and science. He entered a Canada-wide physics contest in addition to his class studies and placed first. A photographic memory was part of it. Norman Paul, a Toronto entrepreneur and pharmacist who knew Sherman well in later years, tells a story of presenting the Apotex founder with a lengthy legal document when he was seeking his advice. "Barry picked it up, quickly scanned each page, close to his eyes, like he was a scanner, and after said, 'Norm, it's fine, but there is a spelling mistake on page forty-two.' And he was right."

Sherman and Ulster's friendship was built on some fundamental beliefs. One of them was that there was no God, not the most popular belief in a community with religion so stoutly at its centre. Over the years, if someone said "thank God" in his presence, Sherman would rail against the notion, telling anyone who would listen, "There is no God!" He opened his memoir by announcing to the reader, "From my earliest years I have been an atheist. I find it incomprehensible that countless persons, including some of apparent intelligence, believe not only in [the] existence of a Supreme Being, but in very specific and seemingly preposterous mythologies."

Joel Ulster, and later friends and business partners like Fred Steiner, would just shake their heads at the comments that came out of Sherman's mouth. Sherman used to tell people he had no emotions, but Ulster saw through that. The two would have long talks while studying, something Sherman under-took in earnest in his last year of school. Ulster, who was not studious, hit the books just to be close to his good friend. Ulster had girlfriends in those days and credits himself with getting his friend interested in girls; Sherman started going on the occasional date. And though neither Sherman nor Ulster was sporty, Sherman particularly not, the two young men played a weekly game of tennis.

Sherman became a regular fixture at the Ulster family home. It was calmer and less chaotic there than at his own house, where his mother had taken in boarders, one upstairs and one downstairs, to support the family. Joel's father, Ben, was an entrepreneur who owned several movie theatres in Toronto, so-called "grindhouses" that showed back-to-back movies all day, including some racy films. Ben Ulster took an instant liking to Barry. "He will win the Nobel Peace Prize one day, and I am going to fly all of us over there to see him accept it," Ulster's father would say. When Joel balked at going with his family on a holiday ski trip to the Catskills in New York State, his parents paid for Barry to come and keep Joel company.

There was a deep loyalty between the two of them, and Sherman and Ulster made it clear that each would always stand by the other, no matter what. Though Ulster was the more athletic of the two, to the extent that either was athletic, he had a failing mark in gym class in his final year, which would have stopped him from graduating. Sherman found the grade book when no one was around and gave Ulster a passing grade. At the end of Grade 13, while Joel was travelling in Europe during the summer break, he received a telegram with his school marks from his father. He worried for hours before opening it. Both had done well, but Joel's father began his message with the news of the Sherman boy's results. "'Barry leads Ontario with 14 firsts.' That was my father writing to *me*," says Ulster. "I loved that!"

In the 1950s in Ontario, Canada's biggest province, students wrote a series of exam papers at the end of the year and were graded against the standard of "firsts." A first was a mark of over 75 percent, considered an A grade, at a time when that sort of mark meant much more than it does today. A headline in the *Toronto Daily Star* from August 23, 1960, read, "Forest Hill Boy Gets 14 Firsts," and the story described how Bernard Sherman "topped" all Grade 13 students who wrote the tests. Two other boys from Forest Hill Collegiate received twelve firsts. Ulster got eight. He was happy with that and delighted for his friend, who, if plans hatched over long study sessions in high school came to fruition, would be his future business partner.

Sherman was particularly interested in flexing his entrepreneurial muscles after an experience working for the provincial government during his Grade 12 summer "processing useless information in an obscure office" in the basement of the Ontario legislature. But what sort of business would be the right fit?

The answer, or at least the start of the answer, came from Uncle Lou. Lou Winter, the younger brother of Sherman's mother, was an energetic though mercurial man who had graduated from university with a degree in biochemistry. Today, pharmaceutical companies and medical laboratories are commonplace; in 1960, they were not. Lou Winter ran two companies. One was Winter Laboratories, a medical testing lab that mainly performed pregnancy tests on urine samples dropped off by women at pharmacies. This was years before the arrival of home pregnancy tests. The other business, a new venture when Sherman graduated high school, was Empire Laboratories, a distributor of generic prescription drugs purchased from American manufacturers. Generics are copies of brand name pharmaceuticals, sold at a fraction of the cost.

Sherman went to work for Uncle Lou for the summer. Sherman was eighteen; Lou Winter was thirty-six. Despite his temper—Winter was prone to rages and would get red in the face when an employee did something he did not like—they got along well, and Winter gave his nephew Barry a hybrid job, picking up urine samples from pharmacies for testing by the lab and delivering Empire's packaged generic drugs to many of those same pharmacies.

Lou and his wife, Beverley, were starting a family. By 1960, the year Sherman started working summers at Empire, they had two-year-old Tim, who had been adopted, and Jeffrey, a newborn. Two more baby boys, Kerry and Dana, would be born in the next two years. Barry Sherman was just out of his teenage years when his Winter cousins were toddlers. It was a busy household, and Lou worked long hours at his two businesses. There were obvious signs that the Winters were doing well, including a stately stone house on The Kingsway, one of Toronto's wealthiest neighbourhoods, a Rolls Royce, and a small yacht.

Internationally, the concept of the generic drug was taking hold, and it was clear to anyone who followed the industry that there was money to be made. The manufacturers of the original drug—called Big Pharma now, a term not yet coined in 1960— did the lengthy and expensive clinical testing and product development. The generic firms copied the drug, but there were legal issues that had to be resolved. A company could not just steal another company's intellectual property. Some compensation had to be provided. Morris Goodman, a Canadian pharmacist and one of the fathers of Canada's generic industry, notes that brand pharmaceutical companies called him a pirate. He never considered himself a pirate. In fact, the feeling he had from governments was often the opposite. "I was acting legally in conjunction with the Canadian law," he says. Canadian governments told him, "'Go after it, because we want lower prices. We want people to be able to afford more drugs.'" Years later, Goodman would have the distinction of being the "only person to ever fire Barry Sherman."

Working in favour of people like Morris Goodman, Lou Winter, and, eventually, Barry Sherman was that, in a system where governments and private companies paid for a big proportion of the cost of drugs people were prescribed, lower cost was a good thing. The question—and it was a question governments would wrestle with and make decisions about that would both propel Sherman forward and infuriate him—was how to achieve that without destroying the innovation efforts of the brand name companies.

Barry Sherman's father had died when Barry was just ten years old. Lou Winter was not a surrogate father, but he was someone Sherman looked up to. As time passed, Winter gave his protégé more and more responsibilities, though mindful that Sherman was still a student. Sherman and Ulster both had enrolled at the University of Toronto. In his "Legacy" memoir, Sherman recalled, "I specifically chose Engineering Physics [now called engineering science] because it was reputed to be the most difficult of programs related to mathematics and the physical sciences." He ranked fourth in the program in first year, third in second year, second in third year. In his final year, he graduated top of the class and was awarded the Wilson Medal, the highest honour in that discipline. "It seems that the tougher the going got, the better I did," Sherman wrote. In these early years, Sherman told friends that his long-term goal was to work at NASA.

Meanwhile, Ulster enrolled in the honours arts program, spent a year studying law, then accounting, looking for something that would click. The friendship of the two young men continued to strengthen. One of the criteria in the courses they both chose was that they had to pursue a university sport. Neither had any interest in football, hockey, or basketball. Then they discovered that table tennis was an approved sport on the university's compulsory list. They signed up. "It was perfect for Barry. You know, I never saw him run once. Just not his nature. Ping-Pong was the answer," Ulster recalls.

There was a belief in the extended Sherman/Winter family, which Barry Sherman articulated on many occasions, that the men in the family had a short lifespan and nothing could alter that. A good diet, exercise, none of it signified in Sherman's life. Breakfast for Barry was often a handful of Smarties and raisins. The fatalism didn't apply to the women in the family, and so it was a shock when, in 1962, Lou Winter's wife, Beverley, was diagnosed with leukemia. Following her first round of treatment, and leaving behind four very young boys, two still in diapers, Beverley and Lou flew to Bermuda for a three-week rest and vacation. What happened in their absence would be a harbinger of what was to come in Sherman's life. Opportunity. Risk. Reward.

Sherman had been working that summer at Empire, where the company was making its first attempt to manufacture its own pills. Previously, Empire had purchased generic pills wholesale from a US supplier and distributed them. The governments of the day were flexing regulatory muscles, swooping in on generic companies and running tests to see if their products were safe and effective copies of the brand product. Generic firms believed that the brand companies were putting government up to this. Barry Sherman's job that summer was to help the full-time employees set up the manufacturing line. As Lou and Beverley relaxed in Bermuda, Empire was starting to manufacture a generic form of Aspirin under contract to the now defunct but then very large Towers department store chain. It was a big contract and one that was predicted to make Empire a lot of money. A call came in from the Towers buyer. Sales were larger than expected and the buyer predicted they would rise even higher. A great deal more of the ASA tablets (ASA, or acetylsalicylic acid, is the active ingredient) would be needed. Apparently, the lower-cost version was flying off the shelves. According to his memoir, Sherman took the initiative, contacted the company that supplied the bulk ASA to Empire, and "negotiated the purchase of a substantially increased quantity at a substantially lower price."

"I also organized around-the-clock production to fill the orders," Sherman wrote. When it came into the small Toronto factory, the ASA was mixed with fillers and compacted into tablets using a tabletting machine that used pressure to form powder into pills. The relatively slow-moving machine was archaic compared to the machines Sherman would have at his disposal in the future: computer-driven punches that would each turn out five thousand tablets a minute. Still, it got the job done and earned him praise.

"Uncle Lou was very pleased with what I had done," Sherman wrote. "Although I did not know it at the time, these summers at Empire Laboratories would later prove to be of critical importance to my future career."

Lou and Beverley came back from Bermuda refreshed. Beverley's leukemia was in remission. Lou returned to his business and Beverley, feeling better, was busy with the children. Photos taken over the next few years captured numerous images of Tim, Jeff, Kerry, and Dana: on a dock in cottage country, all wearing short pants and matching velour jackets; on a beach, again with all of them wearing matching summer shorts and collared short-sleeved shirts; seated together in front of the large oak door of the Winter home in Toronto. A photo of Lou, wearing glasses reminiscent of the ones Barry Sherman wore and laughing with Beverley, is an indication that his infamous temper had settled as he aged. In the family albums, there are lots of photos of Lou and Beverley hugging and kissing, smiling. In one particularly nice picture, the boys, wearing the velour outfits again, are snuggled close to their mother at a beach.

Having graduated from the University of Toronto as an engineer in 1964, Sherman tried something different that summer. Instead of working at Empire, he took a job at the Spar Aerospace division of de Havilland Aircraft in Toronto. His knowledge and abilities with math landed him a plum summer assignment working on vibration issues encountered by satellites being developed in Canada. It was an exciting time in the world of space and aeronautics, with the moon landing plans under development in the United States, and Canada working in tandem with the Americans to develop satellites to study the atmosphere and create an orbiting communications network. At the end of that summer, Sherman travelled to Boston to begin studies in astronautics and aeronautics at the Massachusetts Institute of Technology. For Sherman, it was both physically and mentally a great distance from pharmaceuticals and Toronto.

When he returned to Boston for his second year, he did so with the knowledge that his Aunt Beverley's leukemia had returned. She was being treated at Toronto's St. Joseph's Hospital, but the situation was dire.

Just a few weeks into his sophomore year, in the middle of the night, when Sherman was asleep in his room at MIT, he heard his telephone ring. He feared it was news from Toronto that his aunt had died.

It was his sister. "It's Uncle Lou," Sandi said.

Lou Winter, aged forty-one, had been working that afternoon at the Empire offices in Toronto's west end when he suddenly fell over. An aneurysm in his brain had burst. His employees called an ambulance and he was rushed to St. Joseph's Hospital, a fifteen-minute drive further west, but Lou Winter died soon after arrival. Sherman flew home to attend his uncle's funeral. He did not believe in God, but he understood the meaning to family of a funeral and knew it was important that he be there.

After the funeral, he visited his now terminally ill Aunt Beverley in hospital on the evening of November 9, 1965. He recalled in his memoir how the lights in the hospital went out. Not being a superstitious man, Sherman was not worried but rather curious. Emergency systems clicked on. He began to ask questions, intrigued by what had happened. It turned out that an improperly set relay circuit on a transmission line from the Adam Beck II hydroelectric power station on the Canadian side of Niagara Falls had tripped, sending a power surge into the electrical grid that caused blackouts on the eastern seaboard of the United States—New York State, New Jersey, Massachusetts, Connecticut, New Hampshire, Vermont, and Rhode Island—and a big swath of Ontario. Power remained out for thirteen hours. Newspaper accounts describe traffic and public transit chaos, but there are also stories of people on the jammed streets of Toronto giving up on getting home and popping into bars for a drink by candlelight. A myth, eventually debunked, was that the Great Blackout of 1965 gave rise to a baby boom. Sherman returned to Boston and his classes, only to fly back three weeks later to attend Aunt Beverley's funeral.

His little cousins were seven, five, four, and three years old when their parents died. In later years, whenever the boys' uncertain future—some had troubles with substance abuse, some the law, and all had a hard time finding their place in the world—was discussed, the four boys would always be referred to as the "orphaned cousins" or the "Winter orphans." The immediate question after the deaths of their parents was who would raise the boys. According to a 2008 *Toronto Life* article, Beverley's brother (now deceased) was under the impression that she did not want any of her own family involved. There also appears to have been no discussion about whether Barry or Sandi, who were both in their early to mid-twenties, could look after the children, though some people interviewed for this book have suggested they should have. In testimony as part of the lawsuit the cousins eventually brought against him, seeking a $1-billion share in his wealth, Barry Sherman said there was "nothing" he could have done at the time. "I couldn't adopt them myself. I was a kid myself." In reality, it would have been highly impractical. Sherman was twenty-three years old, single, and living in Boston, working simultaneously on a master's degree and a doctorate. Sandi was also just starting out.

A local couple, Dr. Moishe "Martin" Barkin and his wife, Carol, who had their own children, took in the four boys and eventually adopted the children, using money from the estate to raise them. But while Sherman had no interest in being thrust into parenthood, he did have an interest in the Empire companies Lou Winter had created and where he had worked for two summers. After Beverley's funeral, Sherman delayed his return to Boston. He had a sense that the business was in trouble, and he wondered, as he recalled later, if there was something he could do to help.

Lou Winter's will had appointed the Royal Trust Company as executors and trustees of the estate, with instructions to oversee the affairs both of Empire and the four children, should both Winter and his wife die. Three days after Beverley died, Sherman wrote a letter to Royal Trust. He had a plan. Opportunity was on the table, risk was certain, the reward could be substantial. He proposed that he would purchase all of his deceased uncle's assets, including Empire and related companies Winter had created. He was "anxious to protect the value of the said assets for the benefit of the children of Louis and Beverley Winter," Sherman wrote. He suggested that he would take over immediately as general manager of Empire, putting his studies on hold, and that he would be given the first opportunity to purchase all the assets in January, just two months later. Sherman gave Royal Trust a twenty-four-hour time limit to consider his offer. It was rejected.

Sherman went back to his studies in Boston, leaving behind for the time being any thought of a career in pharmaceuticals. Years later, when Sherman was a veteran of court actions, testifying in patent cases about one drug or another, his lawyer

Harry Radomski would typically begin by leading him through his curriculum vitae, with a sharp focus on Sherman's academics. Sherman would describe how he was awarded both a master of science degree in aeronautics and a doctor of philosophy in systems engineering after just a little more than two years at MIT. His grade point average, Sherman would tell the court, was a "perfect 5.0." The cumbersome title of Sherman's doctoral thesis, "Precision Gravity Gradient Satellite Altitude Control," for which he eventually received a patent from the US government, always raised quizzical but respectful eyebrows. Another paper he penned for an earlier course was titled "Tethering a Satellite to the Moon." After all of this was said on the witness stand, Sherman would pause and say to the judge, "I guess you could say I am a rocket scientist." That would get a predictable chuckle from the judge and anyone sitting in the gallery, a welcome relief from the tedious discussion of whether a particular active pharmaceutical formulation was done in a manner that would circumvent a Big Pharma patent.

It was surprising to some who knew Sherman in the 1960s that he dropped his dream of working for NASA and returned to Toronto to make another bid for Uncle Lou Winter's company.

"I had decided that I did not want to seek employment as an astronautical engineer," Sherman recalled in his memoir. "I was interested in both science and business and I also wanted to return to Toronto to live." A deciding factor for him was that he wanted to be his own boss. One summer, when he was fifteen years old, Sherman had joined the student militia of the Royal Canadian Artillery. The physical challenge of training was bad enough, he recalled in his memoir, but worse were the drill sergeants. "I was and always have been reluctant to submit to any authority." The one bright light for Sherman during his military summer was the opportunity, as he described it, to engage "persistently in aggressive and disrespectful debate" with the military chaplain.

With the NASA plan behind him, Sherman was back in Canada in 1967, checking in on his mother and sister. He called Joel Ulster, who by this time had given up on law and was working towards becoming a chartered accountant. Ulster was married to a nurse, and they had three very young children, with a fourth on the way. "Uncle Barry," as his children called Sherman, was a hit when he visited their house just north of Toronto, romping around on all fours pretending to be a jungle animal and taking an interest in them that would last his whole life. Sherman wanted to get married and have children himself, but not yet. As far back as high school, Joel and Barry had agreed that if they could find a business that was a good fit, they would see if their partnership, first forged during a newspaper puzzle contest, could work in the real world. When they became friends at Forest Hill Collegiate, they would fantasize about the companies they would run and conjure up names using the first letters of their first names, like JOBA Enterprises, or BaJo Ltd. Now, Sherman had an idea, and he wanted Ulster involved. Both knew that to pull it off, they would need financial help from their parents.

Sherman drove over to Empire Laboratories, the group of companies he had tried to purchase two years before. A few of the executives he had known were still there. The new boss, put in place by Royal Trust on behalf of the Winter estate, was a university chemistry professor named George Wright. "He may have been a good chemist, but absolutely incompetent when it came to business issues," Sherman later recalled in a deposition for the cousins' lawsuit against him and Joel Ulster. Sherman said he came to that conclusion by chatting with people at the company, asking questions about revenues, expenses, and, most importantly, their product line. Whereas Empire had been on the cutting edge of the fledgling generic market a few years before, it had not introduced a new product since that time. He also found that they were supplying product to the other new generic company in Toronto, Novopharm, and that Novopharm was then selling the product in stores and undercutting the price Empire was charging. And it turned out Empire president Wright had a plan that to Sherman's young but sharp business mind made no sense.

"George Wright told me that his plan to save the company was to make oral contraceptives for sale to India," Sherman recalled in his deposition. "Completely off the wall idea that made no sense whatsoever. So it was apparent that the company would be closed down and there would be no value at all within a matter of months." Profits from Empire, what little there were, belonged to the orphan cousins. Though his conduct was continually called into question in the cousins' later court action, Sherman never wavered in his response. He believed that it was a good business opportunity for him, and if he purchased it from the estate, that would give the four Winter brothers money for their future.

Sherman called Royal Trust, which was now two years into its job of managing the Winter assets and overseeing the financial affairs of the orphaned cousins, who were being raised by the Barkin family. This time, Sherman made an offer that included what a senior judge fifty years later would refer to as a "sweetener." Sherman stipulated that the four cousins would one day be able to work at Empire and each would have the right to purchase 5 percent of the company shares, provided certain conditions were met. Royal Trust agreed to sell. Sherman and Ulster's offer of $450,000 was $100,000 higher than the only other offer. They would assume responsibility for $200,000 in company debt, and the actual payout to Royal Trust would be $250,000—paid for with a $100,000 loan from Sherman's mother and a $150,000 loan from Ulster's father. When the purchase deal was done and Sherman and Ulster had control of Lou Winter's company, the two men, both in their mid-twenties, looked around the four walls of their acquisition and took a deep breath.

"We're going to be millionaires," Sherman said, his eyes widening behind his glasses. The next day, combing through the company documents and examining the product line, he sat back in his chair and looked at Ulster.

"We're going to be bankrupt."

THREE

CLUES

BERNARD CHARLES SHERMAN'S BODY LAY on a stainless steel autopsy table in a modern coroner's suite in North York, in Toronto. Natural light filtered through opaque glass blocks not too dissimilar to the glass blocks in the house on Old Colony Road that brightened the pool room. Waiting in a cool storage locker in the next room was the body of Sherman's wife, Honey. Barry was seventy-five when he died; Honey was seventy. Their bodies had been discovered the day before at their home, a fifteen-minute drive to the east. The Office of the Chief Coroner of Ontario, which is attached to the Centre of Forensic Sciences, is one of those anonymous glass and concrete building complexes, and even though one would pass within three hundred metres of the buildings when driving from Apotex to Old Colony Road, the couple likely never would have realized they were passing near it.

On Saturday, December 16, pathologist Dr. Michael Pickup had been assigned to conduct the autopsies. He was the forensic pathologist who visited the death scene on Old Colony Road the day before. A story in Toronto's leading tabloid newspaper that morning stated that police believed it was a murder-suicide. It was Pickup's job to deliver his determination. Following protocol, Toronto Police detectives would be on hand to make notes on the results and to ensure the paperwork was done for what is known as "chain of custody" for any samples that were taken from the bodies. Ontario had a relatively recent troubled history with forensic pathology. This fifty-thousand-square-metre building, completed five years before, was in part built as a state-of-the-art response to serious failings discovered in many botched cases over the previous two decades. The work of pathologists and coroners, and sometimes police, had been found lacking. Child deaths were misdiagnosed and a serial killer and rapist stayed on the loose for years, to name just a couple of the wrongs this building and a more focused approach to forensics were supposed to cure. Things were supposed to be better now, more methodical.

Pickup was a medical doctor and a staff pathologist who had qualified as a forensic pathologist seven years earlier. With the high-profile nature of the case, it would have been more likely that Dr. Michael Pollanen, Ontario's chief forensic pathologist, was at least in the room for the autopsies, but he was unavailable. (Neither Pickup nor Pollanen would agree to be interviewed for this book. The description of what happened in that autopsy room is pieced together from sources with knowledge of the case.)

The role of the pathologist in conducting an autopsy is to examine the body, take samples, including toxicological samples of fluids such as blood and urine, and, if possible, determine how the individual died. The fact that a heart stopped beating does not explain how a person has died; it is a symptom caused by something else. In the case of a heart attack, for example, the heart stops because one of the coronary arteries pumping blood to it has become blocked.

Pickup's job was to learn why Barry Sherman's heart stopped. What were the root causes and any compounding factors—disease, drugs, alcohol—that led up to the death? He would do the same for Honey Sherman later in the day. His examination would include a careful inspection of the surface of the body to see if there were any markings that would help the police determine what happened in the Shermans' house. A full post-mortem can easily take three to four hours.

Among the police present were divisional officers, local detectives who "caught" the high-profile case when it was called in, and members of the homicide squad, who that day were present only in an advisory and support role. The case was classified only as "suspicious."

Pickup began by taking photographs of Barry Sherman's body. At the neck, there was evidence of abrasions, indicating that something had been wrapped around it. From his visit to the scene, Pickup knew that both Barry and Honey Sherman were found with a man's leather belt looped around the neck. Pickup used a scalpel to surgically open the neck. From his knowledge of pathology, he knew there was one key anatomical area that, though it would not tell the entire tale, would provide a strong clue about what happened.

Inside a person's neck there is a horseshoe-shaped bone located between the chin and the thyroid, just above the Adam's apple, if you are looking from the front. The bone, called the hyoid bone, is anchored by a series of muscles, and one of its functions is to help the tongue move and allow the individual to swallow. Pickup examined the hyoid bone on Barry Sherman and noticed it was not broken. For Pickup, this was a key finding. When a person is strangled violently, the bone typically snaps, similar to how it would be broken in a judicial capital punishment hanging where the body is dropped two or three metres. The sudden tightening of a rigid ligature, such as a metal wire, would have the same effect. That his hyoid bone was intact was, for Pickup, an indication that Barry Sherman may have committed suicide. In suicidal hangings, which typically lack a long drop (think of a person putting a noose around his neck and kicking the chair away), the hyoid bone is rarely broken. Pickup took biopsies of the damaged skin around the neck where the belt had been looped, and removed the hyoid bone for further testing, recording his findings as he proceeded. Moving down the body, he made other observations as the detectives looked on.

It was evident by even the most cursory inspection that Sherman, the well-known billionaire and founder of Apotex, had not taken care of himself. A poor diet and lack of exercise were evident in pockets of fat and little muscle tone. This was the person police thought had overpowered his wife in another part of the house, strangled her, dragged her down a flight of stairs, and positioned her beside a pool, holding her in a seated position with a leather belt around her neck? A woman who weighed about the same as he did and whose body, once examined, revealed considerable bone density, an indication that she was strong. Then, according to the police theory, Barry Sherman killed himself by hanging from a very low railing? It did not make sense. Something else struck Pickup. Circling Sherman's wrists were abrasions of some sort. It looked as if something, perhaps a rope or plastic zip tie, sometimes called a zap strap, had been pulled tightly around both of Sherman's wrists. That would also seem to contradict the suicide theory. Pickup could not determine if Sherman's wrists had been tied in front or behind his body. But it did seem that at some point, his wrists had been bound.

In addition to what Pickup saw at the death scene, detectives had provided him with photographs taken of the bodies before they were removed from the pool room. In the photos, Barry Sherman's hands were not tied, and police had found no evidence of any ties or rope in the pool room. A mystery. Using a special camera that takes high resolution images, Pickup photographed Sherman's wrists on all sides. Then, taking a razor-sharp scalpel, he removed the skin around the wrists and put it in a special sample container for more analysis. That would be done at the Centre of Forensic Sciences, next door to the coroner's building. These biopsies were necessary because they could tell him if the wrist markings were recent or old. When living tissue is injured, it goes through minute changes as the healing process advances, from inflammation to eventual healing. They looked recent to him, but he wanted scientific confirmation.

After a break to make notes, Pickup began the autopsy on Honey Sherman, with the police detectives watching. Whereas Barry Sherman had no evidence of violence on his face, Honey Sherman did. She had a fresh injury to the face, where there were abrasions but no bruising, an indication that she had died immediately after being struck, or she was struck after she died, because bruises need blood circulation to form. Pickup could not tell how the injury occurred. She could have been struck with a blunt object or been thrown to the ground, or, as some speculated, her face could have been injured when her body was taken downstairs to the pool room. The skin around her neck had abrasions similar to her husband's. Pickup discovered that her hyoid bone and the thyroid cartilage just below it were intact, the same discovery he made in the autopsy on her husband. As he had with Barry Sherman, Pickup removed the hyoid bone for further testing. Looking at Honey's wrists, he found markings similar to those on Barry's wrists. He photographed the markings, then removed for biopsy testing sections of skin from around both wrists and from her face and neck. Pickup also made notes on the overall condition of the body. She was overweight but, unlike her husband, there was significant tone to her muscles.

From Pickup's examination of both bodies it was evident that the Shermans died of "ligature compression," forensic speak for strangulation. Some sort of ligature had been wrapped around their necks, closing off the trachea and larynx, making it impossible to breathe. How forcibly this was done was unclear. Just because they were found with belts around their necks did not necessarily mean those were the instruments by which they died. However, the belts had been brought from the death scene, and by making a comparison to the markings on each neck it seemed likely that they were the ligatures used.

Several doctors in the forensic community in Toronto, upon hearing news that the deaths were caused by ligature neck compression, had the same thought. If the owner of a drug empire was going to kill his wife, then kill himself, would he not have found a simpler way to do so?

That Saturday morning, before Michael Pickup began his examination, when Barry Sherman's oldest friend and original business partner, Joel Ulster, was flying in from New York, Toronto had woken up to a startling headline in the *Toronto Sun*: "Murder-Suicide Suspected in Deaths of Toronto Billionaire and Wife." The reporter who wrote the story was a veteran, Joe Warmington, the self-styled "Night Scrawler," who has a reputation for being too close to police and some politicians, including Toronto's late crack-smoking populist mayor, Rob Ford. But

Warmington also has a reputation for getting it right when it comes to police stories. In Saturday's piece, beside photos of Barry and Honey at a black-tie charity event, Warmington wrote,

> Sources say police were working Friday night on the theory the demise of the billionaire Apotex founder and his wife, which has stunned the city and those who knew them, may have been a murder-suicide.
>
> Sources close to the case believe Honey may have been killed in a secondary location in the $6.9-million Old Colony Rd. house and then moved to the location where she was later found with her deceased husband.

Warmington quoted someone he described as a "police source," saying, "Forensics need to be done and post-mortems on the bodies, but at this stage it appears there was no forced entry and no evidence of anybody else in the house."

In an explanatory piece Warmington wrote for his paper six weeks later, he told his readers how the Friday night unfolded for him, leading to the dramatic story on Saturday's front page. In his first draft of the story, written on Friday evening, the day the Shermans were found, his planned first paragraph was "They were executed." He had been standing outside the police tape at the Sherman house when someone he described as a "witness to the death scene" told him the Shermans both had belts wrapped around their necks and that "it was an execution." Back at the office, Warmington pounded out his story and was about to hand it over to the copy editors when his phone rang. It was a police source. "It was not a double murder. It's a murder-suicide, with him killing her, dragging her body to the pool, hanging it and then hanging himself," the source said.

In a hold-the-presses moment (or, in the case of modern on-line journalism, a don't-press-Send-yet moment), Warmington bought himself a few more minutes and changed his draft. In the story that went online in Saturday's paper, he included a comment from Inspector Bryan Bott, the then head of homi-cide, who said, "At this time we are not searching for any sus-pects." Warmington also quoted police sources saying "there was no forced entry and no evidence of anybody else in the house." While the rest of the Toronto media described them only as "suspicious deaths" in their initial stories that Saturday morning, by the afternoon, around the time Michael Pickup was completing his second autopsy of the day, the rest of the media were falling in line with Warmington and the *Sun*. By late afternoon on Saturday, the *Toronto Star*, *The Globe and Mail*, television and radio, all quoted confidential police sources saying that the active theory was murder-suicide.

Friends of the Shermans in Toronto and beyond reacted strongly. Businessman Frank D'Angelo, the flamboyant entre-preneur who had been backed by Sherman's millions in ven-tures ranging from beer to movie production, told several reporters he was beyond crushed. "He was the best friend I ever had," he told the *Toronto Sun*. "I don't want to say anything until we understand what happened here. I have no way to cope to tell you how I am feeling right now."

The *Toronto Star* reported comments from Sherman's employees at Apotex: "Dr. Sherman gave his life to the singu-lar purpose of our organization—innovating for patient affordability. Patients around the world live healthier and more fulfilled lives thanks to his life's work, and his significant impact on healthcare and healthcare sustainability will have an enduring impact for many years to come. As employees, we are proud of his tremendous accomplishments, honored to have known him, and vow to carry on with the Apotex purpose in his honor."

Murray Rubin, who had owned a pharmacy chain that did business with Sherman as far back as the 1970s, was asked about the possibility that it was a murder-suicide. He bluntly told *The Globe and Mail*, "That is impossible."

There were others who paused and wondered. Maybe there was something to the murder-suicide story. Who knew what happened behind closed doors? Rumours flew. And unbeknownst to the Sherman family, Toronto Police began preparations to go before a judge for a search warrant to obtain medical records on Honey and Barry. Perhaps one was depressed? Or had cancer? Working on the theory of murder-suicide, police followed that sole line of inquiry, producing a sort of tunnel vision. That kind of single-focused investigation can have a negative effect on a case, because everything that is learned is viewed through that lens. And "the forty-eight-hour clock"—known in homicide investigations as the most consequential time in which to develop theories, examine clues, and seek suspects—was ticking. What was not known publicly then was that, at exactly the same time, many top officers of the Toronto homicide squad were involved in a fast-developing probe into the serial killing of gay men in Toronto by a landscaper named Bruce McArthur. The week before the Sherman deaths, detectives had a break in the case when they surreptitiously obtained photos from McArthur's desktop computer in his apartment. The photos would be instrumental in eventually convicting him of eight murders. It is not unreasonable to conclude that from December 7, 2017, until the McArthur arrest on January 17, 2018, detectives who normally would have been part of the Sherman investigation were preoccupied with a high-stakes operation to prevent more murders. The reduced police resources meant that detectives on the Sherman case were often not homicide detectives at all but drawn from the fraud squad and other units within the large metropolitan force.

While police assigned to the Sherman case watched over the Old Colony Road home, an uneasy and frustrated group of relatives and friends gathered late Friday afternoon at the home of Barry and Honey Sherman's daughter Alexandra, known as Alex. People first had to comprehend the fact that the Shermans were dead, then process the rumours that grew stronger into Friday night: that police believed Barry had killed Honey then taken his own life. One person present described their emotional state as "a daze, everyone was in shock, crying and asking questions, all at the same time."

Daughter Alex and her husband, Brad Krawczyk, lived in Forest Hill, not far from where Barry had grown up and just three blocks away from a building site where the Sherman parents were about to construct a mansion. Months later, Alex would play an important role in the search for answers in the Sherman deaths and an equally important role in the charitable affairs of her parents. But in December 2017, the thirty-one-year-old was focused on her career as a registered nurse working with the homeless, and on raising her family. She and Krawczyk, who worked for the Sherman family trust, had a four-year-old son, and weeks earlier, in November, their daughter had been born. Alex had been expecting a visit from her mother, who wanted to cook latkes for Hanukkah with her grandson—Alex and Brad's four-year-old son—and had wondered why neither parent responded to text messages she'd sent the previous day and that morning. She learned the terrible news from her older brother, thirty-four-year-old Jonathon, who'd been told by their aunt, Honey's sister, Mary Shechtman.

A shaken Alex called their sister Kaelen and asked her to come to her house in Forest Hill. Meanwhile, Jonathon informed their sister, Lauren.

Lauren, forty-three, the oldest and unmarried, lived in Whistler, BC, but was on vacation with her son in Mexico. She made plans to return immediately. Kaelen, the youngest at twenty-eight, was in Toronto and headed over to Alex's home. Jonathon had been in Japan with his husband, Fred, the previous week. When he'd called Alex about their parents, he told her that he'd just arrived that Friday morning at his cottage, about two-and-a-half hours northeast of Toronto. He said he would head back to Toronto. By the early evening, the three siblings had converged at Alex and Brad's home, joining other family members and friends.

In the midst of the hubbub, longtime friends of the Sherman couple who were in attendance had quiet discussions about how the four siblings would deal with the sudden reality that they each had an equal share of their father's fortune, estimated at roughly $4.7 billion. From conversations the Sherman friends had had with Barry and Honey over the years, they believed that none of the Sherman children were particularly good with money, though Alex had inherited their father's dislike of ostentation and was intent on following her own distinct track in life, as separate as possible from the Sherman fortune.

The day their parents' bodies were discovered, Kaelen had been busy arranging an expensive "destination" wedding in Mexico for the following spring. She had met a young man on an online dating site two years earlier and they had grown very close. Kaelen called the young electrician—now working at Apotex courtesy of Barry Sherman—her "knight in shining armour." Money was rarely withheld by Barry when the children put in their requests, which they did often. All four children were already living extremely comfortable lives, courtesy of their father's generosity; their mother did not agree with Barry's lavish approach towards their children. She believed it was the wrong way to raise children and secondly, she had observed over the years that Barry bestowed riches on their children and did not do the same with her. Of late, Barry was changing his approach to at least one member of their family: he told Kaelen to have repairs done on her existing car rather than buy a new one. People close to Kaelen say that Barry was displeased with a skyrocketing credit card bill his youngest had accumulated.

Friends of the Sherman couple say Lauren and Jonathon, the oldest two, had received tens of millions of dollars from Barry at an early age to invest in real estate and businesses. Lauren devoted some of her money to a children's party event planning company but in recent years describes herself online as "an advocate of mental, physical and spiritual health" and provides yoga instruction in a small studio in her home; she also offers counselling to people suffering from trauma, depression and other mental health issues. Jonathon had been involved in several businesses and was now running a self-storage firm, apparently financed by Barry. He lived with his husband on a wooded country estate north of Toronto and, according to a family member, had a gun collection which he used for target practice, and was known as someone with much more expensive tastes than his notoriously penny-pinching father. Barry drove an old car and flew economy; Jonathon drove a Tesla and flew first class. In contrast, Alex and Kaelen had received more modest financial contributions from Barry when they turned twenty-one, plus help purchasing homes, cottages, and condominiums. Kaelen, through a series of companies headquartered at Apotex, purchased several residential properties in

Toronto (each cost between $2 million and $4 million), which she rents out to tenants. Sherman friends say Barry supported Kaelen financially in this venture as a way to provide her income she could consider her own. Following university, Alex had travelled to Canada's north to work with Indigenous people and then settled on a career as a nurse at a shelter for the homeless in Toronto. Though she and her husband had a nice house, they were not conspicuous consumers. Both drove a Toyota hybrid vehicle and tried to maintain a modest lifestyle.

It was to Alex that the family looked for strength that Friday, when news of the deaths reached them. In a time of crisis, it would have been more usual to gather at the Old Colony Road home, but that was now a crime scene, though what the crime was remained a mystery. At Alex's house, visitors looking for distraction were happy to hold the new baby or play with the toddler, who ran around oblivious to the unfolding drama. There was discussion, which intensified each hour that weekend, over what exactly had happened. In the first few hours, with so few details available, some theorized that somehow the Sherman couple had been accidentally electrocuted near their pool. But as more details reached the family from people who had seen the bodies that morning, the conversation turned to murder, and who had done it. People's suspicions about who had done it ranged from the Sherman cousins, angry at having lost a major lawsuit against their former benefactor, to Barry's friend Frank D'Angelo, the latter theory being that D'Angelo and Barry Sherman had become involved with underworld people and that Barry and Honey were killed as retribution. Both theories were hotly denied in the months to come from the cousins and D'Angelo. Mourners who arrived bringing condolences and food found solace in Alex, but not in Jonathon, at least not immediately. When Jonathon and his husband Fred arrived shortly after

5 P.M., Jonathon hugged people who were waiting outside, then walked into his sister's house and threw himself on the floor, crying, "Oh my God, oh my God." He remained sitting on the floor and called out, "I need a drink," say people standing nearby. A bottle of Scotch was produced. Later, Sherman friends, including Bryna Steiner, who had arrived with her husband, Fred, say Jonathon leaned against her, crying on her shoulder. Others recall that Jonathon was completely composed later in the evening. His sister, Alex, sat on the couch with her new baby, saying little for long stretches of the evening. It was clear to other mourners that, as is often the case, people grieve and deal with shock in completely different ways.

Among the mourners was Jack Kay, one of Barry Sherman's closest friends and the man who had helped him build Apotex. Kay, who would for a time take over Apotex following Sherman's death, had been with his wife in New York for the previous two days and had just returned to Toronto in the early evening after receiving a panicked call from Alex. Had Kay been in Toronto on Thursday, he would have noticed Sherman's absence from the office suite they shared and most likely would have gone looking for his friend.

Not all close members of the Sherman family could be there that Friday afternoon and evening. Barry's sister, Sandra Florence, and her husband, Mike, were at their winter home in Palm Desert, California. On hearing the news, they had rushed to get a flight back on Friday but could not get on a plane until the following day. Honey's sister, Mary, who had been at her winter condo in Florida, arranged a private jet and flew home early Friday evening. When a car dropped her off at Alex's home, she came in and announced her presence by yelling and crying. At one point, Mary walked up to Bryna Steiner, Honey's oldest and dearest friend, and screamed at her, not stopping until others told her to calm down. Not normally a drinker, Mary had downed several alcoholic drinks while en route from Florida to calm her nerves, and mourners whispered to each other that she was drunk. Other than Barry, no family member was closer to Honey than Mary. Honey had looked after her when they were growing up and protected her from the wrath of their stern and unpredictable mother. Honey and Barry had financially assisted Mary and her husband, Allen, according to Sherman insiders, investing in a retail jewellery business that subsequently went bankrupt, owing Sherman and other creditors roughly $40 million; and helping the couple purchase a series of residential properties in Toronto, which Mary rented out to tenants, providing a steady source of revenue. (Mary disputed this in a July 2019 email to me in which she maintained that she invested in real estate "using my money and getting mortgages from the bank." As well, she wrote, "I also helped Honey & Barry clean up real estate "messes" created by others so Barry would not lose money. He ended up pocketing hundreds of thousands of dollars/millions, from losses he would have otherwise had. Nothing between Honey, Barry and myself was ever formal or written down. We just all contributed what we could when we could.")

That night Mary made a claim to anyone who would listen that Honey had promised her a gift of $300 million. It was one of a series of odd statements that family members made during this understandably confusing time. Kaelen was heard to say that she was finally going to purchase the new car she wanted because her father had recently given her the okay and "that is what he wanted me to do." Kaelen ordered a new Infiniti QX60 sedan within a week. And when she arrived the next day, daughter Lauren reportedly commented, "Well, if it had to happen, it was not the worst time in their lives to be murdered—they had finally gotten to know my son." Among the friends who showed up to give support in those terrible first few hours were Kaelen's fiancé and his parents. Their family had been getting to know the Shermans in advance of the spring wedding and had been expecting Barry and Honey in two days at a Sunday Hanukkah brunch at their home north of Toronto. Just a few days before, Honey had texted the fiancé's mother to ask, "what's the dress code?" Casual, Honey was told.

At about 8 P.M., a detective from the Toronto homicide squad arrived. He asked to speak to family, and they gathered around him in a room at the back of the house. Three siblings, Alex, Jonathon, and Kaelen, and Honey's sister, Mary, and Jack Kay followed the detective into the room. Mary turned around and screamed at Kay, "He said just family!" Kay, who had worked alongside Barry Sherman since the early 1980s and had a brotherly connection with the Apotex founder, was taken aback. He withdrew from the room.

The detective spoke briefly. He said he could confirm that two bodies had been found in the Old Colony Road home and that they were investigating the deaths. He said he could not tell them more at this time. Asked why he was so late in coming to speak to them, the detective, according to a family member, said that he had received the call earlier in the day but had to pick up his children from daycare and feed them before driving to Alex and Brad's house. That admission struck family members as an indication that the police did not consider this a high priority case.

Alex, who witnessed Mary's antics with both Bryna Steiner and Jack Kay, and heard her claim about a $300-million promise from Honey, told Mary that if she was going to stay, she would have to refrain from any outbursts as it was too upsetting, particularly with young children around. It was the beginning of a major rift in the family that would deepen over the next weeks and months. Mary was later disinvited from her niece Kaelen's wedding and cut off from the Sherman family fortune.

The histrionics of Mary aside, what dominated the discussion among the Shermans and their friends that Friday evening were the comments they heard police make to TV cameras outside the Sherman home. While it would be hours before the bombshell newspaper reports that boldly suggested murder-suicide, there was enough in the early police comments—no forced entry, no search for suspects—to outrage the people following developments on social media, television and radio. Those who knew the Shermans well found the "no forced entry" comments particularly odd. Honey always left her side door unlocked. And as Barry's friend Joel Ulster put it, "the 'no forced entry' comment is just ridiculous. How do you get in Barry and Honey's home? You just knock on the door and they let you in, that is the kind of people they were. Nice, welcoming people." The Sherman children, particularly Alex, wanted answers but did not know where to begin. That feeling intensified when, late on Friday evening, Alex received a call from a relative of the late Rochelle Wise. Wise and her husband, David Pichosky, were a Toronto Jewish couple who had been murdered in Florida in 2013, and the case remained unsolved. The relative of Rochelle Wise knew Alex and wanted to deliver a simple message: hire a private detective. Wise's family had become frustrated with the efforts of the Florida police and had hired a private investigator, who had been helpful, though charges had never been laid. Alex was told the Sherman family needed to do the same to have any hope of solving the crime.

Putting pressure on the police might also help, it was suggested. Alex called Senator Linda Frum, a family friend, and implored her to help persuade the police that the theory of murder-suicide was preposterous. Frum, through her network of contacts, made the situation known to the chairman of the Toronto Police Services Board, which provides oversight on police activities. Mayor John Tory, a friend of the Shermans, was also contacted, and he later received public criticism for weighing in.

Saturday morning, the story in the *Toronto Sun* went off like a bomb in places where people gathered to mourn the Shermans, particularly at Alex and Brad's home. In the air, approaching Toronto on a flight from Florida, was Harry Radomski, a veteran litigator who had been at the forefront of Barry Sherman's patent battles. Beside him was Karen Simpson, his wife. Radomski had come in from the golf course on Friday at 12:30 P.M. and received a call from Jack Kay telling him their good friends were dead. By mid-morning Saturday he was at Apotex, meeting Kay and other senior company officials to figure out how to deal with the pressing business of running a complex company whose commander-in-chief was suddenly gone. Radomski's phone rang. It was Alex. "What do we do?" she asked. "How do we deal with this?" she said, referring to the murder-suicide theory. Radomski is a civil litigator, and he knew the situation called for someone experienced in criminal law, someone who would know how to deal with police and, if necessary, hire private investigators. "I think we should call Brian Greenspan," Radomski told Alex. Greenspan, one of Canada's top criminal lawyers, had once assisted Radomski and Sherman in one of Apotex's pharmaceutical battles. Within the hour, Greenspan was retained by the estates of Barry and Honey Sherman.

One of Greenspan's first actions was to make contact with the coroner's office to ensure that the Sherman bodies, once the official post-mortems were done, would remain on site at the complex. He wanted a second set of autopsies. Then, at 4

P.M. on Saturday, and with the help of Greenspan and the public relations department at Apotex, the four Sherman children released a statement to the media.

> Our parents shared an enthusiasm for life and commitment to their family and community totally inconsistent with the rumours regrettably circulated in the media as to the circumstances surrounding their deaths. We are shocked and think it's irresponsible that police sources have reportedly advised the media of a theory which neither their family, their friends nor their colleagues believe to be true. We urge the Toronto Police Service to conduct a thorough, intensive and objective criminal investigation, and urge the media to refrain from further reporting as to the cause of these tragic deaths until the investigation is completed.

Retired doctor and former deputy chief coroner Dr. Jim Cairns was sitting on his couch Sunday morning looking at his bike, which was nestled softly on a special mount attached to the wall in the front foyer. He and his wife, also a retired doctor, lived in Orangeville, a seventy-five-minute drive northwest of the big city, and since leaving government service, Cairns avoided downtown Toronto as much as possible. The bike he was staring at was a retirement present to himself, a Colnago racing bike with a retail value of $20,000 (Cairns was able to get it wholesale).

Lean, with a shock of snow-white hair and a mischievous glint in his eye that could turn steely, the retired Cairns was bored. Not many years ago, he'd had his fingers in all the big crime cases in Toronto and beyond. The previous morning, he had read the Saturday newspapers and cast a keen eye over the story on the apparent murder-suicide of the Apotex billionaire and his wife. Exactly the sort of case he loved being involved in when he was on the job.

"There is no possible way this could be a murder-suicide," Cairns said to his wife, Jenny.

"Relax, Jim," she said. "You're retired."

Cairns looked at the newspaper again and shook his head. Ten years retired, he still wondered on a daily basis what his next act would be, other than hundred-kilometre cycling trips. Snow was falling—more heavily here, north of the city—and it would be months before the native of Ireland, transported to Canada as a young man, could hope to be out on those two wheels. His cell phone rang. Cairns did not recognize the number.

"Jim?" the voice said. "Tom Klatt."

Cairns remembered him. He had known Klatt when the gruff-sounding detective was a member of the Toronto Police homicide squad. Now he was working as a private investigator, a common gig for retired detectives. Klatt explained that Toronto lawyer Brian Greenspan had been hired by the Sherman children to put a team together to conduct a sort of shadow investigation. The children wanted to disprove the murder-suicide theory. With the official autopsy complete, Greenspan and Klatt wanted Cairns to join the team, not on a full-time basis, but for one job: to locate the best possible forensic pathologist to conduct a second set of post-mortems. They had no access to the detailed results of the first autopsies, but, as representatives of the Sherman family, they were entitled to examine the bodies once they had been released for burial. Given that a funeral was being arranged in the next few days, and with knowledge of sensitivities in the Jewish faith regarding a quick burial, Klatt said they would have to act fast.

Greenspan, a veteran lawyer who had a string of high-profile cases on his resumé, would hire additional retired detectives to work on the team. Money was no object. Cairns was told that the Sherman children, heirs to literally billions of Apotex dollars, wanted answers.

Cairns hung up the phone and looked at Jenny, who just shook her head. The retired deputy chief coroner was back on the job. He began making calls. Greenspan and Klatt were concerned that an Ontario pathologist, even if he or she did not work for the government, would feel that the job put them in a conflict of interest and would not want to butt heads with Ontario's current chief forensic pathologist, Michael Pollanen. Cairns's network of contacts included pathologists around the world, and a US pathologist would be a good choice. The first pathologist he turned to was Dr. Mary Case, the chief medical examiner for St. Louis County, Missouri, who was also a professor of pathology at Saint Louis University. He reached Case on Monday morning, and as Cairns would later describe it, her voice was "buzzing" with excitement.

"Jim, I was about to call you," Cairns recalls her saying. "You don't realize it, but this case from Toronto is the big talk among the profession here in the United States. If this is a murder-suicide by hanging, it will be the first one recorded in history."

Case told Cairns she would have liked to do the second postmortems but could not undertake the job for several weeks. Due to the upcoming holidays, there was just no way she could get away to Toronto. She gave Cairns the names of three other US pathologists. He called each one. They declined, because of the holidays and because they were worried they were not licensed to perform an autopsy in Canada. Cairns called Klatt and said he wanted to call Ontario's former chief forensic pathologist Dr. David Chiasson. Cairns knew him well. Klatt agreed.

Unlike Cairns, Chiasson was still working. Though he had retired from government service, he was now a senior forensic pathologist at Toronto's Hospital for Sick Children and a professor of pathology at the University of Toronto. Cairns reached Chiasson between clinics he was giving on Monday afternoon, explained the situation, and asked the pathologist to take on the job. Chiasson thought about it on his train ride home at the end of the day, then called Cairns Tuesday morning to accept. Arrangements were made for him to do both post-mortems the next day, Wednesday, December 20. Chiasson contacted Michael Pickup, the first pathologist, who agreed to attend and answer any questions Chiasson might have. Klatt and Chiasson informed the Toronto Police that they would be performing second autopsies and told the detectives they were welcome to attend. The police declined the offer.

FOUR

FINDING HONEY

HONEY REICH WAS NOT OUT OF BED YET. It was almost noon, but Bryna Fishman was not surprised. She adored everything about her friend: her gutsy up-for-anything attitude, her laughter, the smile that warmed cold rooms, the way she always took an interest in Bryna's life. But Honey's tardiness was sometimes too much to take. For that reason, when they were heading out for an afternoon or evening adventure, Bryna would set a time and she would pick up Honey, not the other way around. She felt that was the lesser of two evils; better to get to Honey's house and get her going rather than waiting at home for her to eventually show up. On this particular day, in the summer of 1967, Bryna had arrived at the Reich house in the Toronto neighbourhood of Bathurst Manor at the prearranged time and learned from Honey's mother that her oldest daughter was still in bed. "I'm getting up," Honey called downstairs from her bedroom. A few minutes later, Honey appeared and performed her "morning" ritual. Boil the kettle. Make a cup of tea. Slowly, carefully, swirl the tea bag on its string, dipping it in and out of the hot water. Then, taking two Turtles chocolates out of a box she kept on the counter, she would dunk the Turtles in and out of the tea before slowly eating the softened caramel-pecan-and-chocolate treat. Only after that was she ready to go back upstairs and get dressed so that the two nineteen-year-old girls could head out on the town, enjoy the weather, and make plans for the future. Both were studying psychology at the University of Toronto and hoped to follow that up with teachers' college.

Anna Reich, known to everyone as Honey, was born in 1947 in a displaced persons, or DP, camp in Austria. These camps were set up after the Second World War to provide temporary housing for survivors of the Holocaust. Her parents, Naftuli and Helen, had been freed by Allied forces from a Nazi work camp in Poland. They were among the thousands who lived in one of these settlements overseen by the US Army, the United Nations Relief and Rehabilitation Administration, and the Central Committee of Liberated Jews. The Reichs then emigrated to Canada with the help of a Jewish agency and set up home in Toronto, where Mary, Honey's younger sister, was born. The Reichs opened a mom-and-pop shoe store in Toronto's west end near the intersection of Keele and Dundas Streets. Reich Shoes gave the family a comfortable, but far from wealthy, existence. The Bathurst Manor area, ten kilometres north of Keele and Dundas, in North York, was and still is a predominantly Jewish neighbourhood. First developed in the 1950s, it became home to many displaced families from Europe who hoped for a better life in Canada. As Mary would recall years later at her sister's funeral, the family did not have a lot of money and so they let out parts of their home to boarders, as Sara Sherman did after Barry's father died.

"Our parents bought a house and rented out every square inch of it," Mary told mourners. "Our house, there was a front room with a piano in it—we didn't realize it was really a hall. Then there was a kitchen like people have kitchens, and then there was our bedroom, but we didn't know it was a hallway with two fold-up cots."

Bryna first met Honey on campus at the University of Toronto, and they were friends from then on. Their exploits started with Honey getting an idea and then coaxing Bryna to go along for the ride. On a trip to New York in the late 1960s, Honey and Bryna found themselves in the lobby of their hotel, two attractive young women, with long dark hair, wearing relatively short skirts. Several young men approached Honey.

"You two ladies want to go to a party?"

Bryna turned away. "Honey. We are not going. We don't know who these guys are. We could wind up dead."

Honey smiled at the men and grabbed Bryna's arm. "We're going!"

"I'm not going," Bryna said. Honey tugged on Bryna's arm again. "Yes you are." Fifty years later, in the condominium where she lives with her husband, Fred, Bryna Steiner smiles at the memory. "Honey was fearless. I loved her for it. We went, and lived to tell the tale. In a million years, if I was on my own, I would not have gone. She was not afraid of anything. They could be mass murderers and she would have gone."

On a trip to Chicago together, where they stayed with Bryna's aunt and uncle, they went on a restaurant dinner date with two young men arranged by an American cousin.

"Do you live in igloos up there in Canada?" one of the men asked.

Honey gave Bryna a sideways look and muttered quietly, "Is this what we're stuck with?"

Honey started speaking French, and Bryna took the cue and joined in. Neither knew more than a few words of French, which had just become Canada's second official language, so they made most of their dialogue up. The dinner ended early, and Honey and Bryna laughed all the way back to the aunt and uncle's house. There would be other trips in the near future, and one in particular, a winter trip to Florida, would change the course of Bryna's life.

When they finished their undergraduate studies at university, the two young women enrolled in teachers' college. Both wanted to teach in the public school system at the elementary level. Conforming to the stereotype, Honey's mother kept telling her to "marry a nice doctor," but Honey wanted to teach and was in no hurry to settle down. Three days into their course, Honey Reich announced that she was dropping out. "They are talking to us like we're five-year-olds," she told Bryna. She suggested they enroll in another form of teachers' college available at the time. They switched to the Ontario College of Education at the University of Toronto, completed their studies, and began working at separate Toronto schools.

Bryna taught for only one year, because she moved to Detroit and her credentials were not accepted there. Honey taught Grade 5 for five years at a school in Etobicoke, a borough immediately to the west of Toronto. Bryna Fishman and Honey Reich's friendship continued to grow and would flourish over the decades to come, even at times when they were not living in the same city.

In the late 1960s, when Honey was completing her teacher's training, she wanted to keep busy in the summer. She always wanted to be on the go, according to Bryna, once she was out of bed, and was interested in new challenges. That saw her registering as a candystriper, or volunteer, at Toronto's Mount Sinai

Hospital. There, she met a nurse named Cindy Ulster, and the two struck up a friendship. Cindy was the wife of Joel Ulster, a Toronto man who had just purchased a generic pharmaceutical company called Empire Laboratories with his best friend, Barry Sherman. Cindy Ulster would soon make a very important introduction.

The media stories immediately after Honey's death spoke of her philanthropy, but only in generalities. People who were actually not that close to her personally commented on her tireless work for Jewish causes. There were few specifics, however, and few stories that allowed readers much more than a passing understanding of her character. Many who knew her were understandably reticent due to the police investigation and a fear that what was said about her might somehow affect the outcome of the probe. In my discussions with people, in trying to get them to talk about Honey, I would often use the example of the Kennedy family in the United States. People spoke openly about the wealthy Kennedys, a family that suffered more tragedy than most, I said, so why not talk about the Shermans?

Fred Waks, a businessman who has a prominent role in fundraising in the Jewish community, spoke at the Sherman funeral. When I later approached him for an interview, he was reluctant at first, but after receiving the blessing of the Sherman children, Waks emailed me explaining why he would speak. "I hope to shed some light on a couple who my wife and I were fortunate to be very close with," he wrote. "I've declined many interviews but I'm really tired of reading commentary from people I know did not understand the Shermans or were only acquaintances."

Our chat was arranged for a Monday morning in the spring, four months after the Shermans died. The night before our interview, Waks's assistant cancelled it. When I tried to reschedule, Waks's clipped response was "Sorry, will not be rescheduling." I pursued the issue, and Waks told me, "It's actually my family" who believed that he "shouldn't, after considerable deliberation." Waks then sent a package to my office that included two copies of *The Canadian Jewish News*, one a special edition published after the Shermans' deaths, highlighting their generosity, the other a two-year-old issue almost entirely devoted to Fred Waks.

Waks was not the only one reluctant to speak. The then Ontario health minister, Eric Hoskins, who was the first to announce the Sherman deaths on social media, had indicated he would speak to me, but then cancelled, saying it was a "personal decision" he made not to give any interviews on the subject. Rachel Nisker, a friend of Honey Sherman who played mah-jong and golf with her, said she had been horrified by the "public defamation" the Shermans received in the early days of the police investigation. "I think the world should know how great they are," she told me. But when it came to sitting down for an interview, Nisker said she couldn't do it: "My head and my heart are at odds . . . I really don't have a comfort level with it." Again, no real explanation for not speaking.

It was Canadian Conservative senator Linda Frum, a friend of the Shermans, who first provided me with a detailed interview. Then Frum and my own friend Bonnie Druxerman convinced two ladies known as the "golf girls" to speak to me. They were among Honey's closest friends, and all of a sudden the stories and laughs and keen insights tumbled out. After ultimately spending many hours speaking to numerous confidants, including Honey's best girlfriend, Bryna Steiner (formerly Fishman), I have decided the initial reluctance of some to speak was born out of a fear that, by talking about Honey Sherman in detail, the truth would come out: that she was a very real and quite normal person, a billionaire who kept a cheap cooked chicken from Loblaws and a Costco jar of Moishes pickles in the refrigerator to snack on; a mother who had difficult relationships with her children; a golfer who would bang her club when she had a bad shot; and a friend to many who, despite her incredible network and tireless efforts in the charitable world and her own generosity to her friends, was always worried she would be left out. "Please include me," she would say.

The decade-old Lexus SUV headed south on Interstate 79. Honey Sherman, feet in sandals because they were less painful than shoes, had the pedal to the floor. Which was surprising to her friends Dahlia Solomon, in the passenger seat, and Anita Franklin, in the back seat with three sets of golf clubs and Sherman's giant suitcase pressed against her. Wedged between the seats was a large green box of Nature Valley granola bars. Whether in Toronto or on the road, Sherman always travelled with a box in the car, to munch on when she was driving and to hand out to people begging at stoplights. It was surprising how fast she was driving that day, because not far back they had been stopped by a state trooper and given a speeding ticket. Sherman was still chuckling over that episode. The trooper was very short. There was some debate in the car over his precise dimensions, but it was generally agreed he barely topped five feet, and it was comical to see him staring up at them through the open window. This was not Sherman's first speeding ticket, and it was not their first golf trip.

"Are we going to stop?" Solomon asked.

"No," said Sherman, smiling.

Franklin stayed silent. She knew better than to get involved. The destination was Kiawah Island Golf Resort, in South

Carolina, just south of Charleston. Home to some of America's top public golf courses, with dramatic views of the coastline. It's an island separated from the mainland by the Kiawah River, and inland are meandering lagoons and salt marshlands. Bald eagles soar above, bobcats roam the wetlands, and, offshore, dolphins play. On some holes, golfers have to be careful not to drive the ball into the giant water hazard: the Atlantic Ocean. Door to door from Toronto to Kiawah, it is eighteen hours of straight driving. Franklin does not drive on the highway. That left Sherman and Solomon to share the task, with Sherman insisting on doing most of it.

The three women met when their kids were little. Franklin had actually known Sherman when they were both at the University of Toronto, but Franklin found her too loud and their friendship did not click. It was not until they found each other again in the late 1970s that they became close. Sherman, Solomon, and Franklin each had at least one child of roughly the same age, and the carpooling needs of a busy schedule drew them together, either driving to Hebrew school or to after-school sports, dance, or musical activities. When the kids were still small, they all travelled as families together, taking ski trips and visits to Florida and going to the beach in the summer. Once the children were adults, Sherman, Solomon, and Franklin began taking golf trips on their own, often two or three a year. This November trip to Kiawah would be their last trip as a threesome; they returned to Toronto just over a month before the Shermans died.

There was a chance Sherman might have to leave her friends early, as Honey and Barry's daughter Alex was expecting her second child any day. Sherman said they would be fine; the baby was not due until several days after their planned return. If they received word the baby was coming earlier, Sherman would fly back from Charleston and Solomon would drive back with Franklin. Their relaxed conversation about that issue and many more was typical for three good friends on a road trip. The Shermans were millionaires when the three ladies met, then became billionaires. But Solomon and Franklin said you would never know it, the way Honey acted. "She was just a regular girl," Franklin says.

The trip began on November 5, 2017. Sherman picked each of them up before 9 A.M., remarkably early, given her track record. Her SUV had recently received extensive repairs. While driving back from a trip north of Toronto a few months before—Honey at the wheel, Barry in the passenger seat—they hit a deer. Many of their friends, including Bryna and Fred Steiner, suggested that Honey get a new vehicle. She did a *lot* of driving, and after all, she could afford whatever type of car she wanted. As she often did, Honey delegated the trip to the repair shop to Allen Shechtman, her sister's husband. After Honey paid the $5,000 repair bill, she proudly showed the Lexus off to her friends. "Good as new," she told the golf girls. As they always did on a trip, each woman put $200 in a kitty for incidentals like lunch and coffee on the drive down. Sherman driving, they headed south, through Buffalo and on to South Carolina. Sherman did not like to stop, and if they did, it wasn't for long. Conversation included their children, their husbands, their next trip to Pebble Beach, previous trips, including a golf expedition to Ireland, and a deep discussion of trade issues between Canada and the United States. When any issue was broached by her friends, Honey would drill down on the subject, asking questions about the topic and what her trip mates thought of the issue. Music was rarely played; it just got in the way of the conversation among the three friends, who referred to themselves as Thelma, Thelma, and Louise, a nod to the road trip movie *Thelma and Louise*. They checked out one discount mall on the way, tried on a few shirts, and each bought something, because, they all agreed, this was what you did on a road trip when you passed a mall.

"We were brutally honest with each other," Franklin notes. Sherman had a habit of insisting her girlfriends buy clothes one size too small, and she did the same. On one of their shopping trips, there was a fierce discussion.

"It fits!" Sherman said.

"It doesn't fit," Solomon said.

Sherman walked over and tugged at the fabric of the shirt Solomon had put on. "It fits."

Sherman then selected a pair of pants and tried them on.

"Honey, it's up your ass," Franklin said.

The three women roared with laughter. Sherman bought the pants. A billionaire with drawers full of brand new, never-used designer wallets at home, Sherman paid with cash from the oversized wallet she always carried: battered, brimming with receipts and notes, and held together by a thick rubber band.

Back on the road, Franklin mentioned, inadvertently, a restaurant many kilometres ahead on the route that promised great sandwiches, and Sherman made sure they found it. "Inadvertently," because on previous trips they had learned not to fuel their friend's single-minded desire to seek out something new, especially a particular fast food place. A battered and fried "blooming onion" was one unhealthy treat they had tried, unsuccessfully, to avoid years before. This time, it was a sandwich joint that Sherman was set on. Four hours later she pulled to a stop at the restaurant, and while Franklin and Solomon were getting out and stretching, Sherman was already in the lineup.

"Hello!" she said to the order taker. Her voice boomed around the small restaurant, a little raspy from her throat operation due to cancer, but still the loudest in the diner. "What do they order here the most?" The clerk mumbled something about a large sandwich that was popular. "We'll take one. And onion rings."

By the time Solomon and Franklin walked in, the order was well on the way to being made. It arrived with three drinks and a large plate of onion rings. As always, Sherman had her go-to drink: Diet Coke, with a little ice and a wedge of lemon. And they were on the road again.

An email Sherman sent to her friends a month before the November golf trip reveals that she was, as always, the trip planner. As her friends said, the Shermans could probably have purchased the whole Kiawah Island resort, but when Honey travelled with her girlfriends, in fact when she did most things, even for charity and business, she was economical. Once, when boarding a flight, Barry and Honey walked past some Apotex executives sitting in first class. The Shermans, on their way to the economy section, went by with a smile. "I hope I can fly first class one day," Honey joked. (They did fly first class, but usually only on overseas flights.) Her email to Franklin and Solomon before their November trip laid out in detail, virtually all in lower case, what she'd planned: "all is done—can cancel up to 1 week out—so that means this coming Monday October 30—total cost for the 3 of us including the golf (and accommodations) is $4,035 US. we r not staying at the hotel—it was far more expensive—we have a lovely 3 bedroom, 3 bath villa overlooking the ocean with a balcony—recently refurbished—full kitchen so we can grab a breakfast & a snack &/or lunch."

Sherman's email sets out her plans for golf each day, plus dinners, with each paying her own way. Yes, her friends thought some of Sherman's behaviour—ordering food for them before they sat down, for example—was a bit control-ling, but over the years they had come to accept that this was just the way Honey Sherman was, and they loved her.

They drove through rain, sleet, and snow on the northern part of the journey. November was rutting season, and they saw a lot of dead deer on the highway, particularly when the road travelled through heavily treed areas. Sherman drove very fast despite having recently struck and killed a deer and having just received a speeding ticket from a state trooper. Solomon was "shit scared" they were going to have an accident. Another of Sherman's habits was to play "gas roulette," seeing how long she could go after the gas gauge showed empty. At 3 A.M., just shy of their final destination, Sherman took an off ramp and pulled into a gas station to fill up before they entered the resort. Solomon emerged from the passenger seat to stretch her legs and looked at Sherman and Franklin.

"Thelma and Thelma?" she said to them. "Next time we do this, Louise isn't coming. I will meet you by plane."

They checked into their villa and, as was their practice, drew straws. Sherman, and it always seemed to happen this way, ended up with the lesser of the three rooms and settled in hap-pily. Despite having managed to get going relatively early on day one of the trip, Sherman had not completely lost her teen-age habit of sleeping in, and Franklin and Solomon knew they would be in charge of waking her up at 8 A.M. They would get up earlier and have breakfast and coffee, then one of them would go into Sherman's room to rouse her. Sherman just poured a cup of coffee into a travel cup, grabbed a yogurt, and they would head out with their clubs for eighteen holes. At home, the three played at Oakdale Golf and Country Club, and they were per-petually trying to get better scores. Breaking a hundred was the target, although all three had surpassed that years before, after a road trip to the Peek'n Peak resort, in New York State, where they hit thousands of balls with a pro.

On this trip they stuck to Sherman's schedule, golfing each day and dining together at night. Sherman played each day despite her considerable physical ailments. In the preceding decade, she had pushed through throat cancer, two hip replacements, a shoulder replacement, perpetually sore feet, and severe rheumatoid arthritis that, of late, was causing painful nodules to appear near her finger and toe joints. Her friends called her "the bionic woman," because there was so much titanium in her body and because of her incredible stamina and strength. After her cancer diagnosis in 2015, Honey drove herself to radiation appointments at the hospital. What amazed her friends during golf games was that their billionaire friend would at various points wander off into the brush or a shallow gully, pull out a plastic grocery bag, and begin collecting golf balls lost by other golfers. This despite having hundreds of brand new golf balls in her Toronto home and Florida condominium. At times, when Honey struggled to pull herself out of a gully with a bag of balls, her friends would have to give her a hand. They were used to helping her and happy to do it. On this trip as for all others, Sherman had packed too much, and due to their friend's infirmities, Franklin and Solomon helped carry her luggage.

"She brought fifty pairs of shoes. I am not kidding you. We told her, never again!" Solomon recalls, laughing. Adding to the weight on previous trips was the hoard of newspapers Sherman had been amassing, sections she had not had a chance to read due to her busy schedule. Her friends had recently cured her of that habit, saying it was simply too much to carry.

There was still plenty of evidence Honey had an insatiable appetite for information and in place of the papers on this trip she talked, listened, and asked questions.

Each night at Kiawah, the three women sat on their balcony and giggled and chatted. No alcohol. Each had a couple of Diet Cokes and ice.

"We never ran out of things to talk about," Franklin says.

Their final day of golf was Friday, November 10. The plan was to put in a full round of golf, then head home. Sherman loved to golf and was frustrated she was not improving. She saw every opportunity to golf as a chance to have a better outing.

"She was a nice golfer," Franklin recalls. "She has limited motion, so all of her balls were straight. She never went sideways."

Water features were her undoing.

Scene: A Kiawah golf course. Sherman hits a ball up and into the pond. Solomon and Franklin have just hit their balls cleanly, landing them on the fairway on the other side.

"Goddammit," Sherman says, hitting another, and another. "You girls are better golfers than I am." Then another shot, and the ball is over.

"Good shot, Honey," Solomon calls.

"I'll tell you when it's a good shot," Sherman grumbles, before adding one of her favourite lines. "Even a blind squirrel can find a nut."

Further on up the course, and the three women have been joined by another golfer to make a foursome, a "nice man" who has been drinking perhaps a bit too much vodka. Franklin believes he had "a quart" in him by the time he hit his first ball. Solomon, to be polite, is chatting with him, and her voice, as booming as Sherman's, can be heard metres away while Sherman is trying to concentrate on her putt.

"I can't stand that goddamn Dahlia," Sherman says, doing her best to keep a smile off her face. She makes the short putt. In friendly golf, a "gimme" is a putt that is so close to the hole that a golfer just picks the ball up under the assumption that nobody misses a two-inch putt. Not Sherman. It slows the game, but she insists on taking every shot.

The round over, a quick bite, and Sherman got behind the wheel of her Lexus and pointed the car north, back to Toronto and the cold of the coming winter. Solomon and Franklin had changed into warm clothes. Sherman stayed in her golf skort and had slipped on some sandals. They talked non-stop for the first few hours. Solomon recalls how Honey always had a story. If she had been to hear someone give a talk in the previous few months, she would recount what he or she had said. Or she'd give them vignettes from trips. She and Barry had met the Pope on a visit to Italy. She told them that story, adding in details of a unique bridge she saw on the trip. Or she would talk about art, Banksy and Basquiat. Never about money, or where she stayed, or what she purchased. Franklin recalls, "I would always write to Honey after a visit and say, 'It was such a pleasure talking to you. I always learn something.'"

They arrived home at 5 A.M. Solomon had driven the last five hours with her two trip mates fast asleep. Before all conversation in the car stopped at midnight, they'd discussed plans for the next trip.

Sitting in her living room beside Franklin six months after the Shermans died, Solomon recalls a Yiddish saying: "*Mann tracht und Gott lacht.*" Translation: "Man plans and God laughs."

FIVE

THE FIRST 48

THE SECURITY CONTROL ROOM AT Apotex headquarters in Toronto was a repurposed closet—long, narrow, and windowless. Five surveillance monitors were attached to a white cinderblock wall, with cables feeding into the main computer. The view on the monitors changed frequently, recording on a computer hard drive movements in hallways, rooms where scientific studies were being carried out, the manufacturing section, where millions of doses of various drugs were made, and the executive suite from which Barry Sherman, Jack Kay, and others ran the multi-billion-dollar business. It's a thirteen-building complex. Outdoors, cameras were trained on the parking lots and the streets around Apotex.

Andrew Dawson's job was to watch all the monitors in the control room and look for anything odd or unusual. Dawson was a part-time security guard working his way through university, with plans for a big career in computer science. He and other shift security workers were also under instruction to conduct hourly "wellness checks" whenever a senior executive was working late in the evening or on the weekend, dropping by the executive's office and saying a quick hello. That was usually either Sherman on the first floor or the company president, Jeremy Desai, on the second.

Security is important in the drug manufacturing field. There are always concerns about theft of intellectual property and the theft of products that would yield a high price on the street. At any given time, for example, Apotex has storage drums filled with $1.3-billion worth of active pharmaceutical ingredients to make painkillers—hydromorphone and other opioids—locked behind concrete-and-steel walls more than half a metre thick in the highest-security facility of its kind in Canada. The door to the main storage facility weighs 4,500 kilograms and has a fingerprint lock that only two people can open. There are also concerns of a more minor nature. Dawson had been helpful several years earlier in capturing the "fruit thief," an Apotex employee from the pill production line who had briefly dated the Shermans' youngest daughter and, after they broke up, was believed to have been stealing sandwiches and fruit from the executive suite refrigerator. It seemed the man had become used to using the refrigerator when he was close to the family. He was caught on a security camera and was fired.

Like many others in the eleven-thousand-employee company, Dawson was shaken by the news two days before of Barry Sherman's death. He had read all the media stories, particularly the reporting that stated "police sources" believed it was a murder-suicide. Dawson refused to believe that. He did not know Barry Sherman well, but he'd often had interactions with him at Apotex. All had been positive, though he did recall that while some days Sherman would be chatty, on other days the Apotex boss would pass him in the hall, head down, some papers in his hand, clearly preoccupied and not pre-pared to stop and talk. They did have one inside "joke" together. Both liked tomato juice. When Sherman found out that one of his security guards liked the same beverage he did, he brought in extra and told him to help himself. "You've got good taste," Sherman told him.

It was the security camera footage at Apotex that was of interest to a very tired-looking Toronto Police detective on the morning of Sunday, December 17. She had been buzzed into the building after she showed her identification badge and had begun to explain to Dawson and his supervisor what she was after. Dawson was surprised the police had not come sooner. It had been two days since the bodies were discovered. Though security and policing were not his true calling, he had watched enough crime dramas to know the drill. Two promi-nent billionaires found dead in their home under very suspi-cious circumstances, according to the papers. That is what's known in the police world as a "red ball" or a "media case," two terms used to describe a high-profile investigation that will develop under the critical eye of the public, the media, politi-cians, and the family—in this case, a very wealthy and well-connected family. Dawson had also heard, and he was pretty sure this was common knowledge, that the first forty-eight hours in a murder investigation were key. Now the papers were saying that police believed it was a murder-suicide. But still, in case it was a double murder, and, judging from what he had read, quite a violent one, why were the police only now coming to look at security footage? The movements of people leading up to their death was quite important, Dawson thought. Then again, if it was a murder-suicide, maybe their movements were not a big deal. These were just some of the thoughts going through the young security guard's head as he helped the detective understand what viewpoints and cover-age were available from the cameras.

"I have been up three days straight," the detective told Dawson. She had been working on the case since the bodies were discovered on Friday just before noon. Now it was Sunday. She had brought a mass data storage device with her so she could take away a digital copy of the last four days of footage. Dawson offered to go through the video and make printouts of a few key sightings if that would help, and the detective agreed. Dawson had been on a daily shift since the previous Thursday. He knew from chatter around Apotex that the Shermans had last been seen on the Wednesday. Apparently, the couple was building a mansion, and early on the Wednesday evening they had met in an Apotex boardroom with the team of architects that was design-ing the home. Out of a sense of duty—he thought somebody should do this—Dawson had checked many of the video feeds since he came on shift. He wanted to see when the Shermans left on Wednesday and whether anyone followed them.

With the detective sitting in the control room, Dawson set the computer to the time codes he had noted, then he displayed the video for those time codes. Sherman had been working in his office at Apotex since late morning on the Wednesday. Shortly before 5 P.M., Honey Sherman and a group of men, pre-sumably the architects, entered the Apotex reception area. Dawson could tell from an exterior camera that they had come in separate vehicles. Barry Sherman met them and they went into a boardroom. At about 6:30 P.M. the meeting concluded and Barry Sherman walked his wife and the architects out. He was apparently staying later, which was normal. Honey Sherman left in her gold Lexus SUV, driving south on Signet Drive, the road that fronted the main Apotex building. The architects left in their own vehicle. Sherman went back to his office to continue working. At around 8:30 P.M., Sherman left the Apotex building and got into his rusting 1997 two-door silver Mustang GT convertible. Sherman's parking spot was the closest to the front door, beside the space, empty at this hour, belonging to his longtime second-in-command, Jack Kay. As his wife had done earlier, Sherman drove out and turned south on Signet Drive. Due to the media coverage of their deaths, Dawson now knew where the late boss of Apotex lived, at 50 Old Colony Road. That would be a typical route for someone who had to get onto the southbound lanes of the nearby expressway before turning east to get to his home.

Dawson gave the detective the printouts of screen captures showing time codes and the arrival and departure of both Barry and Honey Sherman. Dawson also copied the four days of video footage the detective requested onto her mass storage device. Police, he figured, would have the resources to efficiently comb through all of it in great detail and quite quickly, looking for any clues in the comings and goings at Apotex that might shed light on the mysterious deaths of his employer and his wife.

That weekend, Dawson noticed people he had never seen before in the parking lot around the Apotex headquarters. They were men, some scruffy looking, in teams of two, sometimes leaning on a car in the parking lot. Whenever a senior executive left the building, the men would get in their car and follow. The men were part of a large security team employed by an Israeli company recommended by Bank Hapoalim, the Israeli bank Apotex used. With the Shermans dead, the four trustees Barry Sherman had left in charge of his estate decided that there was a risk of violence and had hired a team of men who at one time had guarded Israeli prime minister Benjamin Netanyahu. They were not armed but had experience in self-defence and martial arts and used a sophisticated communication system to keep in touch. Beginning that weekend, the four heirs—Lauren, Jonathon, Alex, and Kaelen—and others, including trustees and senior Apotex executives, had an application called Octopus installed on their phones. If any of them needed help, they only had to touch the app, which would alert a quick response team, in addition to the bodyguards assigned to them.

When he turned over the video of the four days leading up to and including the day the Shermans were last seen alive, Dawson did not realize that due to a security function, the footage from the Apotex cameras could only be viewed on the Apotex system. More than a month later, in January 2018, Toronto Police detectives on the Sherman case contacted Apotex again. "We just got around to looking at the footage, and we can't read it on our system," the detective said. "Can you help?" Dawson and others at Apotex were again surprised. Given the high-profile nature of the case, they expected police would have immediately combed through the footage. Dawson and his boss got to work, converted the file, and provided police with footage they could view.

A similar situation occurred with the video from the home across the street from 50 Old Colony Road. The homeowners had approached police on the Friday the bodies were discovered. Time was of the essence, as the homeowners' system kept only seven days of video. Each day, another day of video was overwritten. A uniformed officer guarding the house had promised to send an officer over. Saturday, the homeowners asked another officer, who again promised someone would be sent across the street. Still no officer came. Sunday, the couple was leaving for a ski trip. They asked again, this time calling a number they were given for a detective working on the case. Finally, a detective arrived to take a copy of the previous seven days of video just before the couple left on their trip. The couple had viewed some of the video and had noticed that on the Thursday, the day before the bodies were discovered and one day after the Shermans were last seen alive, a dark, four-door car drove west on Old Colony Road at 9:11 A.M., and parked on the street out front of the Sherman residence. They watched the grainy footage as a man got out of the car, and walked back and forth to the Sherman front door. The couple recorded the time codes and in total the man appeared to enter the house three times, for a total of twenty-nine minutes inside the house. Finally, he returned to his car and drove off west. The couple could not make out the man's face or the license and style of car.

It is possible, say others who later saw the video, that the man only stood outside the door, not entering the Sherman house. The couple never thought to look at the Wednesday video, which presumably shows when the Shermans arrived home and if anyone was following them. Still, they thought the Thursday video was important. As news reports had revealed to them, the Shermans were dead in the basement at that time. Six weeks after the couple had handed over the video, a police detective arrived at their home to show them blurry photos of a man and a woman captured by another video camera on the street. No explanation was given by the detective. The home-owners said they had seen a couple walking on the street on the Monday, but the photo appeared to show a different couple.

"What about the man who went into the house on the Thursday?" one of the homeowners asked the detective.

"What man?" the detective asked. She went on to explain that she had been working non-stop, had significant daycare issues to deal with in her family, and that she had to "rely on my team" to scan the video and tell her what was on it.

The mystery of that Thursday deepened a year later when a neighbour down the street told me that at the exact time when that man was standing at the Sherman door, a police officer came to her door in response to what he described as a "911 call" that police believed had come from her house. She had not made a 911 call and both her telephone and home security alarm provider confirmed that. The officer did not say when the call was received or whether it came from a landline or cellular telephone. This fueled speculation by members of the Sherman family that the call may have come from the Sherman house roughly ten doors away and that it was somehow linked to the murders. Was it possible that the man in the dark sedan parked in front of the Sherman house was a plainclothes police officer following up on the 911 call? Or was it something as routine as a person trying to deliver a package, or see a house listed for sale? As with so many things in the Sherman case, one revelation led to another mystery.

The funeral of Barry and Honey Sherman was set for Thursday, December 21. Normally, it would have been held at Benjamin's Park Memorial Chapel, a Jewish funeral home. Big though Benjamin's was, it was anticipated that more than seven thousand people would attend the Sherman funeral, such was their popularity in the Jewish community and in the business world, both in Toronto and internationally. The funeral service would be held instead at the International Centre, in Mississauga, a place typically home to trade shows. In the previous few days the centre had hosted a Christmas celebration called "Jingle and Mingle" and a giant trade show featuring footwear and clothing. By Wednesday morning, the day before the funeral, staff had begun to set up 7,500 chairs with the help of Benjamin's, which would convert the aircraft-hangar-size space into a funeral home and run the service.

Dr. David Chiasson was at the coroner's office early that

Wednesday. When Dr. Jim Cairns, Ontario's former deputy chief coroner, had asked him on behalf of the Sherman family to conduct the second autopsies, Chiasson had been of two minds. On the one hand, he enjoyed a challenge, and judging by the news reports describing the mysterious deaths, this was going to be both a fascinating post-mortem and one fraught with scientific questions that would be tough to answer. But on the other hand, he had dealt with a great deal of politics when he was Ontario's chief forensic pathologist, and he did not enjoy that side of a high-profile job. He was not entirely sure he wanted to face that kind of stress again. But he'd made his decision, and he hoped he could shed some light on what had happened to the Sherman couple. He was also being well paid for the work, as were Cairns and the former police officers on what appeared to be a steadily growing private investigation team.

Chiasson had invited both Dr. Michael Pickup, who performed the first post-mortems, and the Toronto Police detectives working the case to the second autopsies. The police, a mix of divisional and homicide officers, had declined. Pickup agreed to go. He did not request permission from his boss, Dr. Michael Pollanen, and later Pickup would catch heat for not at least informing Ontario's chief pathologist.

Chiasson faced a major hurdle in taking on the assignment. Conducting a second autopsy is very different from doing the first. When a first autopsy is done, the body is in the condition it was found in at the death scene. The first post-mortem disrupts the body through major incisions, removal or cross-sectioning of organs, and the removal through biopsy of parts of the skin to determine the age of bruises or cuts. Having Pickup present was key to Chiasson being able to conduct a successful second set of post-mortems. As with the description of the official autopsy, neither Chiasson nor Pickup would agree to be interviewed. This account is pieced together from people with knowledge of what happened that day.

It was important to Chiasson that he not misinterpret anything done in the first round the previous Saturday. Pickup told Chiasson that he had not finalized his report. In fact, the official autopsy report would not be finalized for more than a month. Pickup had not reached a conclusion on the manner of death, and three theories were being considered: murder-suicide, double suicide, and double homicide. Pickup had made a determination of the medical cause of death—ligature neck compression—but he was not prepared to state with 100 percent certainty what caused the compression. Blood and oxygen flow had been cut off by something being wrapped around their necks, but the police had not made a determination as to the type of ligature, although the leather belts were a strong candidate. The medical cause of death had been released by the Toronto Police to the public late Sunday night. The public was told that the homicide squad was overseeing the investigation, but police said it was not classified as a homicide.

When reporters inquired over these first few days, police would say only that the investigation was continuing. To be fair to the Toronto force, at no time did Toronto detectives say publicly and on the record that they believed it was a murder-suicide. But privately, police sources continued to tell reporters that murder-suicide was the working theory, which inflamed the family and friends of the Shermans. While Jim Cairns had been looking for a second forensic pathologist, the Shermans' bodies had remained in temperature-controlled storage at the coroner's building. Embalming and visitation are not part of the Jewish funeral custom, so it was possible to conduct the autopsies on Wednesday and have the funeral on Thursday.

Winter was setting in. On Old Colony Road, a police forensics team continued to go through the house. A special city truck had been brought in to help officers search through the sewer drains, but no explanation was given to the media about the purpose of this. Officers were also seen walking over the snow-covered roof of the house, but again no explanation was given to reporters. In fact, the Sherman house had been one of many broken into in the neighbourhood over the past two years by bandits, still on the loose, who gained access through second-floor windows and doors. In the Sherman house, burglars entered through a skylight. It is quite likely that police were looking to see if anyone had tried to do so again.

If he was going to do a second set of post-mortems, Chiasson wanted it done right, and that meant having experienced investigators in the room to make observations and notes. When Michael Pickup performed the official autopsies on the Shermans the previous Saturday, Toronto Police detectives were present. Joining Chiasson from the private team that morning were former Toronto homicide detectives Tom Klatt, Ray Zarb, and Mike Davis. Also present were two former forensic identification officers, now retired, one who had been with the Toronto Police and the other with the Ontario Provincial Police. The former ID officers were in the room to make detailed observations and to ensure the chain of custody for any samples taken, which Sherman lawyer Greenspan insisted on. Even though this was an unofficial investigation, Greenspan wanted anything discovered by his team to stand the legal test of a criminal court, if it came to that.

Shortly before 9 A.M., Barry Sherman's body was wheeled in. In the days when Chiasson had conducted autopsies for the province, it had been in the old coroner's office in downtown Toronto. This would be the first time he performed a post-mortem examination at the new state-of-the-art building in Toronto's North York. The task ahead of him was formidable. It was like being asked to complete a jigsaw puzzle with half the pieces missing. The process of conducting an autopsy involves cutting the body open, removing organs or sections of organs for analysis, and taking fluid and other samples, including skin biopsies. Dr. Pickup's autopsy, which had determined that both Shermans had died by ligature neck compression, had been typically invasive. The other problem was that, unlike when he had conducted official post-mortems at the direction of police investigators, Dr. Chiasson had no access to the scene where the body was found. That was why Dr. Pickup was present.

The younger doctor told Chiasson he wanted to be helpful. Physically, the two men were polar opposites. Pickup was young, slender, with dark hair, a big smile, and tortoiseshell glasses. Chiasson was a big man, almost completely bald, with a salt-and-pepper moustache and an almost perpetual scowl. Both men wore sterile medical gloves. Pickup produced a folder containing photos and diagrams and spread them out on a table. The photos showed the scene where the bodies were found as well as pictures taken during the first autopsy. Chiasson looked them over, and as he worked, he referred to the photos.

From his conversation with Pickup, and from the police news release, Chiasson knew ligature neck compression had been determined as the medical cause of death. He was curious to see the condition of the horseshoe-shaped hyoid bones in both necks he was going to examine. Though not conclusive, the condition of the hyoid bone would inform his determination. There were those in the forensic pathology world who believed that to make a ruling of murder by strangulation it was imperative that the hyoid bone be fractured. But twenty years earlier, Chiasson and Michael Pollanen, now the province's chief forensic pathologist, had authored a study that proved this was not the case. They found the bone was fractured in only one-third of the cases of homicide by strangulation. In the other two-thirds, an intact hyoid was found to be related to several factors, including the pressure that was used on the neck, the condition of the hyoid bone to begin with, and the type of ligature that was used. The softer the ligature wrapped around the neck, the less likely the hyoid bone was to fracture. Compounding this, and creating further confusion, was how age factored in. In the two-decade-old study, Chiasson and Pollanen had found that the older the victim, the more likely the hyoid bone was to fracture in a homicidal strangulation.

Barry Sherman's hyoid bone had been removed in the earlier autopsy by Pickup. But through information provided to Chiasson that day, he came to understand that neither Barry nor Honey's hyoid bone was fractured. Chiasson wondered if that was why police thought it was a murder-suicide. As he had shown with his research years before, a murder with a soft ligature could leave an intact hyoid. Later in the day, Chiasson looked at the death scene photos Pickup had brought to the autopsy suite. The Shermans were in a seated position, legs outstretched away from the pool, with jackets on but pulled down off the shoulder. A belt was looped around each person's neck, with the end of each belt fed through the buckle and the end then looped or tied around the metre-high railing they were positioned against. The leather belts would qualify as a soft ligature. If pressure was applied firmly but not suddenly, the hyoid would likely not fracture. Chiasson, who would later discuss his findings with Cairns, did not see how the murder-suicide theory could work. While it was theoretically possible that one of the two had strangled the other and then staged the body, the other person could not have died by strangulation simply by looping the belt over the rail and sitting down. There would not be enough weight or downward force. The retired detectives present in the room agreed.

During the dual autopsies, Chiasson also paid close attention to the wrists. When he began his examination of the bodies, he had noted that skin biopsies had been taken from the wrists, which Pickup had done to determine the age of the markings. It appeared they were fresh, but a laboratory test would narrow the time frame. The bodies had remained undiscovered for two days, however, which might skew the timeline. Chiasson consulted Pickup's photos. From the abrasions that were present in the photographs, it looked, and Pickup agreed, like some sort of rope or plastic tie had bound the wrists. Checking the police photos of the death scene, Chiasson did not see any indication that there were ropes or ties near the bodies. Others in the room speculated that the Toronto Police were searching the sewers to see if—and this seemed a fruitless task—ropes or ties had been flushed down a toilet and into the sewer system.

As Pickup had done several days before, Chiasson took fluid samples to check for the existence of drugs, beyond what a seventy-year-old woman and seventy-five-year-old man would be expected to have in their systems. Those samples were rushed to a US lab, and the results were back in forty-eight hours, weeks before the backlogged Ontario laboratory used by the police reported on their results. Chiasson's samples showed there were no drugs in either body ("on board" is the pathology slang) that would have killed the pharmaceutical mogul or his wife.

It looked to Chiasson as if the Shermans were the victims of a bizarre double murder by persons unknown. In discussions with Pickup and others that day, Chiasson got the impression that the police detectives present at the first autopsies had made up their minds that it was a murder-suicide, with Barry strangling Honey, then hanging himself. That notion—and this became a hotly discussed topic among lawyer Brian Greenspan, the private detectives, and Chiasson over the next few days— seemed, at least on its face, ridiculous. It was quite possible the police had formed this theory because Honey Sherman had injuries to her face and Barry Sherman did not. According to that theory, Barry had struck his wife to subdue her, then strangled her. But Chiasson knew there could be a wide range of reasons why one would have injuries to the face and the other did not. The attackers could have injured Honey Sherman, for example, and for some reason not hit Barry Sherman. As some of the private team speculated, perhaps attackers had demanded something from Barry and beaten Honey to try to convince him. The fatal flaw in that theory was that the wound to Honey's face occurred either immediately before or after death, as no bruise formed.

When Chiasson and the private detectives reported their findings to Greenspan, the conclusion was this: it was a professional hit. Some person or persons had murdered both Shermans in a deliberate and apparently professional attack, then had staged the bodies to make it look like they had killed themselves, or like one had killed the other. For some unknown reason, Barry Sherman's body had been arranged almost as if he were in "repose," the word one source later used to describe the serene way he was positioned: one leg crossed over the other in a relaxed-looking fashion, glasses not at all askew. If the killers had struck on Wednesday night and intended to make it look like a murder-suicide, one possible reason for doing that, the team decided, was to buy the killers time to escape. The ironic part of this theory was that, due to a perfect storm of inattentiveness on the part of the Sherman family, friends, realtors, and business and charity colleagues, it was not necessary, as other than the few people who emailed or called, nobody had physically checked on the couple for two days.

Chiasson's findings from these second autopsies would not be considered by the Toronto Police for almost six weeks. It was the beginning of an awkward relationship between the Sherman family and the police. Though Greenspan and his team offered information to the detectives, the police showed no interest until a *Toronto Star* story outlining the findings prompted them to contact Chiasson. As a result, the funeral the next day took place under a cloud of very public suspicion that Barry Sherman killed his wife then hanged himself.

On the day of Chiasson's autopsies, Justice Leslie Pringle of the Ontario Court of Justice was presented with a request by the Toronto Police to access telephone records held by Rogers Communications, a provider of cellular telephone, television, and internet service. It was the first batch of at least thirty-five separate requests for judicial authorization for search warrants or production orders in the Sherman investigation. The documents underlying all the requests to Pringle remain sealed by court order, but it is likely that the production order served to Rogers (one of the few made public during three *Toronto Star* challenges for access to the records where we were allowed to see the target of the production order) was for the cell phone records of Barry and Honey Sherman. Redactions to the document prevented us from confirming this. In Canada, as in the United States and many other jurisdictions, police need a judicial authorization to access private information, including data from cell phones. Modern cell phones can yield many clues in a police investigation, not just the obvious history of calls and text messages. The iPhone Honey used and the BlackBerry that was Barry's constant companion would tell the police, through GPS, where each of them was at specific times of the day and night, or at least where the phone was.

To obtain the records from Rogers, a judge had to be satisfied that the police had probable cause to access the records. Three kinds of judicial authorizations are available to police: to enter a private property, police require a search warrant; to access phone or, for example, banking records, police need a production order; and a third type of warrant gives police the authority to wiretap a person's phone.

For all warrants, a judge or justice of the peace must review an "information to obtain," or ITO, and determine if the information police have in the document justifies issuing a warrant. An ITO is a police document setting out everything the police have learned to date that would convince a judge to issue a warrant or production order. For example, if the police wanted to obtain records proving that a person had purchased a knife at a particular hardware store, the ITO could include the synopsis of a police interview with the owner of the store saying that, yes, Person X was in their store on a given day and bought a knife. The other piece of information the police are required to put before a judge deals with the type of offence being investigated. Using the knife example, if police believed that someone had been stabbed in a bar fight, police would tell a judge they were investigating a case of attempted murder. While the majority of the thirty-five Sherman ITOs remain sealed at time of writing, enough has been released to show that in the early days, police were seeking Barry and Honey's medical records. They were also seeking from someone a series of telephone and banking records, and, intriguingly, information from two airline loyalty programs. Other than the medical records, the seal extended to the owner of the other records being sought. Police were interested in someone's flights and bank records. Whose, they did not want anyone to know. The documents obtained by the *Toronto Star* in a series of court applications in the months after the Shermans died show that when the police first sought search warrants and production orders, they were investigating only that "Honey Sherman was a victim of a murder." It would be well over a month before one of the police applications identified both Barry and Honey Sherman as murder victims.

What was also surprising to anyone taking a hard look at the first days and weeks of the Toronto Police investigation were the many actions *not* taken by detectives. Police were well aware that Dr. Chiasson, a veteran forensic pathologist, had conducted a second set of autopsies, yet for five weeks they did not contact him to determine his findings and conclusions. In the case of samples and fingerprints taken from the death scene, there was no attempt for many months to obtain DNA samples and fingerprints from people who had recently seen the Shermans or been to their house. That is considered good detective work that helps exclude innocent people so that police can focus on any unidentified DNA found at the crime scene, which in turn could lead to a suspect. For example, the personal trainer who routinely visited the house for Monday and Wednesday morning sessions with the Shermans was not asked for a sample of her DNA until late August, eight months after the police investigation began. Some were never contacted at all. The father of the man Kaelen Sherman was engaged to worked in the elevator repair business and, as a favour to Honey, he had spent dozens of hours at 50 Old Colony Road that fall repairing a mechanical dumbwaiter that had never worked. The small elevator travelled the vertical height of the house, ending in Honey's closet. "My fingerprints and DNA would be all over and yet they never contacted me," the father recalled. People who were close to the Shermans were not interviewed for months. Among them was Jeremy Desai—the Apotex CEO who took part in an email exchange with Sherman the Wednesday night just hours before he was killed and would presumably have pertinent information and who was not interviewed for almost two months. Meanwhile, the security camera footage taken from Apotex and footage from two cameras across from the murder scene sat at a police station on a mass storage device for more than one month until it was viewed. Something as obvious as the old-fashioned real estate lockbox looped through the door handle of the Shermans' front door was only checked several days after the discovery of the bodies because Judi Gottlieb, the Shermans' agent, called police to ask if the key was inside. "I called the Sunday night and told police. They hadn't checked it. I gave them the code and they looked and said, yes, the key was there."

None of this information regarding the police missteps was known to the Sherman family or the public in the first six weeks following the December 2017 deaths. Toronto Police continued to investigate the case with a strong focus on their original assumption that Barry killed Honey and then killed himself. When the media asked the police for updates between December 15 and mid-January, police would say nothing. The Sherman family and their friends, when asked to comment, said that murder-suicide was not possible. Beyond the general belief that the couple had a good relationship and it would have been completely out of character for Barry Sherman to commit an act of violence, other reasons to dismiss the notion were put forward. Since it was generally understood that Honey was attacked in another part of the house and moved to the pool, down a long set of winding stairs and then across ten metres of floor, friends said that Barry simply lacked the physical ability. Honey weighed 170 pounds, and it seemed impossible that Sherman could have moved her body. In a bit of gallows humour, it was said by close friends who knew of her toughness and inner strength that if anybody had the ability to kill the other and move the body, it was Honey Sherman.

SIX

BEGINNINGS

"BARRY," FRED STEINER SAID, looking around Sherman's office, "define exactly what your business is." To call the place cluttered would be an understatement. Bankers boxes and stacks of papers crowded every surface. Steiner could see that some of the papers were covered with the scrawl of scientific calculations.

"Well," Sherman said, "it's very simple. I'm a counterfeiter. I take other people's pills and I make them cheaper."

Steiner laughed, running his fingers through the thick, wiry hair he proudly called his "Brillo pad." He was not yet sure what to make of Sherman. When they first met, the previous year, he'd thought, *Well, he seems okay. Bright guy. But he would never be one of my best friends.* He was wrong.

The road that led Steiner into business with Sherman, and to one of his closest friendships, started with the death of Steiner's first wife. Born to parents who fled Austria in 1938 and settled in Detroit, Steiner married at an early age. He and

95

his wife had two children. In her early twenties, she was diagnosed with breast cancer and died a few years later. By December 1970, Steiner was feeling lost. He had two children under seven years old, a boy and a girl, and was struggling to find his niche in a variety of restaurant ventures. He had a teacher's certificate and was a substitute teacher at several Detroit schools, which helped pay the bills.

During the winter holidays, Steiner took his children to Florida for a break, where they checked in at the Newport Beach Hotel. He was a thirty-year-old man who'd had modest financial success but was still looking for his big break. One afternoon by the pool, his four-year-old daughter had to go to the bathroom. He felt she was too old to take her into the men's room, and he certainly could not go into the women's. He spotted two attractive young women—"nice, cute girls"—and asked if they could help him out. The women were Honey Reich and Bryna Fishman, on one of their getaways. They helped Steiner's daughter, after which the three adults spent a pleasant afternoon lounging around the pool. Reich mentioned that her boyfriend, Barry—she called him Chuck, because his middle name was Charles—was flying down later in the week, the four had several dinners together, and got to know each other.

"I looked at Barry and thought, interesting guy, nice guy," Steiner recalls. "But he wasn't my type. You could see he was more of an academic. I was more of a streetwise guy. School was never my thing."

Back in Detroit, Steiner was at a family get-together with his children and his late wife's family, and one of his in-laws was looking at photos from the Florida trip. "Who is this?" she asked, seeing Bryna Fishman's face appear throughout the album. "Just a girl I met down in Florida" was the reply.

Fred and Bryna were married seven months later, on July 4, 1971. Barry and Honey had been married two days before, at a Toronto courthouse, but they waited for Bryna and Fred's wedding before leaving on their honeymoon. The two couples remained best friends until the Shermans' deaths. The Steiners lived for a brief time in Detroit, but they returned to Toronto within two years and have lived there ever since.

Toronto in the early 1970s was an eye-opener for Steiner. It was quite different from Detroit, where riots and gun violence were commonplace. He was teased when he told his new Toronto neighbours that he locked his doors at night. But Steiner was amazed by the welcome he and Bryna were given, particularly by Barry Sherman. One day, he visited Sherman at Empire and told him he was planning to buy a business but had no idea what it would be. He was looking for a sounding board. Other people had promised to invest with Steiner but one after another dropped off.

"Fred, if you find a business that's the right one, then do it. I'll be partners with you," Sherman said. Steiner had no footprint in Canada, no credit history north of the US border, nothing more than a stated desire to succeed. As Sherman would do for many people over the next fifty years who showed similar enthusiasm, he provided financial backing. The business relationship with Steiner would prove the most stable Sherman ever had outside of his own company, Apotex. The deal that Steiner eventually made was to purchase a small firm that delivered coffee, water, and soft drinks to offices in downtown buildings. Joel Ulster joined the partnership at Sherman's suggestion, with each of the three men investing $25,000. It was the early 1970s, and the concept of contracting with an outside company to provide a beverage service to an office suite was becoming big business in the United States, but it was relatively unknown in Canada. The company the trio purchased had 175 accounts. By 2017, when Sherman died, Imperial Coffee had 15,000 contracts across Ontario, supplying product and providing and servicing thousands of high-end coffee machines. All three men were still partners, though Sherman had sold the majority of his shares to Steiner's son Mark at a generously low price. Mark Steiner eventually became president of his father's company.

Most people think of Barry Sherman only as the man who made a fortune as a "counterfeiter," to use his word. Some might also see him as a generic pill guy who dabbled in other businesses, quite often unsuccessfully. But what emerges from interviews with dozens of people who knew Sherman well, or who faced off against him in business, is that Sherman was much more than a "pill guy." He was a risk-taking entrepreneur whose most successful enterprise just happened to be generic drugs. It could easily have been something else. He tried and failed, and tried and succeeded, at many other ventures. His support for Fred Steiner, at a time when other potential investors backed away, is early evidence of his savvy and appetite for risk.

Sherman was only able to give a financial leg up to Fred Steiner in 1973 after an uneven start in the generic drug business that would eventually be his greatest accomplishment. When Sherman and Ulster took over at Empire Laboratories in 1967, Sherman alternated between over-the-moon excitement and fear of the worst. Bankruptcy would mean losing not only the money the two men had put in, but also the greater amount invested by their own parents.

Empire Laboratories, purchased from the trustees representing Sherman's late Uncle Lou's estate, was failing when Sherman and Ulster took control, according to Sherman's

memoir. The orphaned Winter cousins would eventually disagree and dig up information they said suggested the company
was doing much better than Sherman claimed. But according
to Sherman, when he and his partner took over, no new products had been introduced for several years, the building it was
housed in was run down and lacked modern manufacturing
machinery, and the man at the helm, courtesy of the trustees,
was, as Ulster put it, "a disaster." To purchase Empire and its
generic business, the two young men incorporated a company
called Sherman and Ulster Ltd. They paid the Winter estate
$450,000, pooling the money they had with loans from Ulster's
father and Sherman's mother. Sherman was president; Ulster
was vice-president.

Empire's operations were spread out over a five-storey building on Lansdowne Avenue near Dundas Street, an industrial
part of Toronto at the time. The president put in charge by the
estate trustees, chemistry professor George Wright, was not a
strong businessman. Sherman fired him the day they assumed
control. The partners decided that Sherman would handle production, quality control, and product development. Ulster
would handle sales, accounting, administration, and any human
resources issues among the employees.

Manufacturing generic drugs was a fledgling industry at the
time, and a confusing set of government rules controlled their
existence. Morris Goodman, a Montreal businessman who was
one of the pioneers of the generic industry, explains that one of
the main problems he and others in his business faced was that
"doctors did not believe in generics." Physicians were wined
and dined by the brand name pharmaceutical companies, and
their salesmen pushed their brand products at doctors' offices
frequently. Not surprisingly, doctors usually wanted to prescribe the brand name version. Goodman says that if a doctor

did prescribe a generic version and the patient didn't do well, "the doctor blamed the drug." In an ideal world, the generic version would be identical to the brand name product. Using the simplest example, a generic ASA tablet should be the same as an Aspirin. The problem was, at least in the early days, it often was not the same. Government regulators spent a considerable amount of time trying to catch generic companies producing inferior product. Ulster, recalling those early days, says there was always speculation, never substantiated, that brand pharmaceutical companies paid off the government inspectors to perform extra policing of the generic firms that were trying to get a piece of a very lucrative pie.

Similar issues were encountered by the man who would become Sherman's biggest rival, Leslie Dan. Dan had founded the generic firm Novopharm in 1965. A Hungarian Jew, he had come to Canada in 1947 and enrolled in the University of Toronto School of Pharmacy. He was fourteen years older than Sherman and was more established in the pharmaceutical world when Sherman and Ulster emerged on the scene. Their bitter rivalry would be the stuff of acrimonious court battles and occasional headlines in future years. Dan's son, Aubrey, would eventually become an admirer of Sherman, and together they would work on a plan to legally sell marijuana as a pharmaceutical.

Barry Sherman entered the tumult of the pharmaceutical world in 1967 as the twenty-five-year-old owner of a medium-sized generic company and its head of product development. Biochemists and molecular chemists are typically the type of scientists involved in pharmaceuticals. Sherman was neither. His background was in math and physics, and aerospace. "At that time," Sherman recalled in his unpublished memoir, "I knew little about pharmaceutical manufacturing, and virtually nothing about how to formulate a tablet or capsule."

Sherman and Ulster shared a long table that acted as a desk at the Empire office on Lansdowne. When they looked at recent company reports, it was clear there was a problem with quality, not just with the quality of prescription pills but also with the company's relatively simple line of vitamin C tablets, known by the generic name ascorbic acid. James Church, the sales manager, told Sherman that the tablets were soft and broke up in the bottle. Customers were returning them, and revenues from the product, not surprisingly, had taken a big hit. What pharmacy wanted to carry a product that was unstable? What customer, hoping to stave off a cold, wanted to open a bottle and find a jumble of broken pills? Sherman describes in his memoir how he went up to the third floor of the Lansdowne building and spoke to the production manager. The man told him there was nothing wrong with the tablets. He formulated them himself, he said to Sherman, and "every product formulated by him was the best that could be made." Sherman then walked downstairs to the second floor and questioned the packaging supervisor, who told him that, yes, there was a problem.

Within a couple of days, the production manager was shown the door and Sherman promoted Chris Retchford, a young Australian man a few years his junior, who had studied pharmacy for two years back home and then emigrated to Canada. Sherman gave him the title of acting production manager and promised the job would be permanent if he did well. The task ahead, to understand how to manufacture high-quality products, would be critical in Sherman's career. By 2017, Apotex, the company he started after Empire, would be manufacturing twenty-five *billion* doses (pills and other formulations of drugs) a year. At Empire in 1967, Sherman needed to learn how to make one pill and make it right.

His first task was to understand the components of pharmaceuticals. All pills, whether prescription or non-prescription, are composed of the active pharmaceutical ingredient, or API, and "excipients," or inactive ingredients. These are also called binders and fillers. The actual amount of drug, or API, is small. The additives make the pill into a form that can be swallowed and also, depending on the type of medicine, help deliver the active ingredient to the body in a way that allows it to be absorbed properly to have the best effect. Shortly before his death in 2017, Sherman was devising the best way to deliver the various active ingredients of marijuana to the body in pill form.

Working alongside his new acting production manager, Sherman set up a series of trials to see what worked and did not work with the ascorbic acid tablets that were disintegrating in the bottles. The former production manager had left a list of all the inactive ingredients: lactose, microcrystalline cellulose, starch, sodium carboxymethylcellulose, magnesium stearate, talc, and colloidal silicon dioxide. Sherman wrote in his memoir that neither he nor Retchford had any idea of the purpose of each ingredient. They ran a series of trials, compressing all the ingredients with a tablet "punch" but leaving one ingredient out each time. They discovered that only two inactive ingredients were needed: microcrystalline cellulose, which makes the tablets hard but also allows them to break up in the stomach within thirty minutes, and magnesium stearate, which is a lubricant that prevents the tablet mixture from sticking to the tablet punch. Problem solved.

Sherman wrote, "It appears that [the production manager's] approach had been to include a little bit of everything, without doing experiments to determine what was needed and what was not. From that day forward, I personally made all decisions relating to product formulation, based on review of one or more series of comparative experiments."

During this time at Empire, both Sherman and Ulster kept long hours out of necessity. But Sherman also laboured deep into the evening because, and this is confirmed by literally everyone who knew him well, he loved working. In years to come, people would see him on sunny winter days at the Alpine Ski Club, near the Ontario town of Collingwood, sitting inside at a table, his laptop out, typing, his ski boots unbuckled to rest his feet after an obligatory few runs down the slopes with Honey. That scene was replicated many times. When Sherman began dating Honey Reich three years into his time at Empire, she would often drop by the office and they would have a quick meal, usually chicken and fries from Swiss Chalet, then Sherman would go back to his formulations.

If one of the main lessons Sherman learned in those first few years was how to make a pill better (and cheaper, due to fewer ingredients), the new tool he developed involved the law and the courts. In the days immediately after his death, media stories remarked on his "litigious nature," with one well-known lawyer pronouncing Sherman "the most active litigant in any industry in Canada." By his own account, Sherman's first use of the courts to his advantage was in 1971, when a federal official wrote to tell Sherman and Ulster that Empire was being struck from the country-wide list of approved pharmaceutical companies. Inclusion on that list was a prerequisite for selling drugs in Ontario and also for supplying customers, including hospitals.

"We immediately panicked," Sherman recalled in his memoir. The bureaucrat who had written the letter was the chairman of a federal board that oversaw the listing of pharmaceutical companies. It was after hours, and Sherman was unable to reach the bureaucrat at his office in Ottawa. He called directory assistance and asked for a home number, dialled, and the board chairman answered. Sherman identified himself, and while there is no account of the call from the bureaucrat's perspective, Sherman recounts it in his memoir. Ulster's recollection also matches what Sherman wrote. The man was not happy to be disturbed at the dinner hour, but Sherman kept him on the telephone. What the federal board had done, Sherman said, was unlawful, because it had not disclosed the allegations to Empire and provided the company with a chance to respond. He also took issue with the fact that, in Sherman's opinion, these were historical complaints from a time before he and Ulster had taken over.

"It appeared that [the bureaucrat] and his board had never heard of the principles of natural justice with which, according to common law, all judicial and quasi-judicial bodies must comply," Sherman wrote. He warned the bureaucrat that if the decision was not reversed and Empire products reinstated on the list, Sherman would hold the bureaucrat personally responsible. Personal threats were a waste of time, the bureaucrat said, and he hung up on Sherman.

Sherman got in touch with a lawyer he knew, Willard "Bud" Estey, who years later would be named a justice of the Supreme Court of Canada. Estey, with Sherman's urging, went to court and began an application to have a judge quash the federal board's decision. Estey also wrote to the Ontario government and asked it to hold off delisting Empire products, pending the court challenge, which the government agreed to do. Shortly before the court hearing, the federal government backed down and relisted Empire products for sale in Canada.

"This was the first time in my career that I found it necessary to initiate legal action. It was to be the first of many," Sherman recalled.

It was at about this time that Sherman asked his friend and business partner Fred Steiner to come on a tour of a house he was building in Toronto on Beaverhall Drive. Sherman had a contract with the house builder that stipulated certain parts of the construction had to follow a timeline. The plumbing was one of the items, and the toilet in the main bathroom had not been installed as promised.

"I want you to be a witness," Sherman said. He sued the contractor, successfully, as he would with other properties he built. If Sherman believed he was the aggrieved party, and he had a contract, he would take the matter before a judge. The Old Colony Road property, where he would eventually die, was built for relatively little money. Due to his lawsuit for non-compliance with a contract, Sherman would recoup most of the cost of the construction.

The home in Thornhill, north of Toronto, where Joel and Cindy Ulster had settled down was lively. The Ulsters had four children, and were not yet thirty years old. There was a secret in the home that would eventually burst free, but for now it was the picture of domestic, though often chaotic, bliss. Thornhill was a new neighbourhood in the early 1970s, a place with cookie-cutter houses (Mark Ulster, one of Joel and Cindy's boys, says, "Every fifth house was the same") and perfect lawns. Mark recalls how his parents always had friends over, "just hanging around." The adults would get together, and the kids—Mark and his siblings and whoever else was there—would put on a play or some other performance. Everybody seemed to get along. At one point, Joel and Cindy fell in love with the Toronto production of *Hair* and attended it several times. They befriended the cast, and one night they invited them all to the Thornhill house for a cast party. Later, two actors in the play, who were married with children, moved in for several months. Mark says his "crazy hippie" parents and their friends did not quite fit into the area, which Mark took as a sort of badge of honour. Today a successful documentary writer and producer, Mark recalls with fondness how nice it was to have his parents' friends around, and the most popular of them was Uncle Barry, a busy man who still found time for his friend's kids, and a man who would later give Mark a helping hand.

"Barry was just always around," says Mark. "He was very positive. I had always thought that Barry would be a great father, because he was very devoted and would really get down to your level and show interest in you, which was nice." Caroline, Mark's wife, who knew Sherman in later years, recalls his warmth. Photos taken of weekend get-togethers at the Ulster home show Barry and Honey mugging for the camera.

But for all the appearance of a typical suburban family, the Ulsters really were different. The secret in the house was that Joel Ulster was gay and had fallen in love with a man named Michael Hertzman, a Toronto clothing store owner. One day in 1973, Ulster took a walk with Sherman on the streets around their Empire factory and told him his plan to leave Cindy. He had already confided in his friend that he was gay. Ulster recalls that walk, no sidewalks in those days, dodging broken pavement on the side of the road, trucks rumbling past. "He was very supportive," Ulster says. The next day, Joel told Cindy that he could no longer live with her, that he preferred men. Cindy at first believed that her husband was just going through a phase. "It was a huge scandal, because my dad was gay and it was the early 1970s. It was a pretty crazy situation," Mark Ulster says, remembering how it was viewed by others. After all, only a few years earlier, homosexual acts were against the law in Canada. That changed when Liberal prime minister Pierre Trudeau passed legislation decriminalizing gay sex, famously saying, "There's no place for the state in the bedrooms of the nation."

Ben Ulster, who had backed son Joel and Barry Sherman financially, was not at all supportive of his son's decision to leave his family. But Joel had made up his mind. The question was, Where was he going to live? He telephoned Michael Hertzman and told him he had done it, he had told Cindy. Michael asked, "Do you have a place to stay?" Joel did not, and Michael said Joel could stay with him. Following Cindy's wishes—they eventually divorced—he kept the fact that he was gay from their children until they were in their early teens. Mark's brother Jeff recalls his naïveté from those early years: he thought his father merely had a roommate.

Jeff Ulster also recalls how at first their mother would not let Michael into the house after the couple separated. But Cindy was not a housekeeper (she proudly had a poster in her front hall that said "Fuck Housework"), and so eventually Joel *and* Michael would be occasionally permitted to visit, when they would do an "intervention" and throw out accumulated trash from the ongoing parties the house still hosted. Cindy eventually met and fell in love with another man and remarried. She died of cancer in 2013.

Throughout the years, until the Shermans' deaths, Barry and Honey remained close with Joel and Michael. Among the adventures they shared was a train trip on the Polar Bear Express, in Northern Ontario. Photos from the early 1970s kept by Michael and Joel in a well-organized album show the two couples standing in front of a stone monument outside Cochrane, Ontario, the train's southern terminus, Honey in red bell bottoms, Barry in dress slacks. In another photograph, a grinning Honey has curved her body into a pantomime of the polar bear depicted on the side of the train.

Today, Joel and Michael are married and living in New York City. On the walls of their apartment are testimonials to a family life being lived well: dozens of smiling photos of Joel and Michael taken all over the world with the four children from Joel's first marriage and the two children he and Michael adopted in New York. Over the years, Sherman provided financial assistance and mentorship to all the Ulster children. All six are now adults and successful in a wide range of careers.

In the midst of Ulster's personal crisis, Sherman and his partner continued to steer the company to greater heights. Empire was now profitable. New products and better versions of old products contributed to an increase in sales from $800,000 in 1967 to $2 million several years later. Empire was being noticed as a contender in the generic business, and not just by Canadians. Not long before Ulster was preparing to deliver his news to Cindy, a California-based company sent a representative to visit Empire. International Chemical and Nuclear Corporation (ICN) was in expansion mode and wanted to see if Empire would be a good fit. It had recently purchased Morris Goodman's Montreal company, Winley-Morris. Goodman was now president of the renamed company, ICN Canada, and ICN wanted to expand by purchasing other firms. Sherman and Ulster were not sure if they were interested. They had spent several years turning around Empire, and they saw the opportunity for future growth if they continued on their own. On the other hand, the five-storey building on Lansdowne was tired. To renovate would be expensive. Improvements to the chipped, uneven floors alone would be an expensive task. The ideal atmosphere for making pharmaceuticals was completely sterile so that the various ingredients were not contaminated. The Lansdowne location might simply need too much of a capital investment. Sherman also believed that the operations in the building, a factory with constantly moving product spread out over five floors, was inefficient. When they received an offer of about $2 million from ICN, they set to work on the final points of the negotiation, and Sherman took a close look at the documentation provided by the US firm.

"I wanted to be free to go back into the same business," Sherman wrote in his memoir. Ulster recalls how Sherman devised a plan. ICN was stipulating that the shareholders in Empire would not be able to compete in the generic business for two years. What ICN did not know (apparently they never checked) was that neither Sherman nor Ulster, technically, were shareholders in their company. Instead, they each had a personal holding company that owned shares in Sherman and Ulster Ltd., which in turn owned shares in Empire. Sherman withheld the schedule that listed the shareholders in Empire until "the last minute" in the hope that ICN would not figure it out.

"This worked out exactly as I hoped," Sherman recalled. When the dust settled, taxes and debts paid, he and Ulster had each netted about $300,000. Ulster exited the new business, but Sherman stayed on to work as an executive for ICN, until something happened that would occur only once in his life. The ICN Canada president, Morris Goodman, sent Sherman to California for some meetings. The plan was to discuss the future growth of the combined organization. Goodman never heard the details from his American bosses, but it did not go well. Sherman apparently told ICN how to do their work better. "Sherman opened his big mouth," Goodman says. "I got a call saying, 'Fire the son of a bitch.' I don't know what he said."

A few weeks later, Goodman drove to Toronto to meet with Sherman, who, by his own account, knew what was coming.

"I became the only person who ever fired Barry Sherman," says Goodman. "When I fired him, I said, 'You know, I don't like firing people.' Barry said, 'Don't worry, Morris. I was going to quit anyway.'"

Goodman is now eighty-six and still involved in his own business, Pharmascience. His son David is the chief executive officer, and Pharmascience is the largest pharmaceutical employer in the province of Quebec.

After he was fired, Sherman packed up his office and went home. Thanks to his sleight of hand on the ICN deal, he was free to start his own firm. He incorporated Sherman Technologies in 1973, which initially provided equipment for other pharmaceutical businesses, then morphed into a generic firm. Sherman invited Ulster to join him in the new venture, but Ulster declined, saying he was ready for a change. At Empire, the two men had shared an office with two desks and a long table between them. Each day, Joel would open his drawer and find a note from Sherman with suggestions as to what he should do that day, what was prudent not to do that day, or just general observations on the best way to handle Ulster's side of the business.

"He was a very strong presence to say the least," Ulster says. "He didn't know how to stand back and let you do it. He would tell you how to do it."

That rankled Ulster. He understood his friend was well-meaning, but he realized from those daily notes and the extreme effort that Sherman put into business, to the exclusion of all other pursuits, that in the long term they were not suited for a partnership. Ulster also found Sherman to be too much of a risk-taker, and that did not sit well with his more financially conservative attitude.

"We had different objectives," Ulster says. "I wanted to make money, be successful, and then have a life where I could do what I wanted to do, which was a lot of other things. I realized that I loved him, but it wasn't for me."

Best friends, they would continue as partners in some enterprises, but not Sherman's new foray into the pharmaceutical world. Ulster and Sherman were still teamed up with Fred Steiner in his coffee service business. Ulster and his future husband, Michael, who had a successful Toronto menswear store, worked in concert with Sherman in reinvesting some of their funds in second mortgages on commercial and residential properties. Those businesses would do well, and that, plus the cautious investment of his nest egg from the Empire sale, has funded a very comfortable but not lavish life for Ulster.

Ulster's final official contribution was to help Sherman name his new company. They tossed around some ideas the way they had bandied about monikers in school that combined parts of their names. The suffix *tex* was one they had always liked. The original word for a drugstore was *apothecary*, and so it was born: Apo-tex, which eventually became simply Apotex.

The new business he started in 1974 was on a street off Weston Road called Ormont Drive, in an industrial area in the northwest of Toronto. Sherman built a small factory, taking advice from professionals on the best type of materials for the floors and walls, and ensuring they were sealed so that a sterile environment would be easier to maintain than at the old Lansdowne building.

Fred Steiner was in the beginning stage of his own business, and Sherman took him aside and made him a proposition. "Why are you looking to lease space? I will never be able to use five thousand square feet. Move in with me," Sherman said, adding it would be rent free.

Over the next few years, the two men became close friends. As he did with Ulster's children, Sherman took a strong interest in Steiner's son and daughter from his first marriage, and eventually the daughter Fred and Bryna had together. Sherman wanted children of his own one day, but Honey had a series of miscarriages that delayed those plans. Bryna Steiner said she and Honey became pregnant at the same time, when the Steiners were living in Detroit before moving to Toronto permanently. Once a week, they would gab on the phone. Bryna's pregnancy went as planned, but Honey miscarried. After that, Honey did not tell her friend when she was pregnant. Bryna could always tell when Honey was pregnant over the next few years, though, because she would quit smoking and stop playing tennis, fearful of another miscarriage. In 1975, Honey and Barry welcomed their daughter Lauren into the world. She would remain an only child for close to a decade.

At the office, Steiner and Sherman discussed their businesses and politics, but never sports. Topics like sports would produce an explosion. Any mention of the Toronto Maple Leafs, Toronto's professional hockey team, would lead Sherman to opine at length on how ridiculous it was for someone to have an allegiance to a sports club. "That is the stupidest thing I ever heard," he'd tell Steiner. "They are not *Toronto* Maple Leafs. Why do you root for them? What makes you root for one team over another? They are not from Toronto; they are a bunch of people from here, here, and here." So vexed would Sherman get that he would dissect all parts of the allegiance, right down to the name of the team. "And why the 'Maple Leafs'?" Sherman would shout. "It makes no sense."

Discussions about politics resulted in more civil communication. Sherman taught the new Canadian resident (Steiner eventually became a dual citizen) the difference between the parliamentary system and the political structure in the United States. Sherman was a lifelong supporter of the Liberal Party of Canada, and he and Honey would from time to time host fundraisers at their home for local politicians and aspiring national leaders. He felt that the Liberals' stated belief in a wide social safety net was most aligned to his own beliefs, though he hated paying taxes to support that net.

One day, Steiner overheard a conversation that years later he would recognize as the beginning of Sherman's philanthropy. Steiner had dropped by Sherman's office, and they were "shooting the shit" when the telephone rang. Sherman motioned to Steiner to stay; it would be a brief conversation. As Steiner divined from listening in, it was a Toronto rabbi calling, and he had a problem. There was a Hebrew school that had a bus for disabled children. The bus had broken down. Sherman nodded, listening. The rabbi was talking a lot, pleading his case, and Steiner could hear the man's voice, though Sherman had the receiver pressed close to his ear. "Hmm . . . yes . . . hmm, uh-huh . . . yes. How much is it? Okay, I'll give it to you. But on one condition. Do not tell anybody where you got it."

SEVEN

THE TRAIL

THE MAN SEATED ACROSS FROM ME picked the knife up from his plate, and with a deftness that evoked the precision of a surgeon, he gently drew a slit down the centre of his second bran muffin, then buttered each side. The first bite he took was followed by a sharp slurp from his coffee cup. The volume appeared to be more than was intended, and the combination of liquid and muffin sent him into a deep coughing fit. A few dribbles of coffee escaped the corner of his mouth. Flecks from the first muffin, eaten the same way, were scattered down the front of his sports jacket, competing with its checked pattern. There was nobody else in the back corner of the restaurant. I waited.

"Why should I help you?" he asked, drawing out each word.

This was an excellent question. Why help a journalist?

January 18, 2018: a little over a month after the Shermans died. In the diner where we had agreed to meet, the walls were lined with sports and entertainment memorabilia. A lot of

diners have stock "signed" photos of Frank Sinatra and Bobby
Orr and David Copperfield, but these looked authentic. My
breakfast guest was staring at me, doing what my first partner
decades before always called "a cop thing," asking a question
and following it up with silence. I decided to bite. I was close to
getting a story and just needed a little more help.

"I get the real story of the Sherman deaths out," I said, "and
maybe something good comes out of it." I wanted to add something about "the truth" but figured that would sound too much
like a prepared speech.

"You can do better than that," he said.

I looked down at my empty coffee cup, then back up. "The
Shermans have spent a lot of money pulling together this private investigation team. Ex-homicide guys. A pathologist.
Lawyers. I am hearing four to five hundred dollars an hour for
each person on the team. And lots of hours."

I watched to see if he would contradict me on the figure, but
he did not. In my notebook, when I jotted down my recollections after our meeting, I called this man "Zero" as a code name.
"The team has found out some stuff. From what my other
sources say, important information the cops have missed or
maybe just ignored. Why not help me put that information on
the front page?"

I had arranged this meeting looking for a third source to
confirm, and perhaps add to, what I had already learned over
the past two weeks about the manner in which Barry and
Honey Sherman died. When you are pulling together strands
of information that competing parties—police and family—
want to keep secret, that is how it goes. Lots of meetings in
coffee shops and bars. To some extent, journalists are like
salesmen. We are selling our trustworthiness. Zero, my breakfast companion, brushed the crumbs off his lapels. This was

the first time we had met, but he came well recommended as a source with knowledge of this case by several people.

"I don't mind helping you. But I am not *in this*," he said. "Not in this at all. No name. No job identification. Nothing."

"You got it," I said.

"Or you're finished."

I took that in and nodded. Having arrived at an agreement, albeit an uneasy one, we began. No notes. No tape recorder. Just talk.

My journey to this meeting in a Toronto diner had begun two weeks earlier. On January 5, 2018, my boss at the *Toronto Star*, editor-in-chief Michael Cooke, sent me an email. "I don't know if you're looking at the Sherman case—but JH dropped by with some info from someone he termed 'absolutely close to the family.'" JH is John Honderich. He and his family are the leaders of a group of five families that have a controlling interest in Torstar, a publicly owned media company that owns the *Toronto Star*. Honderich is the company chairman. Both he and Cooke are also legendary newsmen with, as the old saying goes, ink in their veins. If *they* sensed a bigger story, it was most likely a bigger story.

Full confession here. When news first broke of the Sherman bodies being found, followed up the next day by the murder-suicide story in the *Toronto Sun* and then my own paper and others, I believed the theory. I knew very little about Barry Sherman and had never heard of his wife, but I did know from thirty-four years of covering and investigating various elements of the human tapestry that sometimes people snap. On my own and with various partners, and as the leader of the investigative team at the *Star* for a big chunk of my career, I have rubbed up against many seemingly bizarre events. Parents who lose it and kill their children. Children who kill their parents. Top executives who are well paid but rob their company or the government blind. Husbands and wives who run out of patience and turn to murder. Religious leaders who sodomize little boys and then are protected by their organization, which covers up the crimes. A cult leader who hacks off a devotee's arm, disappears into the forest in small-town Ontario, and is later found to have killed another follower, after he impregnated all the female members of his cult and fathered twenty-six children.

My point is, bad things happen, and sometimes outwardly good people have a dark side. I knew only that Barry Sherman was the founder and owner of Apotex. I knew nothing about his personal life. On January 5, when Cooke assigned me to sniff around, I knew only what I had read in the media, beginning with the blockbuster article by *Toronto Sun* columnist Joe Warmington the day after the bodies were discovered. When I read that piece, I believed that he was correct in reporting that the police considered it a murder-suicide. While I have often criticized the police over the years, I did not believe that the Toronto Police Service could get something so wrong. This was not, after all, just any pair of deaths. The Shermans were very wealthy people whose deaths, given the way the world works, would likely be given high priority. It seemed to me that the police and the media must have got it right. My wife, to her credit, told me I was wrong.

"Tell me one time when two billionaires died like this in a murder-suicide," she said.

"It happens all the time," I shot back.

"Name one other case," she said. "One case of murder-suicide like this."

I did some online checking and talked to experts I knew in policing and pathology. Nothing. Sure, husbands killed wives and then themselves. Usually a gun was involved for both deaths, or the wife was bashed over the head and the husband shot himself. Sometimes the husband killed the wife then set fire to the house while he was still inside. But with both deaths attributed to strangulation, or "ligature neck compression," this type of murder-suicide just did not happen. If it *had* happened in the Sherman case, the mechanics of it were not clear to me. At the time, the media reports said the couple were found hanging in the pool room, but there was no clarity on the positioning of the bodies. The word *hanging* conjures up an image of being hung from a height, high enough for a drop of some distance and for the legs to swing free. Was that what happened? Nobody was saying. There was another reason the whole murder-suicide or double suicide by strangulation theories did not make sense. Given the nature of Barry Sherman's business, wouldn't pills be the obvious method?

Beyond the initial reporting in December, not much else was known publicly. Yet there was a tremendous interest in the case. At the *Toronto Star*, our reporters, most notably intern Victoria Gibson, had written fascinating stories on the litigious nature of Barry Sherman. In one example, Gibson had unearthed court documents showing that the Shermans' house was the subject of a lawsuit years before and that Sherman had come close to recouping the entire cost to build the home. Stories like that were interesting, but none of the journalism produced in the three weeks since the bodies were discovered had tackled the central issue: Was it murder-suicide, double suicide, or double homicide?

As it turned out, one of my wife's friends knew the Shermans in passing and was close with people who knew the deceased couple. She called to pass on her thoughts. "People who knew the Shermans are saying there is no way, not even a chance, that it is murder-suicide," she said. "You should look into this."

Assigned to this story by my wife, her friend, and now my editor, the question was how to find out what was going on behind the scenes. The Sherman family had buried Barry and Honey and hired a private investigation team to conduct an unheard-of, at least in Toronto police history, mirror investigation. Leading the charge was Brian Greenspan, one of Canada's top criminal lawyers. Greenspan and I had clashed over a number of high-profile cases. Once, he held a press conference outside a courthouse and denounced me because of stories I had written about one of his clients. I was pretty sure Greenspan and his team would be of no help, at least not initially.

The gist of Michael Cooke's email to me was this: our mutual boss, Honderich, who, compared to most journalists, travels in rarefied circles, had been hearing from people who knew the Shermans that the police had it completely wrong. Cooke's note presented me with three pieces of information, but I was not given the source or sources. First, that it was a double murder. Second, the motive might be connected to a land deal "which went badly wrong." Third, that the Shermans may have been murdered as payback for a lawsuit involving bitter family members, cousins who, the note said, "challenged [Sherman] in court and lost . . . and Sherman called in the loans on their homes."

To me, the first relevant question to be answered was the manner of their deaths. If it really was murder-suicide, it hardly mattered if there was a bad land deal or some upset cousins. That would fall under the category of "nice-to-know information," as a cop once called revelations that are interesting but not germane to an investigation. The real challenge was to determine if the police theory of murder-suicide held water. To figure this out, I needed to learn everything about their deaths, including who found the bodies, when they were discovered, how they were positioned, specific details on the cause of death, whether there were any other markings on the bodies, and whether drugs were a factor.

In most cases, in fact in every other case I have reported on, the first source a reporter turns to is the family. In December 1988, a black teenager in Mississauga, west of Toronto, was shot dead by Peel Regional Police officers. Wade Lawson had stolen a car. The initial press release stated that Lawson, aged seventeen, had driven the car directly at officers and the police fired six shots. One hollow-point bullet—designed to have maximum stopping power, because it expands and flattens on impact—struck Lawson in the head. I was a young reporter at the time, just three years into my career. The shooting happened overnight. Early the next morning, working the phones from the *Toronto Star* offices before heading out into the field, I called through to the hospital where Lawson, barely alive, was being treated. With the help of our now defunct switchboard at the *Star*, I was suddenly speaking to Wade's father. He told me how devastated he was, and how angry he was at the police. Before I said goodbye, I questioned him on his son's injuries. Lawson was in critical care and would soon die. The hollow-point bullet had, as its design intended, caused maximum damage. I told Mr. Lawson I had heard from the police that his son had been driving towards the officers. Just to be sure I had the correct details, I asked where in the front of his head the bullet had entered. Mr. Lawson paused, then he told me that the bullet had entered the back of his son's head. It proved a key piece of information, as it was evidence that Lawson was driving away from the officers when shot. The story made the front page the next day. Here was a man who, at the worst possible moment in his life, had spoken to a reporter and answered what in retrospect was an important but very brutal question about the son he loved. (Both police officers were later charged—one with manslaughter, the other with aggravated assault—and acquitted.)

The Sherman family had a vastly different approach. No one in the large extended family—the four adult children, Barry and Honey's siblings, nieces, and nephews—would speak to reporters. At the funeral, which received widespread coverage, son Jonathon railed against the "unreliable news media," saying that his family "had to navigate through a terrifying maze of non-information and unfounded speculation."

For now, it was clear the family would not be providing any information. The story was still out there that Barry killed Honey, and the Sherman children did not want the media's help in discovering if that was true. This was outside my understanding, as families typically speak to the media. I tried to fathom why the Shermans distrusted the media so much. Honey Sherman, according to her golf friends and trainer, not only regularly read the newspapers, the *Toronto Star* was her favourite. Every morning, when Barry Sherman opened his front door to collect a paper from the doorstep, it was the *Star* he picked up. Yet I was aware that my paper had published stories unflattering to Apotex, including investigations by my team that looked at how regulators had discovered impurities in Apotex production facilities in India. The *Star*'s Jacques Gallant had also, just a few months before the Shermans' deaths, published a lengthy piece on the upcoming court challenge by the Winter cousins, who were seeking $1 billion from Sherman.

It was not just the *Toronto Star* writing those stories. Over the years, other media had produced stories that could be deemed negative. One series of stories dealt with complaints of improper lobbying made by the citizen advocacy group Democracy Watch, which alleged it was wrong for Sherman, registered with the government as a lobbyist for Apotex, to host a gala fundraiser at his home for Liberal leader Justin Trudeau in 2015 during the campaign in which Trudeau was later elected prime minister. There was also widespread coverage of Sherman's long battle with a researcher over a controversial drug treatment. Generally, and this is confirmed by Apotex public relations chief Jordan Berman, if Sherman or Apotex was in the news, the coverage was not favourable. Though in all these cases the media was truthfully reporting on actual events, the Sherman children were uncooperative when approached about their parents' deaths.

I set about looking for anyone in the field of policing, private detection, or forensics who might possibly have picked up some information. Even a tidbit I could use to leverage another interview. It is a reality of investigative reporting that a journalist cannot simply call up a source and compel them to provide information. Sometimes, the best way to get information is to tell a source what you already know. This makes the new source more at ease and encourages that person to see it as only confirming, not revealing. I also began speaking to people who knew the Sherman family and had been in touch with them, to find out what the children and other family members had learned from police and the two sets of autopsies: the official post-mortems and the post-mortems conducted by the family's hired pathologist. When I began, I did not even know that pathologist's name. I did this on the premise that a fundamental aspect of human nature is a desire to communicate what you know. When a person learns something, he or she cannot help but pass that information on to others. A good reporter recognizes that and gathers information from the outside in, always tracing and trying to verify, in the hope of getting to the original source and the best information.

One of the people who had helped me over the years on various stories was Dr. Jim Cairns, Ontario's former deputy chief coroner. The native of Ireland had a deep belief that the justice system occasionally needed the assistance of the media to right wrongs or provide a focus where one was lacking. Though retired from government service, Cairns was someone I and other journalists went to for advice, context, and suggestions on how to research a story involving a mysterious death. He had been at the centre of many of the highest profile cases in Ontario history and had consulted internationally for years on suspicious deaths. He had many friends and contacts in the forensic and policing community and kept in touch with them. Despite being retired, he was still in the game. I had phoned Cairns to see if he could help me understand the science of ligature compression, the medical cause of death for both of the Shermans. As we spoke in general about ligature compression and the Shermans, I could tell Cairns was speaking from certainty rather than speculation, and I asked him if he was involved in the case. There was a long pause, and I imagined Cairns, on the other end of the line, crinkling his eyebrows. "Kevin," he said, his Irish lilt strong, "as a matter of fact, I am." With his help, and the help of other sources with knowledge of the case, I gained enough understanding to seek confirmation and elaboration of key details in the deaths of Barry and Honey Sherman.

Twelve days after being assigned to the story, I sat in the diner with Zero. The waiter poured me a fresh coffee. Zero put a hand over his own cup and waved him off. "One's enough for me."

I reached into the pocket of my coat, which was hanging on the back of my chair. I watched Zero tense, then relax when he saw the paper printout in my hand. I unfolded the paper and spread it on the table. It was a photo taken from the internet, a real estate shot, because the house had been listed for sale. The photo was a panoramic view of the Sherman pool in the basement level of the home.

"I don't get it," I said.

"What?"

"All the stories I have read say Barry and Honey were found hanging in the pool room. Hanging from what? The railing?"

"Yup."

The photo showed a stainless steel safety handrail around one end of the pool, its vertical posts bolted close to the edge.

"You can't hang yourself from three feet high," I said.

Zero chuckled. "You've got that right."

I decided to push him a little bit. "Were their legs in the pool? Is that the way they were facing?"

"Huh?"

I said nothing.

"Oh, no, not in the pool. Look, their legs were facing away from the pool. Stretched out in front."

I referred to something one of my sources had said. "Guy I talked to who knows the family said they were 'in repose.'"

Zero's eyes narrowed. "I don't know what the fuck 'in repose' means. They were sitting upright, held upright, legs out front."

"Held up by belts?"

"Yup. Two men's belts."

"Both his?"

"Well, he sure as fuck wasn't wearing two men's belts. One was his. The other, nobody knows where the other one came from."

The waiter came by. I asked for a refill, though I was swimming. Zero allowed another splash. *Keep him drinking coffee*, I thought. *Keep him here.*

Zero took a sip. "Look, *hanging* is the wrong word. Don't use *hanging*. *Hanging* gives the wrong idea." He sat back in his chair, wiped a napkin over his face, then hunched forward and lowered his voice. He asked me if I knew that the family had its own post-mortems done.

"Chiasson," I said, trying the name of a person Cairns had told me had done the post-mortems. "Dr. David Chiasson."

"You have good sources. Yup. He's a big deal, apparently. The whole private team was present, of course, but he was the guy with the scalpel, so he gets the credit. What he found . . ." Zero leaned in even closer. A woman doing a quick mop of the floor had come too near for his comfort. He waited until she had moved on. "What he found was that they were strangled with something soft, as in a belt is soft. Or maybe something else, but most likely the belt. But they were strangled with enough force to shut off the windpipe, but not enough to crack anything."

A medical term popped up from something one of my other sources had said. "Hyoid bone." I said it as a statement, not a question.

This time he looked right into my eyes. "Who have you been talking to?"

I gave him silence back.

"Okay, I get it. You can't betray a source. I like that, for obvious reasons. You are right. The hyoid bone was not broken."

"Hyoid bone gets broken when?" I asked, wanting to see how much he knew.

He picked up a napkin and took out a pen. He drew what I gathered was a neck and then he drew a U shape, the hyoid bone. "To fracture it, from what I understand, you need something really strong, certainly not a soft ligature like a leather belt. It also gets fractured in an old-fashioned hanging, where the person is dropped from a height. That is not what happened here. They were strangled enough to choke off their wind. That's all."

"Which is what happens in suicide?"

"But this was not a suicide. There are other things," Zero said.

"Their hands?"

"More specifically, their wrists."

"I hear there are markings that showed they were tied behind their backs."

"Careful," he said. He put his hands in front of him, wrists together, then put them behind his back, also together. Both times, he turned the wrists so that a different part of one wrist was touching the other wrist. "You try and tell me how they were tied. Nobody knows. There are marks, sort of abrasions from something, but only on one side of the wrists. It is not clear if the wrists were tied in front or in back."

"By a rope?"

"I would not say rope for sure. Could be something plastic made the marks."

Thinking back to something I had seen the military use on prisoners when I covered conflicts overseas, I said, "Like a zap strap? Or a zip tie? You can get them at Home Depot for binding wires and stuff together."

"Yup. And nothing like that was found near the bodies, plastic or rope. So here we have wrists that were bound together hard enough to leave marks, then untied." He put the napkin he had scrawled on into his pocket. "Look, I have given you a lot. I have to go."

Before he could stand up, I asked another question. "Bodies found on Friday. When were they last seen?"

"Wednesday evening around 8 P.M. was the last text or telephone contact from him. Nothing from her, so he was the last one to be heard from." Zero leaned in again. "Okay, I think it was an email from him around 8:15 P.M. Maybe a bit later."

"When did they die?"

"My guess? Late Wednesday or early Thursday. But no later than that. Which makes me wonder, What the fuck were family, friends, and office workers thinking when they did not hear from the billionaire?" This time he stood up.

I got the sense he felt he'd said too much with that last comment. I wanted to talk to him again, so I did not want to be a pest. We agreed he would walk out first. As he was putting his coat on, he came back to the table. "I am counting on you to honour our deal," he said. "What I can tell you is that in addition to the pathologist you already knew about, there is a combined total of a hundred years of homicide investigation experience working on this case as private investigators. From everything that the team has looked at, this is a staged homicide. Likely a contract killing. Those two did not die from sitting under a little railing with belts looped around their necks. Somebody did this to them."

"Then how did the cops get it so wrong?"

"They rushed to a conclusion. Tunnel vision. It was bullshit, but then they got stuck. And they still are."

When he left, I took out my notebook and filled pages of it with the details of our conversation. Then I headed to the *Toronto Star* newsroom. The place had changed a lot in the years I had worked there. Gone were the smoke-filled "get me rewrite" days, the era of editors and reporters banging away on Underwood typewriters and sneaking a drink while they hovered over the latest crime story. Although it was quieter— the office almost had an insurance agency atmosphere at times—the people in it still craved a big story. And nobody ever played a story bigger than the editor-in-chief, Michael Cooke.

He, our lawyer Bert Bruser, managing editor Irene Gentle, and I gathered around the "hub," a long table in the centre of the newsroom. I had written a piece based on my nearly two weeks of investigation. We worked through it, me answering questions from all three and making changes on my printout. What they were initially puzzled by was my description of how the bodies were positioned. In what must have been a macabre sight to anyone nearby, I finally took off my own belt, looped it around my neck by feeding the end through the buckle, positioned myself on the floor with legs out, and held the end of the belt up as if it were tied above my head. A couple of colleagues heading downstairs for coffee whispered to each other when they saw me sitting on the floor with a leather noose. I shrugged and smiled at them.

Cooke looked at me, then down at his printout. He scribbled a few words, changing my description to make it clear. Back at my desk, I made a few changes to the draft based on our discussion, then sent it on to the copy desk. Cooke wrote the headline: "Barry and Honey Sherman Were Murdered." It would soon appear on our website and scream across the front page of the Saturday print edition atop photos of the couple. Additional words under the headline made it clear that this was the conclusion of the private investigation team, according to sources. The first paragraph of the story, or lede, as it is called, read, "It's double murder, not murder-suicide. Barry and Honey Sherman were killed in what looks like a professional, contract killing. That's the conclusion of a variety of experts who have been hired by the family to probe the case."

The story online was read by almost a million people in two days, in Canada and around the world. It was also read by senior officers in the Toronto Police Service, who summoned the homicide and division detectives working the Sherman case.

The order was simple: interview David Chiasson, the pathologist hired by the family. Jim Cairns, who would later fill me in on the background activities the story spawned, said he could never understand why police needed a story on the front page of a newspaper to spur them to interview someone they should have spoken to weeks earlier. Police did get in touch with Chiasson, who spoke to them the following Wednesday. Then police talked again to Michael Pickup, who had performed the first autopsy. Pickup concurred with Chiasson's findings.

At the end of the week, the Toronto Police public relations department announced a press conference to provide an "update" on the Sherman case. Detective Sergeant Susan Gomes, the lead homicide officer, stood behind a lectern in the media briefing room, reading prepared remarks from a sheaf of papers in her hands, rarely looking up. She said that the police had been working tirelessly on the case and that from the start they had considered three scenarios: double suicide, homicide-suicide, and double homicide.

As about fifty journalists looked on, she then delivered the news of the day. "We believe now, after six weeks of work review, we have sufficient evidence to describe this as a double homicide investigation and that both Barry and Honey Sherman were targeted."

Gomes then detailed what the officers under her command had done to date. They had executed twenty search warrants; seized Barry Sherman's computer at Apotex; forensically examined the Sherman home; seized 150 "bulk or packaged items" from 50 Old Colony Road and the Sherman condominium in Florida; and taken 127 witness statements. The neighbourhood had been extensively canvassed, and police had obtained about two thousand hours of video surveillance from commercial and residential surveillance cameras. Thousands of person hours had been spent on the case, Gomes told reporters. As to what they had discovered, Gomes refused to answer any questions.

With the police search over, Gomes said, her team had that morning returned the home to the Sherman family. Over at Old Colony Road, Greenspan's team of investigators were already moving through the house. For the Sherman family and friends, the conversation would now turn from questions about how the police could ever have believed it was murder-suicide to an ongoing debate about who would have wanted them dead. A wide range of theories were bandied about: it was a hit team from the Mossad in Israel; it was an aggrieved business party. More than a year later, in a conversation I had with Greenspan, I asked him how, in his experience, a murder investigation should develop. Greenspan replied, "The classic investigation is you start at the centre and move outwards, eliminating suspects as you go." Whether the police were doing that in the first few months is unknown as, at time of writing, police would not say who they had cleared as suspects and who was still on the list.

Back at the *Star*, after police reporter Wendy Gillis and I had filed the story, I was going over notes in my little office that served as a sort of war room and that a colleague had nick-named the Caper Room. Lawyer Bert Bruser walked in. Bruser and I met when I was a summer intern and had made what at the time seemed like a grave error. I had given a statement to police in a homicide investigation where the victim was a *Toronto Star* employee in our circulation department. Through my reporting on her murder, I had interviewed the man eventually charged with killing her. As I learned the day I met Bruser, I should not have spoken to police without his permission and guidance. Thirty-four years later, he still regularly told journalism students that story as a cautionary tale. Since then, he had been my lawyer, mentor, friend, and quite often antagonist. He sat down in my guest chair and flipped through emails on his iPhone. Bruser never does anything quickly. I put down my notes, looked at his deeply lined face, and waited.

"Good story. Stories, I guess."

Again, I waited. One of the things he taught me was the power of silence.

"But that was the easy part. Now the real work starts. Find out who killed them."

EIGHT

MAKE A BIT OF MONEY

"I CAN'T DIE, JACK," BARRY SHERMAN CALLED out from his office. "The world can't get along without me."

"Barry, you're full of shit," Jack Kay, second-in-command at Apotex, yelled back through the open door of the office next to Sherman's.

"I still have so much to do," said Sherman. "I can't die."

"You're still full of shit," his friend replied.

As would be the case no matter how big the generic firm became in years to come, Sherman and Kay were never physically far from each other, just as it was with Sherman and Ulster at the Empire office years before. It was the mid-1980s now, and Apotex was growing. Even when they constructed bigger offices in a new building, the connecting door between them would always be open, albeit separated by a small experimentation room, where Sherman tried new formulations. A low table held a small incubator, test tubes, and devices to analyze his pill experiments.

"No man in my family has lived past forty-seven, not my dad, not my uncle," Sherman called out. He added thoughtfully, "Then again, Moses lived to be one hundred and twenty."

Once, in the 1970s, Joel Ulster recalls, Sherman smoked a marijuana joint, back when Sherman and Ulster were still partners in the generic drug business. Stoned, out of control for the first and only time in his life, Sherman grabbed a notepad and, as Ulster's eyes widened, began writing numerical formulas, pages and pages, which he pronounced were the secret to immortality. His theory, which had some grounding in science, was that as people age, their cells break down. Sherman's formula would alter the DNA in a human body and reverse the process. He grew more and more excited as he scribbled, as did Ulster. The next morning, Ulster asked his now sober best friend about the formula. "It's complete nonsense, none of it makes any sense," Sherman said. Though he would years later begin working on a plan to make marijuana pills, Sherman never used the drug again.

Sherman had a fatalistic quality. "I have always been very conscious of my personal mortality," he wrote on the first page of his unfinished memoir. Death was a topic he often raised in jest. In an interview for Jeffrey Robinson's 2001 book on the pharmaceutical industry, when asked about what he perceived as his many enemies, Sherman told the author that he was surprised someone had not collected a thousand dollars to "knock me off."

At his desk, Kay smiled at Sherman's gloomy assessment. He had heard all this before. "You have years to go, Barry."

Joanne Mauro, the executive assistant Sherman hired in 1976 as a high school student, who would still be at Apotex after Sherman died, sat outside their offices. She chuckled. The way the two men carried on no longer surprised her, but it shocked newcomers. On more than one occasion, someone had come in for a meeting, overheard Sherman and Kay yelling back and forth about some deal, or God, or politics, and said to Mauro, "Maybe I should come back later?" She would just usher the person into the office.

Mauro, Kay, and the few others who truly knew Barry Sherman had long ago learned that their brainy boss had a dry wit. Anyone was fair game. Reaching over a pile of calculations on his desk one day, Sherman rummaged around and found a sheaf of brown envelopes and the telephone. He dialled his lawyer, Harry Radomski, who worked at a Bay Street law firm in downtown Toronto.

"Harry? We have a problem."

At the other end of the line, Radomski held his breath. Sherman was rapidly becoming his best client, and complaints were rare. In fact, he could not remember a complaint. They worked side by side on cases as Sherman grew his business and battled government, brand name pharmaceutical companies, and other generic firms, using the courts as a cudgel.

"Barry, to begin with, I am sorry. How can I help?" asked Radomski. So closely did they work together that Sherman, though he had no formal legal training, routinely helped Radomski devise strategies to be used in court and sometimes even draft documents for the case.

"It's your accounts," said Sherman. "You just sent me ten accounts."

Radomski took another breath. He did a lot of work for Sherman and was well paid, and he was careful not to charge too much. But he had recently sent quite a few bills, or "accounts."

"Barry, I did. Were they in order? Do you want to go over them?"

Silence. Then Sherman cleared his throat. "You sent ten accounts. In ten envelopes. Next time, if you send them in one envelope, you will save the price of nine stamps."

Radomski exhaled. "Thanks, Barry."

It was a lively office with a mix of veteran employees and young people. Sherman enjoyed giving young people a start in life and a pay cheque, even if they were not going to make the generic drug business their life's work. One of the young people he helped was Joel Ulster's son Mark. He had struggled out of high school, and Sherman had blamed his good friend Joel's bohemian lifestyle for the boy's wayward attitude. At one point, Joel recalls, Sherman took him aside and asked if he could intervene. "You are not doing a good job as a father," Sherman said. To help his friend's son get going in life, Sherman had given him a job at age seventeen. For some time, he had tried to convince Mark to learn the ropes at Apotex and one day take over from Sherman. It would be many years before any of Barry and Honey's children would be old enough to even suggest they should be part of the Apotex succession plan. Mark, not yet twenty years old when the subject of his future at Apotex was raised, and with little interest in pharmaceuticals, said thanks but no thanks to Uncle Barry. He was happy to continue working for a few years at Apotex with Mauro and the other women who made up the office staff, but he did not want to be part of Barry Sherman's plans for the future. "I was a moralistic kid, and I think, looking back to those days, I did not want to sell out," Mark says.

Sherman called Mark into his office one day. As he sometimes did in those early days before automated payroll, Sherman handed Mark a stack of two hundred payroll cheques and asked him to sign the "Barry Sherman" signature. He had neither the time nor the interest to do it himself. Mark went into a closet-sized office off the corridor outside Sherman's office. It was an odd request, but he was used to Sherman and appreciated the trust. In later years, he would realize he was just one of many youngsters who received both trust and help from the Apotex billionaire.

Kay smiled at the activity going on around him and allowed himself a moment's reverie before the next plan or proposal came out of his "brother" Barry's mouth. This was a typical day at Apotex.

The two men shared a brotherly affection for one another, but they could not be mistaken for siblings. Kay was a bull, short of stature but muscular. When I first shook his hand, in 2018, I tensed, bracing myself as men sometimes do, seeing the swell of the seventy-seven-year-old man's biceps. For his entire adult life, Kay has watched his diet and worked out in a gym every second day at 6 A.M. Sherman had different habits, and his body was accordingly soft. But from the moment they met, their brains clicked.

Kay did not begin his career in the generic pharmaceutical world. After university, he trained as a psychiatric nurse at a hospital in Weyburn, Saskatchewan. His specialty in the years he practised was developing an understanding of psychotropic drugs, pharmaceuticals that affect a person's mental state. A brand name pharmaceutical company hired him to be a "detail man," a salesman who travelled around visiting doctors with samples and information, trying to persuade them to prescribe a particular medicine. "Pretty boring after a while," Kay recalls. With a partner, he started his own company, Sabra Pharmaceuticals, which he sold in 1972 to ICN and Morris Goodman, the generic pioneer, who around the same time purchased Sherman and Ulster's Empire Laboratories. Kay moved his wife and family to Montreal and worked closely with Goodman as director of government sales. As one of Goodman's top executives, Kay was put in charge of integrating Empire Laboratories into the ICN portfolio.

Kay was aware of Sherman and knew the story Goodman liked to tell about how he had fired him, but he had only met the

Barry Sherman relaxing at the home of Joel and Cindy Ulster, early 1970s.

Honey Sherman mugging for the camera before departing on Polar Bear Express train voyage with Barry, Joel Ulster, and Michael Hertzman, 1974.

Barry and Honey smoking cigars prior to embarking on Polar Bear Express train voyage in northern Ontario, 1974.

Barry and Honey, mid 1970s.

Good friends and business partners Joel Ulster, Fred Steiner,
and Barry Sherman in Toronto, 1983. By this time Ulster was living
in New York but the trio maintained close contact.

Sherman family, mid 1990s. Foreground: Kaelen, Honey, and Alex. Rear: Lauren, Barry, and Jonathon.

Lou and Beverley Winter's children on holiday in Spain in 1965. From left to right: Dana, Jeffrey, Kerry, and Tim.

Barry and Honey Sherman in the backyard of the 50 Old Colony Rd.
home after playing tennis, early 1990s.

Toronto dinner party in advance of launch of Frank D'Angelo
movie *Real Gangsters*. Starting from left, Honey Sherman,
Barry Sherman, Frank D'Angelo, actors Michael Pare and
Robert Mangiardi. On right side, guests include actors Robert Loggia
(second) and Tony Rosato (third), and at the far end of
the table is Canadian boxing great George Chuvalo.

Barry and Honey Sherman, Bryna and Fred Steiner,
in Florida at Fred's 70th birthday party, 2009.

Honey Sherman, Dahlia Solomon, and Anita Franklin at
Kiawah Island Golf Resort in South Carolina, November, 2017,
one month before Honey and Barry were murdered.

Jack Kay and Barry Sherman in Apotex laboratories, 1999.
(Credit: Dave Cooper, *Toronto Star*)

Flower memorial at Barry Sherman's parking space at Apotex headquarters in Toronto in July, 2018, seven months after the murders.
(Credit: Kevin Donovan)

Fred Mercure and husband Jonathon Sherman in public Facebook post from 2014, hiking in the Yukon.

♥ 3

Jonathon Sherman speaking to 7,000 people at his parents' funeral at the International Centre in Mississauga on December 21, 2017. Sister Lauren on the left, and sisters Kaelen and Alex on the right.

(Photo taken from live public video stream of funeral.)

Barry and granddaughter (daughter of Alex and Brad)
on December 7, 2017, a week before the murders.

Toronto man in passing. In 1982, Sherman was looking for a new director of sales, and he knew of Kay from an industry association. He drove to Montreal to make a pitch, visiting Kay at his townhouse. Money was not discussed. Life and God were. Both men were atheists, though they enjoyed the social and family aspects of the Jewish culture. But Sherman became visibly angry at the notion that a person would believe in God, which he told Kay was "stupid." In his memoir, Sherman wrote that the whole concept of organized religion annoyed him: "I have always felt disdain for organized religion and for the foolishness or hypocrisy of clergymen who sell religion as a source of morality or everlasting life." One of his many observations was that he believed there was a "reverse correlation" when it came to generosity and faith. "Atheists often are enormously more generous than persons obsessively committed to seemingly absurd religious rituals," he wrote. Kay tried, and kept trying for all the years they knew each other, to convince Sherman to be tolerant of people who had a belief in a deity, explaining that it was most likely because they had been raised with that notion.

"Barry, just as you believe there is not a God, there are people who believe there is a God," he said.

"It's an impossibility," Sherman replied.

Their freewheeling conversation moved to the generic business, Apotex, and the job offer at hand. Kay had a good position at ICN, but he was restless. He and his wife had separated, there was some uncertainty over the future of the American company, and he was looking for a change. But would Apotex be the right move? Sherman said that his company would grow and be profitable, because he was devising new techniques to manufacture pharmaceuticals and do it more cheaply than competitors. Margins were very important in the business. At the time, Canada had a system called compulsory licensing, which allowed generic firms to receive a licence from a brand name company to manufacture one of its patented drugs as long as they could prove they were making the identical product. In return for this licence, the generic company, which charged customers less for the drug, would pay 4 percent of its revenues from the generic version's sales to the brand company. It was a kind of symbiotic relationship, and though rocky at times it had generally worked well for many years. In fact, compulsory licensing was a huge boost to the generic industry when it was introduced. As long as they could prove they were making a safe and effective copy of the brand name drug, they could manufacture their own version, sell it for cheaper than the brand, and pay only a small portion of their sales revenues. Eventually, the brand name companies would grow tired of these "pirates" legally poaching from their profit share. They would get the ear of a new government and convince it that compulsory licensing was detrimental to research and development. But for the moment, the system allowed Sherman to develop a profitable game plan, provided he kept his production costs down.

"Why do you think you can be successful when others have failed?" Kay asked.

"I am smarter than everyone else," Sherman shot back.

At the end of a two-hour chat, Sherman stood up. "Jack, come work with me. We will build Apotex, and we will make a bit of money and have fun."

Kay took the job. When he arrived at the Apotex building in Toronto for his first day, he had second thoughts. The operation, in a factory now six years old, was not as modern as Sherman had made it out to be. There was clearly work to do.

With pharmaceuticals so much a part of everyday life today—cold remedies, painkillers, antibiotics—it is hard to imagine a time when they were not. The concept of the medicine-dispensing "apothecary," the word Sherman and Ulster took as inspiration for the company name Apotex, dates back thousands of years to ancient China, Egypt, and other parts of the world. Herbal remedies and some rudimentary chemical compounds were the staples of the early apothecary through the ages. Cures were promised for various ailments, headaches, and ill-defined maladies. Some of the biggest Big Pharma companies in the world today, including GlaxoSmithKline, trace their roots back to the second half of the nineteenth century in Europe. At the time, there was a melding of apothecaries that were using flora like the poppy (for morphine) and the cinchona tree (for quinine) with dye and chemical companies whose scientists were discovering that the products they were making for one application also had a medicinal quality. With this development, particularly in Germany, the modern pharmaceutical industry was born. In probably the most recognizable example of a "wonder drug," in 1897 a chemist at the German company Bayer developed Aspirin, formulating into tablets the salicylic acid found naturally in jasmine, clover, and willow and other trees. It was a marriage of modern nineteenth-century science with knowledge that was more than two thousand years old; the Greeks, most notably Hippocrates, knew about the pain-relieving qualities of willow leaves and bark, as did several other ancient cultures.

In the United States, the Pfizer drug giant was founded in 1849 with a single product that was used to treat intestinal worms, which, the company's historical records note, was "a common affliction in mid-19th-century America." The German-American Charles Pfizer set up the company with his cousin and future brother-in-law Charles Erhart. Pfizer was a chemist; Erhart was a confectioner. Pfizer took the active pharmaceutical ingredient santonin and combined it with an almond-toffee flavouring Erhart had developed and shaped it into a candy cone for a sweeter delivery of the product. The company was instantly profitable. With the coming of the American Civil War between the northern and southern states, the demand for painkillers and disinfectants soared, and Pfizer's profits rose with the demand.

At the heart of all pharmaceuticals are chemicals, something Sherman and Kay understood very well. "It's a chemical business," Kay says simply. Over time, pharmaceuticals, whether brand name or generic, became one of the largest industries in the world. Controversy dogs the business, as it has since the days of the travelling snake oil salesmen who would roam the American frontier offering potions with inflated cure potential.

Today, one controversy is whether drugs are over-prescribed. And there is much debate over the role of pharmaceutical companies in funding academic research. Sherman, particularly with one notable drug treatment he funded in later years, would step firmly into that murky discussion, ultimately with a surprisingly positive result for him shortly before he died. But beyond that, Sherman was uninterested in whether it was ethical to manufacture so many drugs. Was it appropriate for him to manufacture opiate-based drugs at Apotex for use in painkillers that, if used incorrectly, could kill someone? If it concerned him, he never said so publicly or to any of his colleagues interviewed for this book. Not long before his death, Sherman would spend $50 million to purchase a Florida facility to manufacture a generic fentanyl product for sale in the United States; he did it because the law prevented him from exporting Canadian-made controlled substances south of the border. It was a business for him, plain and simple. The doctors prescribed the drugs;

Sherman just made them as cheaply as possible. Yet, with the people closest to him, he shared a deeper belief in what he saw as his role as a generic drug provider. His daughter Alex told me that when her father learned shortly before his death that he was to be awarded the Order of Canada, he was "very proud." She said her father, who she has dubbed a "healing love warrior," was committed to assisting others and "worked hard for Canada's healthcare system in many ways for many decades."

As to Apotex, it was a business Sherman wanted to grow in Canada to provide jobs for Canadians. When other pharmaceutical manufacturing companies left Canada, he responded by adding more production facilities. At the time of his death, Sherman had six thousand employees in Canada and eleven thousand worldwide, including factories in Mexico and India. How he achieved that involved a combination of brinkmanship, risk, and intellect.

Apotex and Sherman would one day engineer a drug to help sustain the lives of a small number of young children suffering from a blood disorder. They would provide generic versions of AIDS drugs and donate them overseas. But the drug that put Sherman on the road to being a billionaire and began the meteoric rise of Apotex to the position of Canada's leading generic company treated much more common afflictions: acid reflux and ulcers. Acid reflux is a condition in which acidic gastric fluid is regurgitated into the esophagus. At its most minor level, it is an uncomfortable feeling we call heartburn. But if it becomes chronic, there can be serious damage to the esophagus. Acid reflux can also be an indication of an ulcer. These conditions affect millions of Canadians. The Canadian Society of Intestinal Research estimates that 13 percent of Canadians have acid reflux, or a related condition, on a weekly basis.

In 1982, the year that Jack Kay joined Apotex, relief came to sufferers when the drug Zantac was launched by GlaxoSmithKline. It rapidly became the highest selling drug in Canada and a huge money-maker for Glaxo. That information—the number of individual dosages sold—was itemized in Section L of a book chock full of prescription data sold by an American company called IMS Health (now renamed IQVIA after a series of recent mergers). The data is purchased from the pharmacies who fill the doctors' prescriptions, and it is a helpful tool for all pharmaceutical manufacturers to track how well a product is selling. Governments and private insurers looking for trends to forecast costs also use the information. But the IMS Health data was expensive, beyond the reach of the fledgling Apotex's purchasing power at the time. In his book about the generic industry, *Trials and Triumphs,* author D'Arcy Jenish quotes Sherman as saying that in the early days Honey Sherman did the company's books, and in the late 1970s, "We were losing $10,000 a month." The early 1980s showed an improvement in their finances, but Sherman was not about to spend thousands of dollars on the IMS subscription. Instead, he and his new employee Jack Kay figured out that they only needed the IMS pages that showed the top sellers. An official they knew in the federal government provided those. They took the top sellers—Zantac was number one—and set about seeing if they could obtain the active pharmaceutical ingredient and manufacture their own version.

"We didn't care what type of drug it was," Kay says.

Just as Sherman had done with those crumbling vitamin C tablets so many years before at Empire, he worked to come up with the correct formulation, a blend of the active ingredient and the excipients, the compounds that would make a pill that would properly deliver the active ingredient to the patient's system.

It took five years of product development and for the federal approval process to run its course before Apotex could bring its generic form of Zantac to market. The key ingredient was a chemical compound called ranitidine. Sherman and Kay found a supplier in Italy, which was then a major source of the chemicals that make up many pharmaceuticals. A little known fact is that most of the drugs we take these days have a connection to the petroleum industry. Ranitidine is synthesized from the chemical nitromethane, a highly toxic substance used both as a cleaning solvent and a race car fuel. Apotex's version arrived in pharmacies in 1987, and the low-cost version was frequently substituted for Zantac. That gave sales and profits at Apotex a huge boost.

"We were dancing," Kay recalls. Their big competitor in the Canadian generic market, Novopharm, owned by rival Leslie Dan, was not even close to getting its version to market. In the world of generic drugs, the first company in makes the big money. The Apotex sales force visited hundreds of pharmacists and pharmacy chains, talking up the product, and individual salespeople made hundreds of thousands of dollars in commissions each from Zantac alone. Kay said he and Sherman watched the revenues climb and allowed themselves a brief pause to marvel at their success before diving into the next product launch.

"We finally did it. We are ahead of our competitors. We are going to make a lot of money. And we had the happiest sales force in the country," Kay says.

As the business grew, it became clear that the acerbic Sherman should concentrate on the science and product development; Kay, with his outgoing personality and street smarts, should oversee sales. Aubrey Dan, son of Leslie Dan, remarked in an interview that when he was a young man working in his father's business in the late 1980s, it was apparent who should be doing which job at their rival's firm. "The more Barry connected with customers, the better we did at Novopharm."

The pharmaceutical world is a cutthroat business. There is a great deal of scrutiny by competitors, and by government, of the companies that make drugs, both brand name and generic. Among the Canadian generic companies, Sherman's Apotex and Leslie Dan's Novopharm were competing neck and neck in terms of product development and revenues at the start of the 1990s, though Apotex would eventually win the race to be first.

Their simmering battles became nasty and public in 1993. Sherman suspected that one of his former employees, a scientist, had given proprietary information on a new drug formulation to Novopharm. Sherman hired private investigators to go through the Novopharm trash. He did not find what he was looking for. Next, Sherman and his legal team went to court to get a rare Anton Piller order, a civil search warrant giving search and seizure power that typically only police have. Jack Kay, who was present during the search at Novopharm, said he watched as the team working for Apotex went through reams of Novopharm company documents and even searched Leslie Dan's office, with Dan standing to one side, fuming. According to court documents related to the case, Sherman found documentation that proved his company's information had gone to Novopharm. The courts awarded Sherman and Apotex $3.7 million in damages, plus legal costs, and ordered that the Apotex research material be returned to Apotex. The already fragile relationship between Sherman and Dan, who were both significant donors to Jewish causes and would often be at the same charity events, was completely broken. Years later, Dan's son Aubrey, a financier and theatre impresario, would become friends with both Jack Kay and

Barry Sherman and work with them on a unique idea to make marijuana pills.

While one company celebrates a success, competitors and government regulators are checking to see if the success is legitimate. In my review of many of the drugs Apotex manufactured, there never seemed to be a simple final answer to the question Who won? Litigation often went back and forth for years. Sherman and Apotex took huge risks. One day they would be down $300 million due to a loss in court after miscalculating a brand name's ability to fight them; a month later, they would win a related battle and be up $600 million. Sherman was aggressive, and as one observer says, "Barry never took his foot off the gas." In the summer of 2017, the year he died, Sherman and Apotex would settle one of his long-standing patent battles and agree to pay $400 million, which would be a big hit to the bottom line at a time when cash was becoming tight. For Sherman, all of this was simply the price of doing business his way.

Zantac alone prompted high-stakes court cases and regulatory challenges. Once both brand name and generic versions of the acid reflux medicine were being sold, the Canadian tax authorities took a close look at documents that both GlaxoSmithKline and Apotex (and later Novopharm) were filing related to the expense of ranitidine, the active pharmaceutical ingredient. Federal auditors discovered that GlaxoSmithKline appeared to be wildly overpaying for ranitidine, which had the effect of raising the company's expenses and lowering its profits and its tax bill.

Canada took GlaxoSmithKline to court. In the years assessed (the early 1990s), Apotex and Novopharm were found to have paid between $194 and $304 per kilogram to the companies that provided them the ranitidine. At the same time,

GlaxoSmithKline was paying between $1,512 and $1,651 per kilogram. Tax auditors did further digging and found that the brand company was purchasing ranitidine from a related company, meaning that the price may have been set artificially high. The case went all the way to the Supreme Court of Canada, which sided with the tax authorities and sent the case back for reassessment and a trial. Before that could happen, Glaxo settled with the federal government, but the amount the company had to pay in fines and reimbursement to government coffers due to the inflated expenses has never been made public.

With the high sales from their version of the acid reflux drug, Apotex was now the number one generic company in Canada. The 4 percent compulsory licensing royalty they were required to pass on to GlaxoSmithKline was a small price to pay. But by the late 1980s, there were strong signs that the days of compulsory licensing would soon be over. That would create much bigger challenges for Apotex, beginning in 1993, and it would give rise to the pervasive belief that Sherman was the most litigious businessman in Canada. While that is most likely true, there was a good explanation for his many court appearances.

But for the moment, the generic Zantac success was savoured and utilized by Kay, the Apotex sales force, and others at the firm. New cars and houses were purchased, trips were taken. They had indeed made "a bit of money," as Sherman had promised in that job interview with Jack Kay in Montreal, and they would earn more and more as the years went by. For his part, however, Sherman remained unimpressed by lavish spending, as he did for his whole life, and it confounded his friends and associates that he did not assume a lifestyle that corresponded with his growing riches. Sherman's choice of car is the most recognizable emblem of his frugality. In thirty-five years, he would have exactly four cars, all North American–made and relatively inexpensive two-door convertibles. All would be repaired multiple times and would show rust and other signs of aging well before each was replaced.

Jack Kay, who has always enjoyed driving a nice vehicle, recalls Sherman frequently expressing concern that employees at Apotex would think the executives who drove BMWs, Mercedes-Benzes, and Jaguars were trying to show off their wealth. He also told Kay that he just did not understand the need for an expensive vehicle. "Jack, you just need four tires and a carburetor to go from A to B. We have employees who cannot afford a car like that, and I do it because I am showing them I am a normal person," Kay recalls him saying.

Ed Sonshine, the founder and CEO of real estate investment trust RioCan, knew Sherman for a quarter century. As a major contributor to charitable causes himself, Sonshine is well aware of the many millions of dollars Sherman contributed over the years to Jewish and non-Jewish causes. What he notes as unusual is that, other than the decision late in their lives to start building a true mansion in Forest Hill, neither Barry nor Honey Sherman seemed to "enjoy their material success. There was something in their brains that was odd."

Sonshine and his wife, Fran, have a condominium in Florida, northeast of Miami, in the same complex where the Shermans had a condo. Sonshine epitomizes the "self-made man." His parents were Holocaust survivors who'd been at the Auschwitz concentration camp, and he was, like Honey Sherman, born in a displaced persons camp. Like Barry, he has worked hard all his life, and though his own fortune pales in comparison to Sherman's, he enjoys the finer things in life. A few years ago in Florida, he was waiting with Sherman outside their condominium entrance for the valet driver to bring his car, a Bentley convertible. Sherman's was a rental, an older, nondescript vehicle.

"My car comes up," says Sonshine, "and then Barry's comes up. He looks at the Bentley and says, 'Did you rent that car?' I said, 'No, it's my car from home. I sent it down here for the winter. A convertible's not much good in Toronto in the winter.'"

Sherman looked at the car. Then back at Sonshine. "Why would you buy a car like that?"

"Because I really like it. It drives great. Look at it, it's a beautiful car. Why not?"

The valet quizzed Sonshine about Sherman, who at the time was a new resident.

"I told him that Mr. Sherman is a very good friend of mine. I said, 'Carlos, he is probably the richest guy in the building. Don't be fooled by that car.'"

Sonshine says it became a "shtick" for Sherman to conspicuously spend so little on material possessions, but he admits that his friend "honestly could not see the point in spending money on material items." Often, when seated in business class on a flight to Florida, Sonshine would see Barry and Honey walk by on their way to the inexpensive seats at the back.

"Where are you going, Barry," Sonshine once asked.

"Economy. It's only a two-and-a-half-hour flight," Sherman explained, holding up the line of snowbirds pulling overstuffed carry-on luggage behind them. "Ed, if I could get a cheaper fare and fly standing up, I would take that one."

In the forty-two years his personal assistant, Joanne Mauro, worked for Sherman, he owned, in chronological order, an Oldsmobile Cutlass, a Buick Reatta, a Chrysler Sebring, and a Mustang GT. All four were convertibles, the one luxury Sherman would allow. Each one he kept for roughly a decade, repairing it constantly.

Mauro had to run an errand one day, and Sherman said, "Take my car," which at the time was the white Buick Reatta.

"There are no brakes!" Mauro said when she returned to Apotex. She'd had to drive at a snail's pace, because she was afraid that whatever lining remained on the brake pads would disintegrate. The Reatta was given away to a local high school's auto body shop after that.

Mauro was sixteen years old in 1976 when Sherman hired her as a summer student to do typing and odd jobs. Throughout that summer and the next, she handled secretarial duties and even did some cleaning. When she graduated high school, she was offered a full-time job by Sherman. She had mused about a career in nursing, but this seemed more fun. It was not unusual for her to be presented with what others at Apotex termed Sherman's "chicken scrawl" on a page but which she could interpret and reproduce on a typewriter as her boss's latest formula.

When Sherman returned from his family trip to the Serengeti, in Tanzania, during which he wrote his unfinished "A Legacy of Thoughts," he handed the handwritten foolscap pages to Mauro, and she typed them up. In those pages, written in 1996, when he was fifty-four years old, Sherman laid out his thoughts on what a person might or should do with their financial gains. "Power and wealth bring no obligation," he wrote. "Given that our instincts give us a desire to help others, particularly those close to us, power and wealth bring an opportunity to derive an extra measure of happiness by acting to help others, be it family, friends, members of our community, our country, or mankind at large."

Barry Sherman would become one of the biggest donors to charity in Canadian history, giving away hundreds of millions of dollars to Jewish and non-Jewish causes, including community centres and hospitals. As his wealth grew, people would approach him hoping he would invest in the next great business: real estate developments, a tax shelter that promised to build a fleet of yachts to sail the Mediterranean, beer production, even a trivia app for smartphones. He would also give millions of dollars to support the children of his friends, and, because he admired the underdog, invest enormous amounts of money in dodgy business dealings. So whenever the issue of his cousins—his late Uncle Lou's children—came up in social circles, it would raise eyebrows. Given Sherman's immense wealth and public commitment to others, people would wonder, Why did he not just give them everything they wanted?

NINE

FAMILY MATTERS

THE MOMENT KERRY WINTER HEARD the news that his cousin Barry Sherman and Sherman's wife, Honey, had been found dead, he had two thoughts, he says. The first, that Barry murdered Honey, then killed himself. Then, as his mind shifted to the bitter, ongoing fight he and his siblings had waged with Sherman, another thought struck him: "Oh my God, I think Jeffrey did it."

Winter was recounting this to me, three months after the Shermans died, while standing at the long "hot table" at a family diner on St. Clair Avenue West, in Toronto, while trying to decide which pasta dish from the line of steaming stainless steel chafing dishes to put on his plate. "Kevin, wait 'til you taste this. Delicious," he said, selecting a heaping portion of lasagna, dripping with cheese and tomato sauce, and ladling it onto his plate. Picking up cutlery and a fistful of napkins, Winter moved to a corner of the restaurant. I followed.

A regular at the diner, and having been featured recently in a TV documentary, Winter turned heads.

"Did you do it?" a man at the table beside us asked Winter.

Winter's eyes widened and he laughed. He nodded at the fellow and then leaned across the table towards me, laying his hand on mine. "Everybody saw me on TV. Everybody. It's what everyone is talking about."

I reminded Winter that he was telling me the story of what he was thinking about his brother Jeffrey. Kerry and Jeffrey are two of the four "orphan cousins" who sued the Apotex founder for $1 billion, an event that upended the already precarious relationship they had with the cousin they referred to as Uncle Barry.

Winter dove into the lasagna. He's fifty-five years old, with dark wavy hair swept back off his forehead. He ate quickly, encouraging me to do the same. Winter speaks with a buttery smooth voice, and he talks in run-on sentences. In another world, I could imagine him being a late-night talk radio host, always with one more story to tell in a stream of chat that, on this day, flows from Sherman to drugs to his days growing up and back to Sherman.

Having heard the news of the bodies being discovered, Winter said it brought to mind his long-standing fear that his brother Jeffrey might one day "go off the deep end" and kill Sherman. Jeffrey had struggled with mental health issues since he was a teenager and can be difficult to manage. In fact, Winter said, he mentioned his concern about Jeffrey to someone just two days before he heard about the deaths. With all that rumbling around in Winter's head, he began panicked attempts to reach Jeffrey, who lives a reclusive life in Mississauga, just west of Toronto. When he heard radio reports that police were at a home in Forest Hill, near where their adoptive parents, the Barkins, lived, he feared that police were there to arrest his brother. Unlike Winter, Jeffrey Barkin had remained in touch with his adoptive parents. (Police were actually in Forest Hill to meet with the Shermans' adult children at the home of daughter Alex Sherman.)

Winter said he kept calling. Finally, Jeffrey picked up the phone at his home.

"Jeffrey, Jeffrey, are you okay?" Winter said he asked.

"Yes," Barkin responded, "why?"

"Where have you been?"

"Well, I've been about," Barkin replied. "What's going on?" When Winter mimicked his brother's response, he did it with a slow, deep drawl.

"Have you heard the news about Barry and Honey?"

"Yes."

"Did you do it?"

"Hell, no. I can't believe you would think I'd do something like that."

Winter said he hung up the phone, and a few minutes later his girlfriend called.

"Kerry," she said. "Tell me the truth. Did you do it?"

"I said no," Winter told me.

"But Kerry, you always talked about doing it," his girlfriend said.

The anger between the brothers and their cousin Barry has deep roots that twist and tangle like old trees growing too close together. The roots spread out into a series of family and business decisions that reach back fifty years into the 1960s. The four sons of Lou and Beverley Winter are, from oldest to youngest, Tim, Jeffrey, Kerry, and Dana. Tim had been adopted when the Winters believed they were unable to have children. Then, soon after baby Tim was brought home, Beverley became pregnant. Three boys were born, one each year, beginning in 1960. Their father, Lou, was the younger brother of Barry Sherman's mother. A university-educated chemist, Lou founded Empire Laboratories in the late 1950s and hired young Barry to do odd jobs when he was in high school. When Lou died suddenly of an aneurysm and seventeen days later Beverley passed away after a lengthy battle with cancer, the four boys were left without parents.

According to an account in *Toronto Life* magazine in 2008, Beverley, who had converted to Judaism when she married Lou, had stipulated that her own family could not take in the boys. She wanted her children raised as Jews. Kerry Winter says that his mother, on her deathbed, called in the trustees dealing with the family business and "added a codicil to her will where she clearly stated she did not want any family members from her side or my father's side coming forward to adopt me and my three brothers." Beverley's brother Wayne Rockcliffe told *Toronto Life* that he and his wife would have been happy to raise the boys, but he believes his sister did not want "us to have what was hers," a reference either to the actual children or to the inheritance that would come from her late husband's generic drug business. Beverley's rabbi found a local Jewish family, the Barkins, who legally adopted the four boys and were given access to funds from the business operations and the eventual sale of Empire to Sherman and Joel Ulster. Dr. Martin Barkin was a well-known Toronto urologist who would go on to become deputy minister of health in the Ontario government and president of Sunnybrook Health Sciences Centre. His wife, Carol, was a schoolteacher.

Rockcliffe, who had a successful career as a chartered accountant, tried to help the Winter boys from afar. He made the calls to get his nephew Kerry into a prestigious boys' school after he had spent time in a juvenile facility in west-end Toronto on drug charges. "I got thrown out of the house at fifteen and landed in jail at sixteen on trafficking charges. I was selling drugs at the time," Kerry Winter recalls. Meanwhile, there was little connection between Barry Sherman and the four boys as they grew. In answers provided during an examination for discovery as part of the litigation between them years later, Sherman stated that he did visit them when he could, but that he stopped because he sensed from the Barkins that they thought he was interfering in the boys' upbringing. Sherman was twenty years old when the Winter (now Barkin) boys were toddlers and was just finishing university in the United States when his uncle died. This was the period when Sherman would make his first foray into the generic world with his purchase, in partnership with Joel Ulster, of his uncle Lou's company, Empire Laboratories. Sherman and Ulster sold Empire to an American firm several years later and Sherman founded Apotex. These points on the timeline—purchasing Empire and selling Empire—would eventually be critical in the two lawsuits launched by the cousins.

As the four boys were growing up, the relationship between them and their adoptive parents was fraught with tension. A split developed that many years later would be displayed publicly in Martin Barkin's obituary. He is described as the "loving father" of Tim and Jeffrey, and Kerry and Dana are not mentioned. From a young age, Dana and Kerry would revert to using the name Winter to demonstrate their displeasure with the sometimes caustic attitude of their prominent father. In an interview, Kerry Winter has said that he and Dana were subjected to corporal punishment—spanking and a belt—by Barkin. "Dana and I were regularly beaten, a lot of physical abuse," Kerry says. "Emotional and physical abuse to the point that I am still seeing a psychiatrist and I am 57." There is no independent confirmation of this, and, as noted, Martin Barkin has since passed away. In an interview by text message, Jeffrey Barkin acknowledged that he and Kerry had very different relationships with their father but would not go into details. When Dana and Kerry moved out, Jeffrey and Tim stuck with the Barkins. Though Dana and Kerry, with their early struggles with addiction, could not have been easy children to manage, there are many accounts from people who were Barkin's colleagues that describe him as having a difficult temperament. Barkin, who had a key role in developing Ontario's health policy in the 1980s and beyond, was well known for his belief that his way was the only way. As one senior official in the Ontario Medical Association, which represents doctors, put it, "The biggest knock against Martin that I am aware of is that he really does not want to listen to anybody else."

Kerry and Dana fell out of touch with their adoptive parents after they moved out, and life settled down at the Barkins' Forest Hill home. Tim (his first name is Paul, but he goes by his middle name), the eldest, who was adopted twice, first by the Winters, then the Barkins, developed an interest in cooking and worked towards being a chef. He is an outlier among the four, seemingly not affected by any demons. Jeffrey had "mental health issues" and "emotional problems," according to statements in the court case between the cousins and Barry Sherman. Those statements were made, respectively, by Kerry Winter and Barry Sherman. At one point, his sister-in-law Julia (Dana's wife) filed an affidavit saying Jeffrey was "under disability" during the case. Kerry openly says his brother Jeffrey was "bipolar" and struggled in early adulthood, but maintained a good relationship with his parents. (Jeffrey told me he preferred not to answer questions about his past.)

By various accounts in court papers, and as stated by Kerry in interviews, none of the four young men had contact with Barry or Honey Sherman until a mutual acquaintance brought Dana and Barry together in the late 1980s. Sherman had learned from the friend that Dana was mired in a cycle of drug addiction and stints in treatment centres and agreed to meet his cousin at Apotex. Sherman's belief was that a good job and hard work could cure all ills. He hired Dana to work in the production plant, but within a month he heard that Dana was dealing drugs to other workers at Apotex. Sherman's next plan involved Dana working outdoors at his latest venture: Deerhurst Resort, in Ontario's cottage country.

Sherman had purchased the Muskoka resort in anticipation of the Ontario government awarding its second casino licence. There was already a flourishing casino in Windsor, across the US border from Detroit, and the well-connected Sherman had picked up the political rumour that Ontario was considering awarding a second licence to a First Nations group that would have ties to a municipality north of Toronto. He set about renovating the tired resort and building a world-class eighteen-hole golf course on the property, and began looking for a First Nations group that would lend its name to the project.

Fred Steiner recalls going up to Deerhurst as Sherman's guest and asking Sherman what he thought about his new course, completed the year before. "Haven't seen it," Sherman said.

Steiner insisted on taking a golf cart and a club and dragging Sherman out to one of the shorter holes to see if Steiner could launch a ball perfectly onto the green. Along the way they passed Dana Winter, who was chatting with some of the female guests. Women who knew Dana, including Sherman friend Bryna Steiner, describe him as having "movie-star looks." He had blond hair, sharp, almost perfect features, and was a charmer. Within a year, Dana was dismissed from the resort because the handsome and charismatic man was sleeping with the female guests and, according to Sherman in an allegation he made at a court proceeding, dealing drugs again.

By the early 1990s, the pattern was set. The three young men, Jeffrey, Kerry, and Dana, would come to Sherman with their plans and he would bankroll them. Tim never did. It is unclear exactly how much the three cousins received from Sherman, but a conservative estimate, based on court records from what would become protracted litigation, suggests that Sherman gave them a total of $15 million. That money went to fund business ventures: Kerry in construction; Jeffrey in several businesses, including sport travel booking and custom music CDs; and Dana in retailing items of jewellery. Court and property records show that Sherman funded their purchases of homes, cottages, and cars. Honey Sherman was not pleased with this and objected to her husband giving money to the cousins, but Sherman said he had an obligation to help his late mother's family.

In answers he provided under oath as part of the cousins' lawsuit the year before Sherman died, with Kerry Winter in the room, Sherman was asked by the cousins' lawyer, Brad Teplitsky, if over the years he was interested in protecting his cousins' interests. Sherman replied, "To some extent, I'm interested in protecting the interests of all human beings."

Asked for his theory on why Dana, Kerry, and Jeffrey were troubled, Sherman appeared to blame them, and possibly their parents and the Barkins, for their ways. "The proof's in the pudding," Sherman said twice during the proceeding, but he did not elaborate other than to say that when he became involved again in their lives in the late 1980s the "boys were in trouble." Drugs, for Dana and Kerry, were the big problem; both were heavily addicted to cocaine and heroin. Jeffrey was not a drug addict, but he was under treatment for mental health issues for many years. At separate points in the protracted litigation between Sherman and his middle-aged cousins, both Jeffrey and Kerry were the subject of motions in court to have litigation guardians appointed because there was a concern that they were unfit to represent themselves. Ultimately, they both continued to represent themselves.

By the early 1990s, Dana's life had begun to blow up in a spectacular manner. With Sherman's support after he lost his job at Deerhurst, Dana moved to western Canada to attend a drug rehabilitation program. Out of rehab, he met Julia Zwicker in a small town in Northern British Columbia. They married and had two children. During that time, Dana stepped back into the underworld and got more deeply involved than he had been in Ontario. The man with the movie-star good looks became embroiled in a case that would leave one man dead and Dana and another man facing murder charges over a targeted killing. In 1994, the body of Landis Heal was found in the woods in Northern BC, shot once through the head with a 45-calibre handgun. Police believed that a man named Tim McCreery killed Heal to settle a drug debt McCreery had with Dana Winter. Winter, police alleged, wanted Heal killed for "ratting" him out to the police over an earlier drug deal. Detectives used what, in police vernacular, is called the Mr. Big ruse and pretended they were fellow drug dealers who wanted to get into business with McCreery. In time, McCreery opened up about the killing to his new "friends," men who were actually undercover detectives. Then McCreery implicated Dana Winter. To assist his cousin, Sherman flew out to BC to hire a criminal defence attorney and put up the $100,000 bond to get his cousin out on bail. Dana thanked Sherman and then disappeared onto the streets of Vancouver.

Dana "was dead a couple of weeks later from an overdose," Sherman recalled in his examination for discovery. The trigger man on the case, McCreery, was sentenced to life in prison.

Now there were three cousins: Tim, Kerry, and Jeffrey. Tim continued his work as a young chef in Toronto. Jeffrey, while at university, had begun to take a strong interest in his own roots and what happened to the generic drug business Lou Winter had founded many years before. Just exactly what had happened to Empire Laboratories? Jeffrey wondered. Was it possible he and his siblings had some pot of gold that was just lying there for the taking? He and his brothers were aware that Royal Trust had been appointed the estate trustee and that Barry Sherman had purchased Empire, but little else was known. Jeffrey's private investigations would end up playing a pivotal role in what was to dominate all of their lives for the next two decades. But it was Kerry who was struggling the most. A drug habit that had begun in high school intensified when he became an adult. Cocaine and heroin were his drugs of choice. Kerry says he got hooked on those drugs while backpacking through Peru following a failed attempt to complete a master's at San Diego State University. Kerry had received an undergraduate degree in London, England at Richmond College and said he was able to manage his addiction during that four-year stretch. But it was when he started travelling in South America and Asia that he began using heavily. "I was a full-blown crackhead. I started using coke in Peru. I put a form called 'paste' in a cigarette and smoked it."

Back in Canada, Kerry Winter began visiting Sherman at Apotex. People who worked in the office in those days, in the late 1990s and early 2000s, recall that Winter was allowed access to the Apotex inner sanctum. One day they were chatting and Sherman said, "Kerry, do you know why I like when you come up and see me? You are so euphoric. You make me laugh."

Winter was often on drugs when he visited Sherman, he said, and his cousin seemed well aware of that and would accuse Winter of being high. As he had done with Dana, Sherman gave Kerry a job. Winter recalled Sherman handing him a pair of boots and telling him he could work in the stockroom, and if he was not clean of drugs in ninety days, Sherman would pay for him to enter a drug rehab program. Winter had reservations about rehab. He had seen Dana go through two Sherman-funded one-month rehab stints, each costing $20,000, and to him it seemed like a "revolving door." He took the boots and worked as an order picker in the Apotex logistics warehouse, driving up and down the giant shelves filling orders for customers.

"On the ninetieth day, I walked into Barry's office and dropped the boots on the floor," Winter said.

Sherman looked up from pages on his desk. "Are you going to treatment?"

"No, Barry. I am clean."

Winter said that Sherman later attended a ceremony at his Cocaine Anonymous group, where Kerry received a medallion celebrating one year of sobriety. Sherman stood up and told the room of addicts how proud he was of his cousin.

"There is a long history where Barry was really good to me," Winter said.

Back in the diner, a server cleared our plates, and I could see she was taking a little extra time. Recounting his memories of conversations with Sherman, Winter became more and more animated, waving his hands, tapping them on the table. Winter spoke loudly and forcefully as he described his more critical thoughts on his late cousin. He could be heard at nearby tables and had caught the interest of other diners. One man fumbled with his phone, leaning a little closer while pretending not to listen. Winter's negative comments about Sherman were in complete contrast to the feelings that friends Fred Steiner, Joel Ulster, Jack Kay, Frank D'Angelo, and others repeatedly expressed about him.

"Here are my feelings about Barry. I am not going to call him a serial killer, a sociopath, a pathological liar. That's for shrinks. I'm not a psychiatrist. I am just a recovering drug addict trying to get through a day. But I can say this: that his idea of friendship, love, honour, loyalty, things that bind people, was a foreign concept. This was a man I don't think had any friends."

Winter said that he and Sherman had lengthy chats about life whenever he dropped by Apotex. He said Sherman had a fascination for Winter's involvement in illicit drugs. Among the questions he recalled being asked by Sherman: "What's it like to take drugs? What's that rush like? What's it like to shoot heroin?"

There would often be a negative spin on what Sherman said, Winter told me. Winter asked him about an Alaskan cruise he'd taken with Honey. His cousin's response, said Winter, was "Fucking icebergs." One day, when Sherman gave him a lift, Winter noticed Sherman's car radio was broken and asked him if he planned to get it fixed. "Fucking music, it all gives me a headache," Winter recalled Sherman saying. By his own admission, Winter was high during many of these conversations, and the accuracy of his recollections, along with Sherman's purported use of profanity, has been questioned by the friends of Sherman to whom I have related this information. They also vehemently challenge a much more outlandish recollection that Winter recently made public.

Winter claims that in the mid to late 1990s, he twice had conversations with Sherman in which Barry asked him to arrange a contract killing of Honey. Apparently, the request came out of the blue. "He asked me in his office at Apotex. I was surprised he would ask me," Winter recalled in an earlier interview I did with him six weeks after the Shermans died. A friend of Winter's told me he recalls Winter telling him of Sherman's request at about the time of the alleged conversation. Winter has said that Sherman would often tell him he was unhappy with his marriage, and that was how the discussion moved, according to Winter, to discussions of arranging a hit man. In Winter's interviews with other media following the Shermans' deaths, one of them a British publication that flew a reporter to Canada, he was definite about this and said that his cousin told him he wanted Honey "whacked." As a result, Winter said, he contacted an underworld connection but never went further with the plan.

Winter said that he'd grown nervous and suggested another approach. "Why don't you just get a divorce?" he said he asked Sherman.

"There is no way she is getting half of my money," Sherman allegedly told him.

I have asked Kerry Winter if it is possible that Sherman was merely asking odd but theoretical questions about hiring a hit man out of some morbid fascination, possibly brought on by Dana's recent involvement in a contract killing or by boasts from Kerry that he "knew people." Perhaps Sherman was just interested in the concept of hiring a killer, just as he was curious about what it was like to shoot heroin? Maybe Sherman was asking, hypothetically, "Okay, are you saying you could have someone killed? Like my wife, for example?" As odd a comment as it would be, Sherman was known to have an unusual sense of humour and an interest in unusual topics.

To the possibility that Sherman was asking a completely hypothetical question, Kerry Winter replied: "Maybe"; "It could have been"; "I've said my memory is not the best, but I know we talked about it."

Winter said he considered setting up a "hit" because during this time he felt increasingly beholden to Sherman, who was funding his businesses and at one point providing him with a $20,000 monthly living allowance.

Meanwhile, Kerry's older brother Jeffrey was digging around in provincial archives, searching for details of the deal that saw Barry Sherman and Joel Ulster purchase Empire Laboratories from their father in 1967. (Jeffrey was seven at the time, Kerry was six, Dana was five, and Tim, the oldest, was nine.) Jeffrey spent several weeks combing through musty documents in long-stored boxes that spelled out, in bare bones fashion, the sale to Sherman and Ulster. As Jeffrey would write in court papers he eventually filed, he was surprised at what he did not find: nothing that spelled out the nitty-gritty of the deal. He began to suspect that his late father's drug business had been worth much more than what Sherman and Ulster paid. The sale was managed by Royal Trust, which had been appointed as trustee for the Winter estate and was to oversee the money Lou and Beverley Winter left for their children. Jeffrey was attending Queen's University, in Kingston, Ontario, during his early sleuthing. Using a legal database, he came up with the name of James Church, a man who worked for Lou Winter as national sales manager and continued in that role under Sherman and Ulster. Jeffrey located Church, who eventually filed an affidavit for the cousins stating that Empire was profitable and well managed when Sherman purchased it.

Sherman, in his "A Legacy of Thoughts" and elsewhere, had described Empire in less than glowing terms: vitamin C tablets were crumbling, the machinery was antiquated, top managers were incompetent. In his affidavit, Church acknowledges that some of the business did drop off when Lou Winter died, but, he said, as national sales manager, he was "never aware of any financial troubles."

In his pursuit of the case, Jeffrey asked Royal Trust if he could see the documents it had on file related to the sale of Empire more than twenty years earlier. Royal Trust refused. Jeffrey retained lawyers and eventually won a court order that allowed him to inspect the documents. One of the items he discovered was a four-page document known as the option agreement. It formed part of the deal Sherman put forward when he purchased Empire. Royal Trust had turned down Sherman's first offer to purchase Empire, and as part of his second offer, he stipulated that if the children of Lou and Beverley Winter "desire," they could be given jobs at Empire upon reaching the age of twenty-one, and, if they were interested, they could purchase 5 percent of the issued shares of Empire after two years' employment. The caveat to this was that Sherman and Ulster would still have to own Empire at the time. However, the two young businessmen sold Empire to ICN several years after they purchased it. When that option was discussed at an Ontario Court of Appeal hearing in 2018, after the Sherman deaths, and when the cousins were still fighting his estate, a justice of the court called the Sherman option "a sweetener" to secure the deal.

Jeffrey Barkin, who was now assisted by brother Kerry Winter, kept digging. They hired private investigators to dig up information, even securing the services of an investigator in Puerto Rico to try to determine (unsuccessfully, as it turned out) the value of an Empire-related holding Lou Winter had there at the time of his death. During this time, according to their own affidavits, they were asking Barry Sherman what he knew of the sale. When they began asking questions about the option, Sherman said, according to their court filings, that it simply did not exist. While this was going on, Sherman continued to fund his cousins' business ventures. He loaned them each, at 7 percent interest, millions of dollars but secured the loans as mortgages against each property they purchased, and also had his cousins sign legal documents saying that if they defaulted on the loans, he could recoup his losses from the money each had been left in their parents' estate. The interest rates were roughly the same as market rates at the time, and it appears Sherman did not collect on the interest charged but rather let it accumulate.

In 2007, the three surviving cousins and Julia Winter, as her late husband Dana's representative, sued Barry Sherman and Apotex. The claim moved through the courts for more than a decade. Essentially, the cousins were asking for $1 billion, a calculation based on 20 percent of Sherman's estimated net worth. Their logic was that had they, as a group (5 percent each), been able to buy into Empire, they would have owned 20 percent between them. And since they contend it was Empire's eventual sale that led Sherman to found the now multi-billion-dollar Apotex, they have told various judges they are deserving of one-fifth of that fortune.

As my lunch with Kerry Winter at the St. Clair Avenue diner was winding down, he explained his point of view.

"You have to understand. My hatred of Barry, my disdain for Barry, was only because of his betrayal and lies. I said to Barry once, 'I don't want twenty percent of Apotex. I don't want anything, Barry. I just want you to tell me the truth. Why do you keep lying to me?' Do you know how many years he kept lying to me about the option agreement?"

Sherman, in his court pleadings, maintained that he never lied. Ultimately, he contended, the option agreement did exist but it was a worthless document. Yet it is a document that generated a great deal of anger and many disputes. Winter said he believed, and still does, that Sherman funded the brothers' enterprises and lifestyle not out of duty but to keep them financially handcuffed to him. Winter has also stated that Sherman's generosity was intended to stop the cousins from pursuing the option issue. The year before the cousins sued Sherman, Winter said he had a conversation with the Apotex founder at a social event at the company. It was the annual Christmas party, and Winter always brought his children, even though he was not working there any longer. He said Sherman gestured for him to come out to the parking lot. They stood against the wall of the building as Sherman spoke. "You know, there aren't too many people in the world that have a Cousin Barry," Winter said Sherman told him.

"Oh, I know that," Winter said he replied.

"Do you know that? I don't think you do. You're thinking of coming after me. You should think twice. Because you won't beat me. You don't know who I am yet."

Winter said he responded, "Barry, I know who you are."

He said Sherman looked at him directly. "I'm good to you. I give you everything you want. Why do you want to come after me? You are getting bad advice from lawyers and bad advice from your friends. They don't have a Cousin Barry. You do. Think twice."

Winter said it was conversations like these and his belief that Sherman had stolen his future from him that led him to have fantasies of decapitating his cousin in the Apotex parking lot and "rolling his head" down the pavement.

"I have been angry at Barry for so many years," Winter said in one interview with me. "I think, more than money, what would have made me happy would have been if he acknowledged my father and mother's contribution to his life and donated money to create the Lou and Beverley Winter wing at some hospital."

One of the questions I asked everyone I interviewed for this book was "Where were you on the evening of Wednesday, December 13, 2017, the time when Barry and Honey Sherman were murdered?" It was a question that most answered readily. I asked Kerry Winter that question the first time I spoke with him, in late January 2018. It was during a telephone call with both Winter and his lawyer on the civil case, Brad Teplitsky.

"I had absolutely nothing to do with Barry and Honey's death. Zero. I want to put that on the record." Winter made that comment immediately after he revealed that he had fantasies of murdering Barry Sherman, and also that Sherman had once asked him to arrange the murder of Honey. Those comments, which Winter made to the *Star*, CBC's *The Fifth Estate*, a British paper, and other media outlets, led his sister-in-law, Julia Winter, to file an affidavit in court questioning his sanity and suggesting that in the wake of the Sherman murders, Kerry had suffered "some form of a nervous breakdown" and could no longer provide instructions to their mutual lawyer. Winter, who appears unfazed by any critique of his actions, told me what he was doing that Wednesday night. He said that after his day job in construction, he attended his regular Twelve Step program for his addiction issues, then went home and "watched an episode of *Peaky Blinders* on Netflix" and went to sleep. A man who attends the same Twelve Step program and has been friends with Winter since childhood confirmed Winter's attendance that evening. Winter said he had an early shift the next morning and was up and out the door at dawn. Twice divorced, he has a girlfriend but she lives on Canada's west coast and he lives alone. He acknowledged there was nobody who could confirm that he spent the entire night at home.

As to his sometimes erratic and angry comments about Barry and Honey Sherman, including those made on prime time television, Winter says he is merely speaking what he considers to be the truth. That includes, he says, his ongoing belief that the Toronto Police are covering for the Sherman family and that Barry really did murder his wife, then kill himself. As for his own involvement in the deaths, Winter says the days of him knowing people in the underworld who would be capable of murder are long past.

"I am six years sober. I'm a wonderful father. I work full time. I haven't done a drink or drug in six years. I view myself as rehabilitated and recovered. I no longer associate myself with street people, drug dealers, criminals."

TEN

BUILDING A BIGGER EMPIRE

JEREMY DESAI HAD A DAY OFF FROM HIS JOB with a generic pharmaceutical company in London, England, in the summer of 2002 when Barry Sherman came calling. A marathon runner with a lean, wiry build, Desai had always been a big believer in karma. Upon reflection, he decided the fact that the phone call to offer him a new direction in life had come on a vacation day was a sign. Time for a change. Desai had heard of the maverick Canadian generic entrepreneur. Big Pharma spent a lot of time trying to stay ahead of people like Sherman and Apotex and had a lot of names for the generic companies. The "dark side" was the one Desai always used when he worked for brand name companies. Sherman was looking for a new director of research and development, and his headhunter firm suggested Desai, who had recently switched to the generic world. Come to Canada for an interview and see what we are all about, was the message from Sherman. Not long after, Desai was sitting in a chair across from Barry Sherman at Apotex's headquarters on a Saturday morning. His sister, who lived in Toronto, had dropped him off with a plan to shop and return in a couple of hours. Desai was dressed in his best suit and tie. Sherman was in jeans and an old shirt that seemed two sizes too small for the billionaire. "We don't do ties here," he said.

The Apotex owner opened a file on his desk and pulled out a neatly stapled collection of papers that included Desai's resumé. After graduating with a PhD in pharmacy, Desai had spent most of his career working in research at various brand name firms, including GlaxoSmithKline, a company whose products Sherman had made generic copies of numerous times. While at those companies, Desai was involved with teams that specialized in finding scientific ways to make patents airtight. Then he had taken a senior job at a British generic company that, like Apotex, was run by an entrepreneur. Sherman flipped through the pages in the Desai folder, then tore them in half and threw them into the recycling bin beside his desk. "All this is garbage," he told Desai. "Talk to me about yourself."

Four minutes into Desai's monologue, Sherman held up a hand. "The job's yours," he said. He explained that Apotex was doing well, but he wanted to take it to the next level, and he was looking to inject a bright light with pharmaceutical smarts into the executive stream. Sherman had a specific goal in mind: to one day produce fifty billion individual dosages a year. "My HR head told me, if I like the person, I have to keep my cards close to my chest," he said. "But what the hell, it's my company. You are my new head of global research and development."

It would take several months before Desai accepted the position, and what happened between that Saturday morning at Apotex and his taking the post cemented a feeling of loyalty. Desai's wife and children (two boys, aged three and nine at the time) were not keen on leaving England. His elderly mother had recently moved into their London house, and she also was reluctant to move to another country. Once back in England, Desai told the headhunter to thank Sherman for the opportunity but tell him he was passing. The following Saturday morning, Desai slept in after a Diwali festival party. When he got up, his eldest son told him a "Barry Sherman" had telephoned and would be calling again that afternoon. When Sherman called, he told Desai that he was at a wedding in Chicago and had heard that the man he believed would be his future chief of research had passed on his offer. "Jeremy, there are only two people who can do this job, you and your twin brother," Sherman said. "And I know you don't have a twin brother. Take a week and give me your final decision."

Desai was flying to New York for the New York City Marathon the following weekend. In the British Airways lounge, he decided he could not run this gruelling race with the job offer hanging over him. Why not take Sherman's offer? Desai had been impressed by how straightforward Sherman was and by his "humanity." He made a snap decision, printed out the offer sheet, signed it, and faxed it from the airline lounge. Just as Sherman had said to Jack Kay twenty years before, Desai says his new boss told him, "You're my guy. We're going to have a lot of fun."

Desai moved to Canada on his own for the first few months, since it was still the middle of the school year. When he returned to England in the summer of 2003 to help with the final packing for the family move, he noticed his mother was unwell. Never one to visit doctors, she had to be persuaded by Desai to go for tests. Within a few days, doctors had diagnosed colon cancer. The prognosis was that she had eighteen months to live. Desai called Sherman and said he was sorry, but since his mother would not be covered by Ontario health insurance, he did not think he could return to Apotex. Sherman did not even pause. Desai was to bring her over with his wife and children, he said, and he would cover her medical expenses and ensure she got the best treatment. Desai's mother lived only six weeks after they arrived in Canada, but Sherman's gesture forged a bond of loyalty between the two men. Both Sherman and Jack Kay attended the funeral. When Desai's sister, the one who had driven him to the Toronto job interview, was later struck by the same form of cancer their mother succumbed to, Sherman again offered to help. Desai's sister battled her cancer for thirteen years, and Sherman supported Desai throughout, never worrying that the man who had become his company president was occasionally missing work to sit with his sister at medical appointments. "Family is family," Sherman told him.

"Barry took away the pinch points and the pain," Desai recalls.

Desai thrived at Apotex and was eventually appointed to the job of CEO as both Sherman and Jack Kay moved out of the day-to-day operations to concentrate on the big picture. As Sherman had done with other key executives over the years, he compensated Desai well, including providing a $3.15-million interest-free loan for the purchase of a $3.175-million Toronto home soon after Desai moved to Canada. In all the years they worked together, Sherman never wavered in his belief that Desai was key to Apotex's growth.

The biggest test of Sherman's loyalty to his protégé came in 2016, when Desai and Apotex faced serious allegations of industrial espionage. Teva Pharmaceutical Industries, the Israeli generic firm that had purchased Apotex rival Novopharm years before, had alleged to the FBI that Desai and a female Teva executive had a romantic relationship and that the executive had emailed Desai sensitive Teva data on a generic drug in development. The FBI investigated and no charges were laid. Teva did not give up. In the summer of 2017, six months before the Sherman murders, Teva sued Desai, Apotex, and the now-fired female executive in a Pennsylvania court. Legal filings reveal that Desai and Apotex vigorously denied the allegations, though Desai admitted that the Teva executive did have contact with him by email and he did have a personal—Desai said it was not romantic—relationship with her. At one point during the legal filings, the former Teva executive was dropped from the claim, with no explanation on the public record. The messy lawsuit was settled in 2019 and the terms of the settlement are confidential.

Throughout the scandal, Sherman stuck by his CEO. Apotex insiders say that any other company owner confronted with that situation would have made Desai a scapegoat and fired him. Not Sherman. His unwavering support of Desai led to whispers in the pharmaceutical community, never substantiated, that Sherman was personally involved in a plan to learn information about his bitter rival's new drug. It was not until shortly after Sherman's death that an agreement was reached with the Apotex board of directors for Desai to resign to "pursue other opportunities." It is likely that, had Sherman not died, Desai would still be the president and CEO of Apotex.

As just one of the many oddities that contributed to the theories spun by armchair detectives after the Sherman deaths, the announcement of Desai's departure from Apotex went out on January 26, 2018, just hours after the Toronto Police declared that the Sherman probe was now a double homicide investigation. Was there some connection? people wondered. "Pure coincidence," an Apotex spokesman said. "We had no idea the police were going to make that announcement."

While there is speculation that Desai was fired, he maintains it was his decision to leave. Barry Sherman was one of the big reasons he was at Apotex. Departures from a company, no matter how they occur, can be difficult. Reflecting on that in interviews, Desai and Kay both noted that Sherman never had the stomach for delivering bad news and would get them to do the firing, making sure that a plan was put in place so the fired employee would be able to get back on his or her feet. "Imagine what their families will think when they go home tonight," Sherman would say, as he gave instructions on how the dismissal should be handled. "We have to remember, when we make these decisions, we are playing with their lives."

The decision to hire Desai in 2002 was just one of a series of moves Sherman made that boosted Apotex to new heights of financial success, beginning in the early 2000s. The company expanded its manufacturing facilities in Canada and began the process that eventually saw Apotex set up manufacturing plants in India and Mexico, hire more chemists to formulate drugs ("bench scientists," as Desai calls them), and bring more lawyers on staff to fight brand name companies and the federal regulator Health Canada in court. Harry Radomski, the outside legal counsel who was Sherman's top litigator, had never been busier. The generic landscape in Canada had changed dramatically in the 1990s. As Radomski recalls, the seismic shift they experienced mirrored what had taken place earlier in the United States, where governments wanted to protect homegrown intellectual property: "The world was changing, and the idea of encouraging innovation through patent protection was in vogue." Meanwhile, Sherman was still looking for new pharmaceuticals to genericize and new ways to bring these cheaper drugs to market.

Suddenly, that became much harder to do in Canada. Prime Minister Brian Mulroney's Conservative government had done away in 1993 with the very comfortable system of compulsory licensing that had allowed Canada's generic industry to thrive. Gone were the days when a generic company like Apotex could replicate a brand name drug and sell it at a lower cost, paying just a 4 percent royalty to the brand company, based on the generic drug's total annual sales. Now, the federal government had linked its drug approval regime to a patent system, giving brand name companies patent protection for twenty years after the drug came to market. Unless the generic company could find a legal way around the patent, they were stuck in a long waiting line. This new system brought constant tension. The federal government wanted to reward the innovation of the brand name companies by promoting sales of their drugs, but the provincial governments and private insurance plans that funded drug purchases preferred the cheaper generic forms.

From 1993 until his death twenty-five years later, Sherman devoted a great deal of his energy to finding ways to use science and the courts to get around patents. Along with his personal skirmishes in court, this intensification of legal action in the pharmaceutical world perpetuated the notion of Sherman as one of the most litigious men in Canadian business history, and certainly the most litigious in the Canadian pharmaceutical world. There are great elements of truth to the first statement, and the second is a simple fact. But those statements come with an important caveat. When Mulroney created the new system, he replaced it with one that mandated litigation if a generic firm wanted to bring out a generic copy. Since Apotex was the biggest of the Canadian generic firms in volume of drugs produced, it stood to reason that it would be the most litigious.

Navigating this new reality required an understanding of how government and drug companies were now expected to interact. Post 1993, once Health Canada had approved what is known in pharmaceutical circles as the "safety and efficacy" of the product, it issued a notice of compliance that allowed the new drug to be made available to the public. For a generic company to try to bring a similar product forward, it now had to file a case in federal court called a notice of allegation, challenging the patent or patents that protected the drug from being copied. Smart brand name manufacturers made sure they had multiple patents on the formulation of the drug, the process used to make it, and other related items, which sometimes even included a patent on how the drug was packaged. But as Sherman and his legal team proved over the years after 1993, there were a number of ways to show the patent was either not valid or that making a copy of the drug would not infringe on the patent. In some cases, Sherman would seek to show that he had made a "bio-similar" drug but formulated it in a different way. In others, he would aim to show that the brand company had really not done anything unique. Radomski says he and his team were sometimes able to demonstrate to a court that "the patent should never have been issued because somebody invented it before," or that, because it was such an obvious creation, "any moron" could have come up with the drug.

Sherman, Desai, and Kay thrived in this atmosphere. All three men enjoyed the challenge. For Sherman, who liked reading and even drafting legal briefs, it hearkened back to the early 1970s, when he had first learned he could use the courts to get what he wanted. It was not unusual for Sherman, pleased with a court pleading he had helped Radomski prepare, to email the document to friends like Fred Steiner, or to his daughter Alex. As he described to business associates and friends, he thought of the courts as a tool, one that he knew very well. Sherman and other Canadian generic leaders believed the federal government had sold out to the powerful Big Pharma lobby and that they had a duty to consumers to fight back. Of course, they also made a great deal of money when they were successful. But their constant mantra in many deputations to government was that they were keeping drug costs down. If they did not, Canadians and the Canadian healthcare system would be paying far too much for their drugs, since a generic version cost only a fraction of the price of a branded pill.

For their part, the brand name pharmaceutical companies maintained that in order for them to innovate they needed patent protection. After all, they argued, it was their scientists who were coming up with the initial drug formulations. This philosophical difference of opinion was at the centre of the brand name versus generic battle.

Canadian court files are filled with hundreds of cases involving Apotex. The battles were lengthy, sometimes taking decades, and they were expensive for both sides. It was not unusual for several hundred million dollars or more to be at stake. Some Apotex won, and the company was able to bring a drug to market and rake in millions of dollars in new sales. When Apotex lost, it often had to pay millions of dollars to the aggrieved brand company due to patent infringement. Over years, motions went back and forth, and there were discoveries and hearings and appeals in front of judges who struggled with the scientific formulas that were hotly debated by lawyers on both sides. Many of these cases continued even after a drug went to market. In some instances, in anticipation of a win he had not yet secured, Sherman took the financial risk of ordering his factories to make millions of dosages of a drug and have them ready for the moment a ruling went in his favour so that he could flood the pharmacies with the cheaper alternative. If a case went against him, Sherman always appealed. He did not give up, no matter the odds.

Lawyer Brian Greenspan, who would eventually lead the private investigation into the Shermans' deaths, recalls with great clarity his discussions with a man he calls "fascinating and challenging." Sherman's patent lawyer, Radomski, brought Greenspan into a case in which Sherman and Apotex were accused of contempt of court in the 1990s for selling a drug in violation of a court order obtained by a Big Pharma company. Greenspan advised Sherman that if he admitted wrongdoing and accepted a fine from the court, it would be a modest payment and he could put the matter behind him. "Barry told me, 'I will never accept doing something I think is wrong in principle,'" Greenspan recalls. The legal battle raged for seven years through various court levels, and ultimately Sherman lost and paid a modest fine.

The man who drove an old car and hated to pay for parking often said that he was fighting these fights for two reasons: one, to grow Apotex and keep jobs in Canada; two, to reduce the cost Canadians paid for their medication. When the difference in price between a brand name and a generic pill could be 5 to 1, or 100 to 1, or 400 to 1, depending on the type of drug, it was hardly surprising that company health insurance firms and provincial drug programs loved generic drugs.

One unusual offshoot of the tension between the desire to drive innovation at the brand name companies and the need to keep drug costs low is that some brand name firms now sell generic versions of their drugs through a related company. It's all about keeping as big a slice of the pie as possible, industry watchers say. "There's a lot of animosity between brand and generic companies," says Barry Fishman, a pharmaceutical executive who has worked on both sides. Fishman, who was Canadian vice-president of sales for brand company Eli Lilly and later ran generic rival Teva's Canadian arm, says there is also a symbiotic aspect to the brand–generic relationship. "But I never saw generics as enemies. I saw them as keeping us on our toes constantly to innovate and come out with new products."

For the layperson, it is nearly impossible to understand how a chemist can invent a new drug and how another chemist (or engineer, in Sherman's case) can come up with what is called a bio-similar version of the drug that is somehow not an exact copy. Radomski explains that in some cases chemists have come up with a way to "pack" the molecules differently. When you add the courts into this equation, and with the understanding that judges are typically not scientists, it becomes even more difficult to understand. Desai recalls how Sherman, if he did not like the ruling he was given, would lash out with a quick comment that made clear what he thought. "Judges are idiots!" he said on more than one occasion. Yet Radomski, a lawyer with no scientific training, says that during his many years in court, he has noticed that some judges have become quite adept at grasping the difficult scientific concepts involved.

Perhaps the best known Apotex battle occurred in 2010 over the generic version of Lipitor, which was then the most popular drug in the world. Lipitor is the brand name version of a drug called atorvastatin. A statin is a drug that reduces fatty acids, or lipids, in the blood. With cholesterol levels rising fast in populations around the world, often due to bad diet, doctors were looking for a way to counteract those levels. In 1985, a scientist at Warner-Lambert's Parke-Davis research facility in Michigan developed atorvastatin and began almost a decade of clinical trials, which were required before the US Food and Drug Administration would approve a product. Other companies had similar drugs, but the team behind atorvastatin believed theirs would prove the most effective. The firm entered into a partnership with Pfizer, and in 1996 Lipitor came to market in the United States. The two-company partnership then sought approvals in international markets. In 2001, Pfizer Canada was granted a notice of compliance by Health Canada and Lipitor began selling to a waiting and very eager audience. Just as Jack Kay and Barry Sherman had combed through documents to find the top-selling drug in the 1980s at the fledgling Apotex offices, they continued to do so decades later. Jeremy Desai had just joined Apotex, and Sherman instructed Desai and his team to make Lipitor a priority. Though he lacked any formal chemistry background, Sherman began conducting his own experiments in an attempt to create a different form of atorvastatin that would have the same effect on cholesterol levels in the bloodstream. Desai says, "Barry came up with an ingenious, alternative form" of the active pharmaceutical ingredient at the heart of the drug. As he always was when he felt he had a breakthrough, Sherman was excited, telling everyone Apotex was going to be successful with the new drug. Jack Kay would urge Sherman to be cautious, reminding him that moving from the laboratory and scaling up to production of millions of pills was a big step. Sherman would laugh and tell his friend he was "full of shit" and then wander off to tell someone else of the plan.

With the Lipitor generic science well underway, it was time for the lawyers to get involved. Radomski and other Apotex counsel started preparing their notices of allegation in federal court, and the battle began. A great deal of money was at stake. Pfizer's Lipitor during this period had earned about $1.2 billion in annual sales. On May 19, 2010, after years of work, Apotex issued a press release announcing that its Apo-Atorvastatin drug was approved and on the market. Sherman had prepared for this day and had shipments ready to go as soon as they received federal approval. According to the release, Apotex had "invented its own crystal form" of the drug, "thus overcoming the patents twelve years ahead of when they were legally set to expire." Apotex estimated in the release that over the next twelve years this would result in "close to $7 billion of cost savings for the Canadian healthcare system."

Kay, who was then the president and chief operating officer (Desai would later take over as both president and CEO), said at the time, "This is a historic moment as provincial governments are struggling with increasing deficits. . . . The risks for companies like ours to develop products and to litigate are huge, but the real beneficiaries are the public and private payers and consumers."

A story in the *Wall Street Journal* describing the product launch noted that Lipitor sales accounted for half of Pfizer Canada's 2010 revenue. Pfizer told the *Journal* that it had foreseen the eventual generic approval, and within two years the company would sell its own generic form of Lipitor.

As successful as Barry Sherman was in building his empire, those around him often had to shield him from the world of regulators. Over time, Kay and Desai realized that having Sherman present at a negotiation with, for example, Health Canada was counterproductive. Desai was better suited temperamentally to participate in the proceedings. Before Desai flew to Ottawa for meetings, the three men would sit in Kay's office and discuss strategy. There was no point sitting in Sherman's office, because the round table there was always completely covered with stacks of files. Desai would provide a briefing, Kay would weigh in, and then Sherman would cut them off. It could be an issue with a brand company, Health Canada, or the very powerful Food and Drug Administration (FDA) in the United States.

"They're full of shit," Sherman would say. "Sue them."

Desai would patiently try to explain his position, Sherman would interject, then Kay would smooth things over, convincing

Sherman to listen to the man he had hired from England to eventually run Apotex. Once, over Desai's objections, Sherman sued the US government, seeking $520 million in damages for slapping an "import alert" on Apotex, which warned American customers to beware of certain Apotex products (the United States is Apotex's second largest market after Canada). The US court filings in that case reveal that in 2009, FDA officials discovered that "Apotex had distributed products in the US market contaminated with hair, glue, plastic, nylon, metal, rust and acetate fibers." Inspections were carried out by the FDA at the Toronto plant in question, and according to the US government's allegations, inspectors found problems with the production system serious enough to warrant the import alert. Regulators on both sides of the border worked with Apotex and the issue was eventually solved, but Sherman sought damages from the Americans for loss of revenue. That losing battle cost an estimated $5 million in legal fees. Desai believes that the suit, which went to an arbitration panel and was ultimately unsuccessful, subsequently caused the FDA to target Apotex. More and more inspections of Apotex's international plants followed in what Desai calls "payback" for Sherman daring to take the US government to court. A series of other negative inspection reviews by both US and Canadian regulators over the years were reported on in the *Toronto Star* by David Bruser and Jesse McLean. Desai, who was interviewed for those stories, explained his belief that "compliance is a journey," given that the manufacturing of drugs on such a large scale imposes constant challenges, including contamination, and all companies have to be vigilant in order to deliver a high-quality product.

For Sherman, though, the regulators, the courts, and the media were always in the wrong. "Barry believed he was always right," says Desai.

The most public fight Sherman engaged in was a nasty conflict over a drug called deferiprone, a treatment for a relatively small group of people worldwide who suffer from the blood disease thalassemia. Books have been written about the decades-long dispute, and John le Carré's novel *The Constant Gardener* appears to have taken inspiration for one of its characters from Sherman's opponent. Libel suits were filed against the media who covered the case, and it led to Sherman's appearance, in a highly embarrassing interview, on the CBS program *60 Minutes*.

Pitted against Sherman and Apotex was Dr. Nancy Olivieri, a Toronto researcher who for a time in the 1990s became a media darling. After years of lawsuits, both sides signed a settlement and agreed not to say anything disparaging about the other. In her book about the conflict, *The Drug Trial*, journalist Miriam Shuchman referred to the saga as "the scientific version of a Greek epic."

Thalassemia is the name given to a group of relatively rare genetic disorders that cause anemia because the red blood cells in the body do not form properly and as a result do not carry enough oxygen through the bloodstream. Thalassemia is most common in the developing world; one research paper estimated that there are about 100,000 people with the genetic disease in India. In Canada, just 250 people are known to suffer from the disease, and in the United States 1,000. In Europe, it is more prevalent; there are an estimated 10,000 people with the disease, with significant clusters in Italy and Cyprus. Conditions like this, affecting only a relatively small number of patients, are called orphan diseases. Treating them calls for an "orphan drug," which, due to the small population at risk, is very expensive to design and produce.

The condition starts in early childhood, and the only known treatment is frequent blood transfusions, typically every two to four weeks. Along with the hardship of frequent transfusions comes a killer: iron overload. This is a situation where both the disease and the treatment can kill you. In healthy circumstances, the human body maintains its necessary iron in balance. But when blood transfusion on a regular basis introduces more iron, the body cannot handle it and the resulting iron buildup clogs the heart, liver, and other organs. It is typically fatal. Without some way to remove the iron, many patients die in their teens. For many years, the best drug was the very expensive Desferal, which is a "chelator," meaning that once it is inside the body, it attaches, or binds, to iron and is then flushed out of the body as waste. The problem with Desferal was that it had to be administered either by a painful regular injection or an uncomfortable infusion over a twelve-hour period several times a week. Some patients were also allergic to it. It was bad enough that young patients had to get blood transfusions every few weeks; having to then receive frequent injections or infusions to lower iron levels was so onerous that teen patients were opting out, getting sicker and dying. The holy grail researchers in many countries said they were seeking was a daily pill.

Nancy Olivieri was a young pediatric hematologist working at Toronto's Hospital for Sick Children in the late 1980s when she became fascinated by the disease. Worldwide, there were pockets of researchers looking for a solution. The drug formulation called deferiprone was one candidate, and Olivieri believed it was promising. Olivieri teamed up with Dr. Michael Spino, a University of Toronto researcher and professor who was doing some consulting work for Apotex and would soon be hired by Sherman to run ApoPharma, his new division that sought to develop its own brand name drugs, not just generic copies. To bring a drug to market required expensive trials, and Olivieri needed funding for tests on deferiprone. At the time, in the late 1980s, Apotex was not the multi-billion-dollar company it would become; sales then were about $200 million. A private company, it did not make public its profits.

The theory was that if a thalassemia patient could take a pill orally, the medication would bind to excess iron and remove it from the body. In an interview, Spino said Olivieri and another researcher had come to him at ApoPharma and asked if he thought Sherman would be interested in funding the clinical tests to study deferiprone. Spino agreed to take the pitch to his boss, though he was not confident he would be given a green light. Developing a new drug can cost tens of millions, or hundreds of millions, of dollars, and Spino was still new to the business, having spent his entire career at universities and hospitals.

He recalls how he tried to almost goad Sherman into funding the research. "Barry, I've come from academia," he said, "and let me tell you what the perception of generic drugs is there. That they're piranhas. The real drug companies do the research and then the generics come in and pick the cherries and make the money off that."

Sherman, Spino says, was deeply offended. "We're saving the public billions of dollars!" he shot back.

"Why don't we do something to show that we are different," Spino suggested. "Why don't we take a drug that nobody's going to develop. It's needed because patients are going to die. Why don't we develop it for the needs of the community."

Sherman scratched his head. "Will it work?"

Spino smiled. "I'm pretty sure I have the evidence that it will work. And if we don't do it, nobody else will do it."

"Can we make any money?" Sherman asked.

"I'm not sure if we will make any money. But we may break even."

Sherman scratched his head again. "Okay. Do it."

That decision began a clinical research project that for many years made headlines for Sherman and Apotex, most of them negative. During the human clinical trials for the drug she had brought to ApoPharma, Olivieri became concerned that the drug was toxic to the liver and ineffective. She wanted to raise those concerns publicly but was told by Apotex that due to the confidentiality section of her contract with them she could not. Apotex researchers believed in the drug and wanted to continue its tests. Olivieri did raise her concerns publicly, writing letters to patients in the trial as well. Apotex informed Olivieri that she was effectively fired from the drug trial program for breaching confidentiality, and the battle was on, raging in the media and the courts for well over a decade. Many sided with Olivieri, at least initially, and there can be no doubt that vitally important issues were in play. Academic freedom was being tested. Also in question was just how much the public and patients should be told while a drug was being tested on humans. Among the notable events in this battle, *60 Minutes* correspondent Lesley Stahl interviewed a very stiff and at times upset-looking Barry Sherman. According to Shuchman's *The Drug Trial*, during the interview Sherman muttered "She's nuts," referring to Olivieri. In an account of the interview provided by Shuchman, Sherman then offered to say "certain things" to Stahl "off the record," and Stahl shot back, "We're reporters, we're not your pals." Just that short exchange led to one of the many lawsuits in the case: Olivieri sued Sherman for libelling her in the interview.

Meanwhile, at ApoPharma, Spino hired Dr. Fernando Tricta, a Brazilian hematologist who for many years had been treating thalassemia patients in Brazil and also in Italy. Tricta was put in a room for three months to review all the testing literature on deferiprone. He disagreed with Olivieri's conclusions. Still, the ferociousness of the controversy, which made daily headlines at one point, affected him deeply. One night, when Tricta was out to see a movie with his wife in Toronto, a fellow theatregoer noticed he was wearing an Apotex jacket. "You should be ashamed of yourself," the woman said.

Not long after that, with executives at Apotex becoming concerned that Olivieri's dispute was ruining the image of the firm, a meeting was held. Some present wanted to stop the clinical trials. Tricta says Sherman listened to all sides, then stood up. "This is a drug patients need," Sherman said. "No other company will do it. It's the right thing to do. We will do it."

Neither side will discuss the intricacies of the case. Olivieri, when asked to speak about the deferiprone research and her own interactions with Sherman, declined an interview but then sent me a dozen emails containing links to studies, reports, legal actions, and other information related to what she said was ultimately a nineteen-year fight. Asked about a thalassemia patient group that, in the final year of Sherman's life, had lauded Apotex, Spino, Tricta, and Sherman for saving the lives of thousands of patients, Olivieri was skeptical and alluded to how patient groups often receive funding from pharmaceutical companies, telling me in an email that as a general rule "inquiries about who (and what companies) funds which patient organizations are never misplaced." Indeed, after checking the financial records of the patient group in question, I discovered that it had received a grant of US$102,000 from an Apotex charity the same year as it praised Apotex and its researchers.

Spino, who is still president of ApoPharma almost two decades after he joined (Tricta is there too, and both men are researching other potential uses for deferiprone), says he, Sherman, and the researchers were hurt by the attacks. He says much of the media portrayed Apotex as a company that, through its research, was "causing death in children for the motivation of money." It was exactly the opposite, he says. To begin with, millions of dollars were being spent with little hope of a return. Eventually, through continued testing after Olivieri was no longer involved, Spino and Tricta learned that the drug deferiprone "protected the heart" more than any other chelator used to remove iron, and that more people survived with it than with Desferal: "It gets into the heart and removes the iron." Additional studies eventually backed deferiprone and it was licensed around the world under the ApoPharma brand name Ferriprox. It was first sold in India in 1994, then in Europe (1999), followed by the United States (2011) and Canada (2015).

The controversy still shows no sign of going away, with competing research papers differing on the health risks to patients. One study published in 2018 by the *British Journal of Haematology* involving five hundred patients determined that deferiprone reduced cardiac iron more than a competing drug. In 2019, a Toronto researcher working with Olivieri examined the clinical studies of forty-one patients and published a paper in *PLOS ONE*, a Public Library of Science journal, stating that patients on deferiprone had an elevated incidence of diabetes and liver dysfunction.

Throughout the years of the Olivieri conflict, Apotex grew, adding its production facilities in Mexico and India. Jeremy Desai says that at the time of Sherman's death, production had just surpassed twenty-five billion dosages (tablets, capsules, or other single-dosage forms) a year, more than halfway to Sherman's goal of reaching fifty billion.

The many Apotex facilities in Ontario are impressive, an expansion beyond the Ormont Drive factory that has been ongoing since the early 1980s. A sign at each facility greets visitors and sets out the beliefs that Apotex seeks to instill in its employees: "I am dedicated. I am non-compromising. I am accountable." Touring a visitor around the plants, scientists, many of them twenty-year employees, show off gleaming modern equipment in well-designed buildings, some with ceilings seventy feet high; rooms with airlocks to keep out contaminants; robots that move product around; heavy drums of raw materials shipped in to be refined into the unformed finished product (chemists call it "the dope"), which will be sent to another factory to become pills. One of the chemists at the facility that processes the raw active pharmaceutical ingredient notes that it refines about five metric tons of deferiprone annually, just as an example of the scale of production. Senior scientists at these production facilities say Sherman almost never visited, but he made sure that they had the state-of-the-art equipment needed to get the job done. Dan Matu, the production manager at Apotex's plant in Brantford, Ontario, who has been with the company since he came to Canada from Romania in the early 1990s, says, "Dr. Sherman created the environment for people to do this work." And tours through the Apotex factories reveal something Sherman and Jack Kay took a great deal of pride in: over eighty different cultures made up the workforce, chemists and other scientists who immigrated to Canada and wound up working for the generic firm.

By the time of Sherman's death, Apotex had revenues of US$1.6 billion a year. As a private company, their actual profit is not made public.

ELEVEN

KING AND QUEEN

BARRY SHERMAN, SPORTING A BROWN checked suit with a diagonally striped tie, sits beside his wife, Honey, both of them perched on director's chairs in a studio. It is October 11, 2017, two months before they will be found dead. A clean white background puts the focus on the power couple. A video camera rolls. As part of an effort to celebrate volunteers and donors, the United Jewish Appeal Federation of Greater Toronto (UJA) is preparing a tribute to two of its most generous supporters: Honey Sherman and her husband, Barry. Honey, wearing a crisp white shirt with a big collar, a black jacket, and a pearl choker, begins by explaining to donors and volunteers how her family, having survived unimaginable conditions during the Holocaust, ended up in Halifax, on Canada's east coast. After some Maritime hospitality, Honey Reich and her family, along with other Jews who had been living in displaced persons camps in Austria and Germany before making the ocean crossing to Canada, boarded a train to Winnipeg. In Toronto, there was a change of plans for the Reichs. A Jewish Immigrant Aid Service leader came on board and offered lodging and jobs to those who wished to disembark. The Reichs got off the train. The memory of that generosity, from people her family did not know, stuck with Honey. She goes on to explain how it was not until years later, when she was newly married to Barry, that she received her first request for a donation to a Jewish cause: just $100. Honey says she told the fundraiser, a friend from childhood, that she would give it her consideration, but she did not donate on the spot: "I disappointed her grossly. I said, 'Let me go home and think about it and get back to you.'"

Honey then describes how she went home, discussed it with Barry, and the next day made an anonymous gift of $1,000. The friend, Honey says, likely never knew she had made such a deep impact. And as stories of Barry Sherman's success in the generic pharmaceuticals world spread, requests for donations intensified. "That's how it started. People started to ask, and we were able to do it."

Barry is watching Honey tell her story. He smiles. His gaze does not waver from his wife. Honey's right hand is lying comfortably on the armrest of her husband's chair, their wrists touching. Now it's her turn to watch Barry speak. The message he delivers is one he has repeated many times to people who have been targets of his often aggressive fundraising requests.

"I don't think any person can be a happy person if he is successful in life and doesn't give back to the communities," Sherman says, smiling. "I would encourage all youngsters to get involved and always make it the focus of their lives and participate in society and to give back, because that is a source of great satisfaction." As Barry speaks, Honey reaches over and makes an adjustment to his tie, which is poking out of his buttoned suit jacket a bit too much for her liking. That small gesture is typical of one part of their relationship. Honey wanted to make sure her Chuck was presentable to the public.

Later in the video, the couple is laughing at a story of the origin of their first large donation. It was to assist in the international Operation Exodus campaign to help Jews from the former Soviet Union emigrate to Israel in the late 1980s and early 1990s. A well-known man in Toronto's Jewish community telephoned the forty-six-year-old Barry Sherman in 1989 and said, "Barry, this is an emergency campaign. . . . Would I be crazy to ask you for a million dollars?" In those days, at the start of Apotex's success, "that was a lot of money," Sherman recalls. He hung up, he says, and talked to Honey. Then he called the man back a few minutes later to say he would write a cheque for the requested amount. The two burst into laughter on camera when Honey reminds her husband that the fundraiser on the Exodus campaign was kicking himself afterwards, saying, "Dammit, I didn't ask for enough!"

The story finished, Honey gives her husband a playful nudge. His suit jacket is riding up at the shoulders. "Now, you've got to sit up straight and pull down your jacket," she tells him. He does.

Over the years, Honey encouraged Barry to break out from his normal wardrobe—"Barry's uniform," Apotex colleagues called it—of white shirt and grey slacks. Barry, by all accounts, cared as much for nice clothes as he did for nice cars. Which is to say, not at all. At one point, in exasperation, Honey even enlisted their friends Fred and Bryna Steiner to take Barry to the high-end menswear shop Harry Rosen to see if the clothiers there could make an impact. The effort met with limited success. Barry Sherman did not think that clothes made the man; rather, it was intellect, drive, and how much you gave back to your community.

The UJA video filmed two months before their deaths was eventually shown the following year as part of a tribute to the Shermans. At the event, on June 8, 2018, organizers announced they were posthumously giving Honey the Ben Sadowski Award of Merit to acknowledge her "outstanding leadership qualities and years of involvement in the Jewish and general communities." Though seen as a high-powered couple—friends dubbed them the "king and queen" of Jewish fundraising—it was their individual and very different achievements that were remembered. Barry Sherman, the leader of a generic drug powerhouse who gave away hundreds of millions of dollars. Honey Sherman, the tireless charity volunteer who sat on boards and asked tough questions to ensure that the family money was well spent.

At the end of the video, Barry describes his take on the couple's separation of duties: "We decided to divide up the responsibilities. She does all the community service work—she has been chair of just about everything—and my time is better spent doing what I can to earn money so I can write the cheques. That's how we have divided it."

Honey nods and looks serious for a moment. It appears, at least to a casual viewer, that she has never heard her husband articulate the arrangement this way, at least not in so public a forum. She nods again, decisively this time. "Fair and equitable," she says.

It's difficult to quantify how much the Shermans gave to charity in their lifetimes. At times, it was done anonymously. Dr. Michael Spino, the ApoPharma president who was involved in the thalassemia and deferiprone research, says that when he first arrived at the company, "We had to force Barry to at least acknowledge Apotex. Barry did not want to be set up as some sort of super person. Honey felt a little bit differently, but Barry just did it because it was right."

Sherman told people, and Spino was one of them, that he believed people should give 20 percent of what they earned to the community. He insisted that all people who were able should make significant financial contributions.

Since Apotex is a private company, there is no way to know what Sherman earned annually, but the Bloomberg Billionaires Index estimated his personal net worth at $4.7 billion at time of death, a calculation largely based on his Apotex holdings. One highly placed insider with knowledge of Sherman's family holding company told me that Sherman had numerous investments outside of Apotex and that his real net worth was closer to $10 billion. A UJA official said that Sherman gave that organization at least $150 million over the years. The public record of press releases and news stories reveals that a series of multimillion dollar donations were made over the years beginning with a donation of $60 million in the late 1990s, to what was eventually named the Sherman Campus, a Jewish recreation and cultural centre built in the north end of Toronto. Sherman friend Leslie Gales explains that this was a very important project for Barry, who grew up at a time when Jewish people were not accepted in other health clubs. Out of that was born the concept of the Jewish Community Centre (JCC), recreational and cultural clubs built in the 1950s and 1960s. Sherman wanted to build new infrastructure on the existing site of an outdated JCC, and friends convinced him to attach his family name to it. After their deaths, a two-acre park in a corner of the campus was named the Honey and Barry Community Park in recognition of their service and contributions.

As noted in the UJA video, both the Shermans volunteered as well as providing funding, Honey much more than Barry. She was on numerous boards, including that of the Baycrest Health Sciences Centre in Toronto, the York University Foundation, the Mount Sinai Women's Auxiliary, and the Friends of Simon Wiesenthal Center. She was also chair of Toronto's Sarah and Chaim Neuberger Holocaust Education Centre. Those who sat with Honey Sherman on boards and travelled with her to Israel to see where some of the donated money was being spent recall that she would ask probing questions. Recently, the mayor of Sderot, a town on the border of the Gaza Strip, commented to a Canadian charity official that he would miss Honey Sherman, both as a regular visitor to his town and as someone who was clearly invested in making sure donated dollars were well spent. The mayor told the Canadian charity official that "nobody asked more or better questions than Honey Sherman." Friends and colleagues also recall how, in addition to asking tough questions, Honey found it important to make a tangible connection to the difficult past of her family. Friend Karen Simpson Radomski, herself a veteran volunteer in Jewish charities and the wife of lawyer Harry Radomski, recalls the trip she took with Honey to Poland, where they joined in the annual March of the Living, a silent walk on foot that traces the journey from the Auschwitz concentration camp to Birkenau, where the gas chambers were located. "It was so important to her to learn first-hand about this part of her family's history," says Simpson Radomski. "I think, for her, there was some element of survivor's guilt. She knew how fortunate she was, and I think that is why she always tried to help others."

Barry Sherman was much less hands-on than his wife, but he did hold various fundraising posts over the years, and as a graduate of the University of Toronto he had a continuing commitment to providing guidance and advice (in addition to donations) to the university's Entrepreneurship Leadership Council. The Sherman philanthropy included major donations to Baycrest Apotex Home for the Aged, and also non-Jewish charities, with significant gifts to the United Way and Mount Sinai Hospital. Alex Sherman told me that "one of the amazing things my parents did was envision the Baycrest Apotex Home for the Aged. . . . They often thought big-picture but also paid attention to the little details that brought comfort and joy in the spaces they created."

The Shermans have also sponsored pharmacy research at the University of Toronto with about $12 million in donations, primarily to the Leslie Dan Faculty of Pharmacy, named for Sherman's greatest rival, the founder of Novopharm. Internationally, Sherman's Apotex Foundation has donated an estimated $50 million in pharmaceutical products to relief groups coping with natural disasters and epidemics.

But what kind of couple were the Shermans? Did they travel together? Read the same books? Gossip about their friends and neighbours? Watch the same Netflix shows? Could they be relied on if you were in trouble? What kind of parents were they? Were they a loving and close couple or a distant one, living a marriage of convenience?

The Shermans' marriage of forty-six years began not long after Cindy Ulster introduced her candystriper friend Honey Reich to Dr. Barry Sherman in 1970. Over the years, the running joke was that Barry was not an especially attractive catch, because Honey's parents had always hoped their daughter would marry a medical doctor. When it turned out that Barry had a PhD but not an MD, Honey told her parents and girlfriends she had decided that was fine. "Close enough," she said. The couple married the next year. Fred and Bryna Steiner, who wed two days later, were the closest "couple" friends the Shermans had. Dinners, parties, and trips to Florida were done together. No matter where they were, laughter dominated their table, with each person holding their own in the lively conversation. Fred and Barry did discuss their business interests and how much they both had to pay to the Canadian government in taxes. Barry, in particular, hated to pay taxes and over the years would engage in a variety of schemes designed to lower the amounts he owed. But Steiner also recalls free-ranging discussions among the four of them about the issues of the day.

When their orders were given and the food arrived, the Shermans' plates were never filled with anything particularly healthy. Fried food was their favourite, the more batter on fish the better. Vegetables were tolerated if the zucchini was fried in a thick batter, served crispy brown. Sherman had diabetes, but he wasn't keen to follow the diet prescribed by his doctors. He had also had prostate cancer and various other ailments. Years later, Joanne Mauro would make an effort to ensure that her boss ate well at least at lunch. She would pick up a healthy takeout meal or, when Apotex was big enough to have a chef and a cafeteria, make sure something green and leafy showed up on his desk. That did not stop Sherman at odd hours figuring out the best route to take through the Apotex building to find the choicest assortment of cookies and chocolate sitting out on employees' desks. Out at a restaurant, away from the eyes of Barry's assistant, the Shermans were freer to indulge in whatever they thought was tasty. And Honey always seemed to home in with laser focus on the plate beside or across from her, particularly if it held french fries.

Neither Barry nor Honey was a big drinker. Barry could barely tolerate half a glass of wine, and Honey was only marginally more interested. If there was a dance floor, Honey would drag Barry onto it, though he did not like to dance or in fact like anything at all about music. He told people music was "pointless," that "it all sounds the same." But if Honey wanted to dance, he danced. Barry also had a mischievous side to him, and he liked to get a rise out of the Steiners. At a certain point in a dinner, he would look at Honey with a sly narrowing of his eyes behind his thick glasses. Then he'd look at the Steiners, then back at Honey. Pushing his chair back from the table, he would nod to his wife and say, "Let's go get laid."

One story the Steiners chuckle over was a visit to Amsterdam's red light district in the 1970s. Honey could not believe what the "women were *doing*," recalls Bryna. In fact, both of the Shermans delighted in showing they had a bawdy side. On one of their Florida trips in the early days, Honey announced to Bryna, "I want to go to that male strip club, the Crazy Horse Saloon." Bryna shook her head. "Honey, you're being crazy." Honey insisted, and the two couples got in a car and headed to the Crazy Horse. Six men, all dressed like the Village People, danced onto the stage and the show began. Barry kept marvelling at their "equipment" as, one by one, the dancers stripped down to nothing. Bryna, who had been coaxed by Honey many times to step out of her comfort zone, tried desperately and unsuccessfully to convince Honey to approach the stage and tuck a $20 bill into one dancer's skimpy waistband. Another time, when Honey found out that some of Barry's male friends would occasionally exchange emails containing photos of naked women and dirty jokes, Honey insisted that the men forward them to her. As Bryna says, "Honey did not want to miss out on anything."

The couples certainly had fun together, but they made a point of being there for each other if help was needed, including a shoulder to lean on. The Shermans also took care of their own parents. Honey's mother and father, for example, had a nice condo in Florida courtesy of the Shermans. Barry and Honey each had a sister, and both were well cared for by their wealthy siblings. In particular, Honey invited her sister, Mary Shechtman, to work on designing and decorating the homes the Sherman couple owned over the years. Mary, according to Sherman holding company insiders, was also given significant financial assistance to purchase real estate, including numerous houses sub-divided as rental apartments and her Forest Hill home where she and her husband, Allen, live. Allen's foray into the retail jewellery business, helped by at least $32 million in Barry Sherman money, ended in bankruptcy. With the death of the Shermans, and the rift that developed between Mary and her nephew and nieces, the Shechtmans were cut off. "My family (Allen and my children) and I have struggled desperately since the incident," she wrote in a May 2019 email to me. "We have never had the luxury of healing properly. We were left on our own and had to put all our energies into surviving. We lost more than we could ever imagine and more than Honey & Barry would ever have wanted for us. They would be horrified, angry and devastated by the pain we have had to suffer and the losses we have had to endure. . . . hopefully we are finally on the road to recovery from the devastation we have had to deal with emotionally, financially and physically." At time of writing, Mary was telling her friends that Allen is driving an Uber and she is planning to start work as a tour guide to make ends meet.

From his early teenage days, Barry knew he wanted to have children. In high school, he made pocket money by babysitting neighbourhood kids. He told his friend Joel Ulster, who married before Barry did and quickly started a family, that he looked forward to having his own. With the Ulster and Steiner households brimming with kids, it would often be Barry sitting on the carpeted floor, amusing the children with toys and games. A standard opening line from Uncle Barry, once the children were old enough to have a conversation, was, "Tell me what's going on." Friends have mused that his affinity with children, particularly when they were babies, grew out of the notion that children were blank slates, filled with promise and potential, which appealed to his entrepreneurial spirit. Adults frequently disappointed Barry Sherman, but young children never did. As future parents often do, the Shermans "test drove" other people's children. To give Fred and Bryna a break, Barry and Honey would sometimes pick up their three children on a Friday and take them for dinner. "Our kids became his kids," Fred Steiner recalls. It was yet another odd part of Barry Sherman's personality that though he spoke so often of wanting children, when he had his own, he saw very little of them.

Having their own children proved more difficult than the Shermans expected. After Honey first miscarried in 1972, it happened several more times before Lauren was born in 1975. Joanne Mauro, who began working as Barry's executive assistant not long after, recalls that Barry or Honey would bring toddler Lauren, a "real cutie," to the Apotex offices. Lauren remained an only child until she was eight. Honey was continuing to have miscarriages, and finally, in the early 1980s, the couple decided to try surrogacy. In the 1980s, paying a woman to use her eggs and her womb to carry a child to term was not common practice in Canada, and it was only just becoming popular in the United States. An American lawyer provided the Shermans with books that described the physical characteristics and education of potential mothers. In each case, Barry's sperm was used, and each of the three surrogates they would engage came from a different US state. The lawyer had the women sign what Sherman told friends was an "iron-clad contract" that would prevent them from ever having a claim on the child or the Sherman fortune. In each case, the mother was flown to Canada for the birth so that the children would be

Canadian citizens. Jonathon was born in 1983, Alex in 1986, and Kaelen in 1990.

The funeral for Barry and Honey Sherman on December 21, 2017 was the first time anyone but the closest of family members and friends had seen the Sherman children in public since their parents' deaths the week before. None had spoken publicly and the only communication was the brief statement they had issued decrying the murder-suicide theory. The four Sherman children came on stage together after Rabbi Eli Rubenstein read the poem "Each of Us Has a Name" by Israeli poet Zelda Schneurson Mishkovsky. Jonathon stepped to the podium first and encouraged those in the audience to take a moment to "breathe and reflect" and to consider the "enormous impact that this is having on everyone gathered here today." Before her brother delivered the first eulogy, Alex Sherman sang a Hebrew song—"Eli Eli (My God, My God)," a hopeful song written by Hanna Senesh, a young Hungarian poet and paratrooper who in 1944, as part of the British Army, jumped into Nazi-occupied Europe and was later caught and executed. She is considered a national heroine in Israel and the story of how, at age 23, she refused a blindfold and faced the firing squad head on, is a powerful tale of bravery. Kaelen, the youngest Sherman, recited the words to the song "You Are My Sunshine," which she said their father, returning home late from work each night, used to sing to them as children. "I would like to take this time to sing it back to him." Lauren, the eldest Sherman child, did not speak.

In the audience were thousands of mourners, including Prime Minister Justin Trudeau, Ontario Premier Kathleen Wynn and Toronto Mayor John Tory, along with hundreds of Apotex employees in blue company T-shirts. Jonathon began by describing his family ordeal. "These last few days have been really fucked up for my family," he told mourners. When his parents were alive, he said they would always take charge and provide comfort in difficult situations. While Barry focused on his work and supporting the family, Honey handled all the organizational details of the children's lives, including parent-teacher interviews, after-school events, and summer camp. "Our mother always had everything taken care of," he recalled. While she was organized on her kids' behalf, Honey was often forgetful of her own things. On a family trip to Israel, Jonathon told the mourners, the family had to retrace their steps after each stop to look for his mother's left-behind wallet, keys, or other items. Her funny ways aside, Jonathon said he and his siblings marvelled at how "stoic" their mother was, displaying so much energy in making sure her children's needs were met while struggling physically. Knowing how difficult it was for his mother to get around on some days due to various infirmities, Jonathon said, it was a significant accomplishment that she was able to train for, take part in, and win a *Dancing with the Stars*–style competition to raise money for a charity.

Jonathon spent part of his eulogy talking about his sisters. He gave the eldest, Lauren, "amazing credit for paving the way" in the family and lauded her "free spirit and your ability to love life." To his sister Alex, he said she was the "heart of the family" and said he will always recall the gruelling, 250-kilometre race in the Gobi desert in 2007 to raise money for an AIDS charity when she gave her walking stick to a villager who she said needed it more than she did. Alex finished the race, but her brother did not as his partner at the time had to pull out. To Kaelen, the youngest, Jonathon said their parents were "teeming with excitement for your wedding" and he vowed she would still have a wedding when she was ready because "that is what mom and dad would want." Later, Fred Steiner would put his hand on

Jonathon's shoulder and congratulate him for how he was taking a leadership role in the wake of his parents' deaths. "Your dad would be proud of you taking charge." There was also an edge to some of Jonathon's comments, which upset other members of the family, including Honey's sister, Mary. In describing a family ski trip to Vermont, Jonathon said his mother let him choose a more difficult run for her after a series of easier trips down the mountain. "When I picked the black run, directly below the chair lift, you were reluctantly gung ho," Jonathon said, addressing his deceased mother before the thousands of mourners. "I'll never forget watching you wipe out on the first turn and slide down the entire run for everyone to see. It was effing hilarious. Until you made me march up and collect all your gear." Mary, and many of the Shermans' friends were taken aback by Jonathon's words, given Honey's infirmities. It was a poorly kept secret in the circles the Shermans travelled in that Jonathon and his mother did not get along. People who knew both Jonathon and Honey said they "hated" each other. In fact, the relationship between Honey and her children was, on many occasions, strained. Lauren, the eldest, confided to one close friend of Honey's that her mother's controlling behaviour amounted to "psychological abuse." Kaelen complained to people she was close to that her mother often told her, "You're fat. You need to lose weight." Some friends of Honey said she, in turn, did not like to speak about her children and, as odd as it may seem given her background, called them "the Nazis" to her sister and close friends—an apparent reference to how she felt they controlled her with constant demands. Barry, friends say, was caught in the middle. He maintained a stronger connection to their children by doing two things: listening and giving them money, although he gave significantly less to the younger two than to Jonathon and Lauren.

With four young children, the Shermans did what most people did and set up carpools to get them to class and after-school events. Golf friends Anita Franklin and Dahlia Solomon had children who were roughly the same ages as the Shermans' kids and recall how both Honey and Barry took part in carpooling. When it was Honey's turn to drive, it automatically meant the children would be late for school. She was always running at least fifteen minutes, often thirty minutes, behind schedule. But the children loved it when Barry drove, because he would talk to them non-stop, drive right past the school, and take them off in a completely different direction, nattering all the way about one theory or another. When it came to involvement in the kids' activities, Honey and Barry were the opposite of helicopter parents. Barry, in particular, rarely attended after-school events his children were involved in. A late riser, it was unusual for him to see them in the morning, and his late-night and weekend work schedule kept him from being very involved. Barry typically worked six days a week at the Apotex office. Sunday, he worked in his home office.

At the funeral, Jonathon—briefly removing his kippah in what onlookers took as quiet deference to his father's atheism and asking others in the audience to do the same—said he could remember every single time Barry Sherman took part in father-son activities with him. "He would come and watch me play hockey or baseball every season or two. But those few games were my Stanley Cups and my World Series."

It was difficult for those who did not know the family well to tell if Jonathon harbours a grudge against his distant father. In his eulogy, he acknowledged the reason his father could not always be there. "We clearly knew why our dad was not always present. He was a pretty busy guy." The theme of Barry being overly preoccupied with work was raised a second and third

time by Jonathon, who noted that Honey was his "first golf partner" and the witness to his only hole-in-one. "Well, Dad was
there, but he was buried in his briefcase, I am sure." And on one
of the "three or four" times that Sherman played baseball with
his son in the backyard, Barry hit the baseball over the fence
and commented that as a boy his friends called him "slugger."
Jonathon, who had learned from his father's friends that Barry
lacked any athletic prowess, said this was an example of one of
his father's best attributes. "You were always so funny."

One part of the children's upbringing that Sherman did focus
on was grammar and spelling, patiently but firmly correcting
each error. In his eulogy, wiping tears from his eyes, Jonathon
got a laugh from the crowd when he apologized to his absent
father for any grammatical mistakes he might make. It was a
running joke among Sherman friends and family that if you
uttered something incorrectly, he would interrupt with the correct phrasing. A few months before he died, Sherman friend
Senator Linda Frum sent an email to Barry Sherman and several others with the subject line "Barry's ancestor?" The email
read, "'I see that you have made three spelling mistakes.'—last
words of French aristocrat Marquis de Favras after reading his
death sentence during the French Revolution." Attached was
an image of Favras, and Sherman responded, "I look a lot like
him. Perhaps I am his reincarnation."

Over time, Jonathon said, he figured out that his father was
a "real-life superhero," because he set an example of what a
"great Canadian" was. He cited his father's success in business
and his philanthropic contributions as reasons to regard him
as being as much a Canadian hero as hockey superstar Wayne
Gretzky.

In later years, Barry Sherman became Jonathon's business
partner in several enterprises, and title records show at least

$127 million in loans from a Barry Sherman-funded company registered against Jonathan's venture into the self-storage business and a group of rental cottages on Chandos Lake, northeast of Toronto, where Jonathon and his business partner, Adam Paulin, had a cottage and owned a small marina. Jonathon believed Chandos Lake was ripe for development and he wanted to expand his holdings to eventually purchase cottages on one quarter of the lake. There were disagreements along the way, with Jonathon as recently as 2015 asking his father to consider investing an additional $250 million in those businesses. Jonathon, who studied civil engineering at Columbia University in New York, wanted his father to listen seriously to his plans. As one person who worked closely with Barry Sherman for years said, "Jonathon wanted to prove he was just as astute a business person as his father. Prove to the world." Barry, in a 2015 email exchange with his son, does not appear overly receptive to the pitch, particularly because Jonathon was criticizing Barry's decisions over the years to back certain businesses, most notably those run by Barry's good friend Frank D'Angelo. At one point in the email chain, the 32-year-old Jonathon tells his 73-year-old father that he understands business concepts because he has "studied accounting and finance." Barry, who is balking at providing his son more money, shoots back, "Please also remember that I have been making business judgments for many decades, often making decisions with which others disagree. The result has been some big losses, but also some even bigger gains. As a result of my decisions, you will likely be a multi-billionaire."

In his eulogy at the funeral some two and a half years later, Jonathon made no reference to any acrimony between them, saying his father was a proud partner in his "little" business, a venture called Green Storage (named "Green" because, according to its website, it has sites powered by solar energy, with electric vehicle charging stations and low flush toilets). Jonathon told mourners that when he and Barry began their partnership, they had the shortest shareholder meeting ever. It boiled down to his father offering "anything, anytime."

Despite Barry's attempts in later years to rein in his son, the elder Sherman was a soft touch for money, and it started at an early age. Friends have recalled how one Friday morning when Jonathon was in Grade 1 at the United Synagogue Day School (now Robbins Hebrew Academy), he went up to his parents' room because he needed a weekly donation for a Jewish charity. Barry was still in bed, but he mumbled from under the covers that his wallet was on the bureau and Jonathon could take what he needed. Later, as the children lined up to drop their dona-tions at the front of the class, little Jonathon stuffed a fistful of bills into the collection jar. Several hours later, a teacher called the Sherman home and told Honey that Jonathon had put nine $100 bills into the jar. Honey told the teacher to hang on to the money, and later she retrieved most of it.

The relationship to money in the Sherman household was intriguing and likely can be traced to Honey's and Barry's upbringing, though each parent ended up with a different approach. Both had parents who at various times struggled financially. As described earlier, Barry grew up in a home where his father, Herbert, was president and part owner of a zipper manufacturing company, and in those days the family was quite comfortable. But Herbert died when Barry and his sister were young, and their mother had to take in boarders to pay the bills. Honey was a first-generation immigrant whose parents had survived the Holocaust and then lived in a dis-placed persons camp in Austria before coming to Canada and starting their small shoe store. Honey was consequently careful with money, and at times she seemed to invent scarcity and need where there was none. That resulted in some oddly controlling behaviour. When Lauren, their oldest, was a little girl, she had a birthday party. Thirty friends came, and it was a big event. After the party, according to other parents who were there, Honey told Lauren she was not ready for her daughter to open the presents. It may be, friends speculate, that she feared Lauren would be spoiled by having so many gifts at once and wanted to appoint a time to open them later when Lauren would appreciate each present individually. The wrapped presents remained set aside at their home for weeks before they were opened.

Unlike most of their well-to-do friends, the Shermans employed very few people to help run their home and daily lives. Whereas some had full-time staff working at their homes, the Shermans only hired someone to water the plants and a cleaning lady once a week. Barry in particular seemed uncomfortable with the notion of employing people of lesser means to do domestic tasks. At an overnight dinner party at the Muskoka cottage of Linda Frum and her husband, Howard Sokolowski, the summer before the Shermans died, Frum was in the dining room clearing the table while her two housekeepers, who had helped serve dinner, were tidying the kitchen. Barry, who had lingered beside the table, looked uncomfortable. "Don't you think it's unfair?" he said, nodding towards the women in the kitchen. "We have so much. We have so many beautiful things, and other people do not. Why should we be served and they do the serving? Who decided that some people have to serve and some people get served?"

Frum was put off by the comment and wasn't sure how to respond. She wondered if he'd had a bad time. She tried to convey to Sherman that her housekeepers were well paid, that she treated them like family and did her best to help them if they needed something. "We ended up having a social justice conversation. I think he was struggling with the idea that the whole evening had been a cosmic injustice."

Honey herself exhibited what could be taken as hypocrisy in her relationship to money. She drove her ten-year-old SUV, which she frequently had repaired instead of buying the latest version, yet on shopping trips with girlfriends she'd buy three or even ten of something, including pricey Louis Vuitton or Jimmy Choo purses, if she was convinced she was getting a good deal. The purses, or perhaps three identical versions of a designer jacket, would be stored in her closets and never used. Yet small, inexpensive items could hold great meaning for her. On a trip to Ottawa a few weeks before she was killed, Honey was awarded a Senate medal in recognition of her, and Barry's, philanthropic contributions. Her friend Senator Linda Frum was with her to make the presentation. Afterwards, Honey misplaced her scarf and spent several hours retracing her steps to recover it. Frum and Leslie Gales, a fellow attendee at the event, assumed—correctly, as it turned out—that Honey was scouring Ottawa not to find an expensive Loro Piana scarf from Italy but rather a $40 scarf from Banana Republic. Several cab trips later, the scarf retrieved, Honey explained to her two bewildered girlfriends, "I love that scarf."

Both Honey and Barry always carried a lot of cash with them. Honey, who never went to a bank, would get spending money from a drawer that Barry kept stocked with $50 and $100 bills. But stories of the Shermans' unwillingness to spend their cash on certain things are legion. Fellow philanthropist Leslie Gales recalls how her young son asked Barry Sherman one day why he was wearing a cheap watch and not a Rolex. Sherman replied, "I buy my watches at a flea market, and for an extra few dollars I get one with the date on it. Why spend money on something you don't need?" When the Shermans were heading out to a restaurant and parking was difficult to find, Barry would do his best to find a free spot. Fred Steiner, who would happily leave his car in a No Parking zone and pay a fine as long as it was not a tow zone, said trying to save a buck was just one of the quirks of his friend. Another was his single-minded focus on his job. One day, at the private Oakdale Golf and Country Club, where the Shermans and Steiners were members, Toronto businessman and philanthropist Lou Bregman asked Fred Steiner to introduce him to Sherman. The two men met and chatted. Sherman did not like small talk, and Bregman was trying to find an opening so that he could get to know Sherman.

"Barry, I never see you around here. Do you golf?" Bregman asked.

"No," replied Sherman.

"Do you play cards?"

"No," said Sherman.

"Do you run around with broads?" Bregman asked, now completely at a loss as to how to get the conversation started.

"No," said Sherman."

"What do you do for fun?"

"I work," Sherman said.

Bregman laughed. "I work too, but what do you do for fun?"

Sherman said what he said to Steiner and others who had posed the same question over the years. "I like to give away money."

RioCan founder and CEO Ed Sonshine says that Sherman's lack of interest in spending his money on himself made him very different from other successful businessmen. One day, Sonshine and Sherman and their wives were at the exclusive Magna Golf Club, in Aurora, Ontario, for a charity dinner and

Sherman remarked on the beauty of the place. Sonshine agreed and said he was a member. Sherman knew that Sonshine was a member at Oakdale as well.

"You belong to two golf courses? You're insane," Sherman said, his eyes wide.

Taken aback, Sonshine said he had worked hard all his life. He was a big supporter of Jewish and other charities, and, yes, he also enjoyed some of the fruits of his labours. "Barry, I didn't steal any money. I didn't inherit any money. I am going to spend it the way I want to spend it."

"You must be insane. That's crazy," Sherman said.

Sonshine asked Sherman what he enjoyed in life. He says Sherman paused and appeared to be giving it serious thought.

"I enjoy work. And giving away money," said Sherman, repeating what he'd told Bregman.

Barry Sherman had a reputation as a workaholic, and it was deserved. But he did join the family on some holidays, including the 1996 trip to Tanzania for a safari. In his memoir, which would years later be entered into evidence as part of his legal battle with his cousins because it contained his version of how he came to launch Apotex, Sherman noted that he did not bring any work with him to Africa and was perhaps for the first time "incommunicado." In his eulogy, Jonathon Sherman recalls their father on that holiday "acting like a lion" to amuse his sisters as they drove around in a jeep on dirt tracks that wound through the open plain, passing giraffes, wildebeest, warthogs, and antelope. There were also many winter excursions with their friends and their children to Florida and to US ski destinations. Sometimes, though, it would just be Honey as the lone Sherman parent. In 1994, the family, minus Barry, took a trip to Steamboat Springs, Colorado, to ski. Dahlia Solomon recalls that Tropicana orange juice was not in Canada yet, and Honey saw it in a grocery store they stopped at on the way to the mountain. "She was always excited with whatever was not sold here. She had to try it," Solomon says.

Honey loaded their shopping cart with ten big cartons of orange juice, plus a monster amount of sliced cheese and white bread. "The kids had canker sores by the end of the week," Solomon says. That's because Honey did not like to waste food, and she insisted on having an "orange juice party" at least once a day. On the final day, Honey saw there was still a fair bit of bread and cheese left, and they had to leave for the airport. "She made cheese sandwiches for everyone. She just did not like to leave anything behind."

At the end of that trip, when they had taken a break from skiing to go trail riding on horseback, Honey's wit was on full display. The ride camp featured some big horses with long hair. Honey climbed aboard one of them and asked the guide the name of her horse.

"Adolf," the guide replied.

Without a pause, Honey asked her friend, "You think he's going to ask for my papers?"

Honey's sister Mary, her friends say, was a big part of the Sherman family's life when the children were little, and that is likely one reason the eventual rift cut so deep. Before she was married and had her own children, friends say "Aunt Mary" helped with carpooling, taking the Sherman children to lessons and play dates, and helping with homework. Once Mary and Allen became parents, there were times when some of the Sherman children joined their family on trips that included golfing in Arizona and Disney World in Florida.

The Sherman home on Old Colony Road was the gathering place for big Passover and Rosh Hashanah dinners. A long banquet table that stretched from the rarely opened front door to the staircase at the rear of the house was set for extended family and close friends. In his eulogy, Jonathon described his mother wearing her "cow" apron and cooking chicken noodle soup with carrots and what he described as "those little illegal eggy things." *Eyerlekh*, Yiddish for "little eggs," refers to not-fully-developed eggs found inside just-slaughtered hens and sold by Jewish delis, against health regulations, to knowing customers like Honey Sherman in a little brown bag.

As the children grew to adulthood, Barry Sherman lavished them with millions of dollars to buy houses, cottages and cars. Friends say Honey did not approve, but it was Barry's way of showing affection. In some cases, he provided them with money to buy income properties in the hope that they would learn from running a business. Friends of the Shermans say that Barry told them that the first two children, Lauren and Jonathon, were given $100 million each at an early age to invest in businesses and real estate. Whether that is true or an exaggeration is not clear. Public records indicate early examples of Jonathon's involvement in real estate. He purchased a large wooded property north of Toronto at a cost of $2 million in 2006 when he was just twenty-three, and developed it relatively recently with the help of a $5-million mortgage from a Bahamas company sources say is connected to Barry Sherman. It is now the principal residence of Jonathon and husband, Fred. It was not just the Sherman children who benefited from Barry's generosity. Before Fred, Jonathon was dating a young Toronto man named Andrew Liss and in 2011 Sherman insiders say Jonathon convinced his father to fund the $4-million purchase of a Forest Hill home on Warren Rd. for Liss. The numbered company that purchased the house is headquartered at Apotex, and Liss is listed as company president and sole director. Over the next few years, as renovations progressed on what became a lavish home, land title records reveal $14 million in mortgages registered on the property, held by a Barry Sherman company. Sherman sources say that in addition to the extensive renovations, there was also major damage from frequent parties at the home. Eventually, in 2015, a buyer paid $11.5 million for the house. That Barry Sherman, who was funding those real estate dealings, would allow this raised the eyebrows of Sherman's friends. "Barry did so many unusual things with real estate," said one. "Offshore companies, putting unexpected people on title. That was Barry." In contrast, the younger Sherman children, Alex and Kaelen, were initially given $1 million each, with instructions to invest the money wisely. Each also received considerable financial help in purchasing a home, but as to bulk payouts, Kaelen and Alex received far less than their older siblings. Whether that decision to provide significantly less money was in response to pressure on Barry from Honey, friends did not know.

Once the children were adults, contact was sparse at times between some of the children and their parents, with Alex being the closest to her parents, particularly her father as they shared a similar approach to money and philanthropy. Something that bothered Barry was that none of them wanted to enter the generic drug industry, something he believed was necessary if they wanted to become part of an Apotex succession plan. Barry was disappointed, particularly as he saw the children of successful businessmen like Fred Steiner and Morris Goodman working happily in their fathers' ventures. Steiner's and Goodman's sons eventually took leadership roles in those businesses. Of all the Sherman children, their youngest, Kaelen, seemed the most emotionally needy. She frequently called her father during the workday, and friends and business associates who were present during those calls say Sherman always answered and provided whatever assistance Kaelen required. In the year leading up to her parents' murders, people close to Kaelen say she seemed more grounded, which they attribute to her engagement to the young man she had met on a dating site in 2015. At a dinner in the fall of 2017 to celebrate the engagement, the young man's father said Barry took him aside and said, "I have never seen Kaelen happier." The couple would marry in April 2018 and separate three months later, divorcing in 2019.

The child Barry seemed to work hardest to become close to was Jonathon, though the two also had frequent arguments about how Barry should spend the money he had made. At one point, perhaps to curry favour, Sherman took the craft beer business and other holdings, including a Mississauga soft drink manufacturing and bottling plant he had in partnership with Frank D'Angelo, away from D'Angelo and gave them to Jonathon.

Later, Sherman sold off the beer-making machinery and returned the Mississauga plant to D'Angelo, who now produces a range of products there. Though Sherman was at times not close with his adult children, friends say he remained closely involved and interested in his still very young grandchildren: Lauren's son and Alex's two children. Photos taken the week before the murders show Barry and Honey at Alex and Brad's house posing with their one-month-old granddaughter. There is also a sweet picture of Barry, lying back on a couch, looking into the little girl's eyes. Still, Jack Kay, who maintains close contact with his own children, told me, "I think Barry really missed out."

Honey, who always wanted to be the centre of attention, liked to go out at night. Barry preferred to work until 8 or 9 P.M. most nights. The majority of the Shermans' outings were related to philanthropy. Honey would triple-book herself on some evenings. If Barry could not join her, her sister, Mary, was his stand-in. When Apotex had a box at the Air Canada Centre (as it was called at the time), and Barbra Streisand was performing, Honey insisted that Barry invite friends and business associates. Jack Kay recalls that everyone but Barry was mesmerized. Barry was sitting on a couch near the bar area, working on his BlackBerry. Kay sat down to keep his friend company.

The Shermans, their friends say, did not sit at home and watch movies or TV together. For starters, the television in their room did not work for many years, because neither wanted to hire someone to hook it up. Honey did like the occasional show on Netflix, with the show *Scandal*, about a Washington-based crisis-management firm, being one of her favourites. Joel Ulster's teenaged granddaughter remembers Honey sitting down with her to go over the latest plot twist when Honey came to visit.

The couple, particularly Barry, maintained a close relationship with many of the children of their closest friends, providing financial assistance to some, business mentoring to others. All of the Ulster children, for example, received some form of help from Sherman over the years, all given with no strings attached. In the months before the Shermans died, Barry was coaching Jeff Ulster on his first foray into the business world. Jeff had until recently been the director of digital talk content for CBC Radio and had decided to leave the CBC to start a business with a partner that aimed to link advertisers with podcasters, something that was flourishing in the United States but not in Canada. When Barry heard that his oldest friend's son was going to abandon the comfort of a salaried position for a start-up, he got in touch and they began regular chats. Their email exchanges show that Sherman, though busy at Apotex, took time and care to assist Jeff.

"Many businesses fail, despite being potentially successful, because the owners run out of money before cash flow turns positive," Sherman told Jeff in October 2017. "When I started

Apotex, Honey kept telling me to close it down before I lost everything, and I nearly did lose everything." Sherman's advice was to "accelerate revenues while minimizing cost, as much as possible, until you reach break even, or are at least confident that profitability lies ahead."

Sherman offered on several occasions to provide seed capital for the new business. "Starting a business is not easy," he wrote to Jeff. He suggested he could provide a substantial interest-free loan for eighteen months, getting shares in the company in return. But Sherman said that, "in reality, I would give you a personal confidential option to buy my shares for $1." Jeff was not comfortable with having Sherman invest or partner in the business, fearing it would complicate his relationship with his business partner. Having just left the security of a salaried job, he did relent and gratefully accept some financial support on a monthly basis to cover his family's expenses in the first few months of the new business. Their dialogue continued until just a few weeks before Sherman died. In all the correspondence, Sherman shows a strong interest in helping Ulster make the right decisions. His questions were on point and helpful. Sherman reminded him in one exchange about the drafting of an agreement: there can be "a devil in the details."

A poignant note in the chain of emails between Sherman and Jeff Ulster comes when Sherman tells Jeff he has realized he hasn't had an update on the other five Ulster siblings. "If they too are in need of any assistance, I would like to know and would be more than happy to help. You are family, and I love you all," Sherman wrote.

As to the strength of the Shermans' marriage, friends say it was shaky at times, with Barry working long hours and Honey wanting more of a social life. In that way, they were incompatible. At one point, about six years before he died, Barry told some of his friends that he was considering leaving Honey. There was no specific reason, friends said, just that they were spending so little time together that he thought living separately might make more sense. Honey's friends told me they were unaware of this, and that as the years passed, Barry and Honey seemed closer than ever.

With the children grown, and with more time to travel, Honey wanted to see the world. Barry told Honey that with his intense work schedule, he could not take the number of trips she wanted. As a result, Honey began travelling several times a year with girl-friends Dahlia Solomon and Anita Franklin and others, including realtor Judi Gottlieb, who joined Honey on some major international journeys. On their trips, each woman was given a job: Gottlieb was the "negotiator"; another woman was the "poet laureate," who would write poems about the trip; another was "quality control." Honey was the "drug dealer," since she travelled with a bag of Apotex samples that included painkillers and antibiotics. As she did in Toronto, Honey also insisted on travelling with a big green box of Nature Valley granola bars. Her plan, which some of her friends felt was culturally insensitive, was to hand them out to beggars instead of money, explaining to her girlfriends, "They need to eat."

Those who travelled with Honey say she had an insatiable thirst for knowledge. Judi Gottlieb credits Honey with providing her, on a trip to India, with one of the most memorable nights of her life. It was in the northern city of Varanasi, which is on the Ganges and is regarded as the spiritual capital of India. There are well over two thousand temples in the city. When Honey, Judi, and four other girlfriends arrived on a trip in 2006, most of the group were bracing themselves for a typical tourist experience. "Honey always kept us honest," Gottlieb recalls. "A lot of the girls just wanted to shop."

It was late in the afternoon when they got there, and the six travellers from Canada were exhausted. The guide who met them at their hotel laid out the plan: they would get a good night's sleep, and in the morning he would take them to the bank of the Ganges, where they would board a boat and see the sights along the riverbank from the water.

"No," Honey said to the guide, "we want to go tonight."

Gottlieb says the guide sized up the six women from North America and shook his head. "You will not like it. It is much better in the morning."

Honey's eyes narrowed, a look her girlfriends had seen before. They knew where this was going. Honey got her way. That night, as the guide took them in a wooden boat along the riverbank they saw families carting their deceased loved ones to funeral pyres, lighting the bodies on fire, and later emptying the grey ash in the sacred river. "It turned out to be the most important thing we did on the trip," Gottlieb says. "Honey had researched and read about it and pushed the guide." The next morning, the guide took them on a boat ride and they watched in amazement as mourners came to the river and bathed themselves in the ash-thickened water. "It meant so much more to us."

Many of the women who took these trips with Honey also attended an annual weekend in Muskoka at Nancy Pencer's cottage. Videos from the events show a Honey Sherman so relaxed that she, with the others in attendance, dressed up with full make-up for the yearly themed costume event (*From Russia with Love*, *Moulin Rouge*, and *Memoirs of a Geisha*) and belted out karaoke show tunes.

The one passion Barry and Honey Sherman did share was philanthropy. They were relentless and sometimes annoying in their pursuit of donations. In addition to all the major charities they supported and raised funds for, Barry made annual requests to his friends and business associates on behalf of a small orphanage in Israel. It was run by a rabbi who had encountered Sherman and somehow persuaded him to be his lead, and possibly only, fundraiser. At the same time each year, Sherman would telephone Ed Sonshine, Leslie Gales, and others to arrange their annual donation to the small charity. Sonshine said it had gone on for so many years that Sherman would simply email a request for $10,000 and say, "Maybe you can do $15,000 this year."

Gales and Sonshine both asked Sherman why he didn't simply make the entire donation. Asking friends for money takes a certain kind of disposition, and Sonshine says he has done it in the past but now finds it distasteful; he is happy to give but does not like asking. Gales says Sherman said to her, "Leslie, no one gift is as significant as the gifts from a community." With Sherman dead, that charity has lost both its biggest benefactor and fundraiser. A Toronto rabbi who acts as the local contact contacted me in June 2019, after having read of my efforts to unseal the Sherman estate files. "Would you know if our charity is mentioned in the will?" the rabbi asked me. I told him that I did not think any charity had been listed in the Sherman will and that, to the best of my knowledge, the estate was divided equally among the four children, with some discretion for the trustees to give money to other family members if they desired. No charity had been designated.

Though generous to Jewish charities, Sherman made it clear that it had nothing to do with a belief in a deity. A few months before his death, he was approached by a rabbi seeking money for a cause. Sherman said he would help the man but suggested they meet at his Apotex office on a certain Saturday in October. "But Barry, that's Yom Kippur," the startled rabbi said. Sherman replied, "That's fine with me. If you are hungry, I'll bring some ham sandwiches."

Sherman had a name for those who did not donate. "He said they had a black heart," Sonshine says. Sherman simply could not understand why a person who made money would not give according to their wealth, says Gales.

Sherman was incredulous that people would refuse him. "You know what?" he said to one friend. "I call really wealthy people and ask them for ten thousand dollars and they say no. To me! Can you believe it?"

As Honey's friend Linda Frum recalls, Honey would not publicly criticize those who did not donate. Instead, she would bestow the title of "good boy" or "good girl" on a person who made a substantial donation to one of her causes.

At the time of her death, Honey Sherman had been enlisted by the UJA's Steven Shulman to create a campaign to convince Jewish real estate agents in Toronto's red hot property market to give donations that corresponded with their growing wealth from commissions on big sales. Judi Gottlieb, the Sherman realtor, has taken over that cause and is working on a plan to get fellow real estate agents to step up their contributions.

Jack Kay says Sherman told him on many occasions that there was no meaning to life but there was an obligation. "Life is what it is," Kay recalls his friend saying. "As long as you leave the world a little bit better than when you came in, you have contributed to the betterment of society."

TWELVE

RISKY BUSINESS

THE BLACKJACK TABLE IN THE CASINO on the Las Vegas strip had an opening. Fred Steiner motioned for Barry Sherman to join him, and they squeezed in between two other gamblers. "Barry, let me show you this game." Honey and Bryna were off wandering around the strip, and they had all planned to meet up later in the afternoon.

Sherman put down a $10 bet and promptly lost. Steiner, who loved to wager on cards and was just getting started, saw his friend back away from the table.

"Where are you going?"

"That's it," Sherman said over his shoulder, walking off. "I gamble every day in business. What do I need this game for?"

To Steiner's knowledge, his friend never gambled again on that three-day trip to Vegas in 1982, nor did he ever bet on cards again. Sherman saw no point in risking a few dollars for a possible reward in a game of chance. Yet when it came to his business outside the pharmaceutical world, he would happily gamble millions of dollars if he had a hunch he was right. That pattern would continue for his entire life. In an email to his son Jonathon in April 2015 explaining why he chose some investments (money to Frank D'Angelo in particular) and not others, Sherman wrote, "I cannot debate this with you. There are no equations used for an analysis. It is simply a judgment call, implicitly based on intuition as to the expectations."

Close friends like Steiner, Jack Kay, and Ed Sonshine, and his entire family, were well aware that away from Apotex, Sherman carried on a high-stakes game with a cast of characters strikingly different from the buttoned-down scientists and bureaucrats he spent most of his life with. Many were larger-than-life individuals who, for one reason or another, had trouble finding more traditional backers. And among these characters, no one was more different from Sherman than Frank D'Angelo.

Sherman once described D'Angelo as being similar to a worn version of a famous movie actor. That was on the occasion when one of his in-laws, who did not like D'Angelo, called him at Apotex to say that "Frank D'Angelo is at a store right now buying a hundred-thousand-dollar Breitling watch with your money." At the time, D'Angelo happened to be sitting on the other side of Sherman's desk at Apotex. Smiling at D'Angelo, Sherman leaned back in his chair and said to his in-law, "You mean the guy who looks like a bad version of John Travolta? Frank D'Angelo? You don't have to worry. Frank is in my office and not buying a watch."

It is difficult for many of Sherman's friends to fathom what the billionaire scientist saw in D'Angelo. He is a streetwise entrepreneur with Sicilian-Italian roots who purposefully puts on the air of a comic-book gangster but in reality is a singer, songwriter, talk-show host, actor, movie producer, restaurateur, former beer baron, hockey goalie, and apple juice maker, to name a few of his activities. Since he started out in the fruit and vegetable business with his father out of high school, D'Angelo has ridden a financial rollercoaster for his entire life. While he may not have the Midas touch, he has made a great deal of luck over the years simply by working hard and being in the right place at the right time. As a hockey-crazed kid, he was at a game in the Boston Garden when Bruins captain Phil Esposito spotted him outside the dressing room, freezing in the cold of the arena and hoping for an autograph. Esposito, who would later become friends with D'Angelo, took the eleven-year-old into the dressing room to meet Bobby Orr and Derek Sanderson. The movies D'Angelo makes, which Sherman bankrolled and executive produced, all feature different but equally rumpled versions of D'Angelo, who, of course, stars in each movie. He's the everyman, the tough guy, the guy with the whole world against him who comes through in the end.

D'Angelo was the first person with any real knowledge of key events who agreed to speak to me when I began investigating the deaths of the Shermans. It took a while to believe that he was not inventing his friendship with the late billionaire. D'Angelo told me, and many others, that he loved Sherman like a brother and that the sentiment was returned. However, others, including Joel Ulster, suggest that Sherman treated D'Angelo more like a son. When I met with Jack Kay for the first of two lengthy interviews with him, I asked him if it was true that Sherman and D'Angelo were pals. All true, Kay said. I asked what Sherman saw in D'Angelo. "Frank is a character's character. What's not to like?" Kay said. "And Frank is an idea-a-second guy, and he works his ass off. Barry liked people who had ideas but didn't have the wherewithal to bring those ideas to fruition."

There were many business outsiders who gained Sherman's attention over the years, but none with D'Angelo's charm, which may have been one of the reasons he and Sherman were friends for more than fifteen years. "Frank was very different from the people Barry related to in his business life and his personal life," Jack Kay told me. While Kay's practice was to play the devil's advocate with Sherman, "Frank knew how to stroke Barry the right way. . . . I would tell Barry he was stupid and full of shit. Frank would tell Barry he was fantastic."

It began in 2001, when D'Angelo's company, D'Angelo Brands, which produced and packaged apple juice and other products, was unable to get a steady supply of the crushed and filtered apple juice necessary to build market share. It occurred to D'Angelo that maybe he needed his own processing plant. A friend told D'Angelo that a very wealthy man named Dr. Barry Sherman owned a bankrupt plant in Tiverton, a community in Bruce County, Ontario. Due to its proximity to the Bruce Nuclear Generating Station and a special deal provided by the power facility, the processing plant was powered by free electricity. In one of his earlier gambles, Sherman had financially propped up a former friend who had a plan to make juice and beer at the factory. The businessman (who Sherman eventually sued successfully) also had a scheme to make a product that could be fed to cows to reduce bovine belching and flatulence, major contributors to global warming. Those plans had come crashing down, and now Sherman's money managers were planning to break up the state-of-the-art machinery and sell it off. D'Angelo got an audience with Sherman and his money managers and presented his plan. He would purchase the processing plant for $5 million (which he did not have) and pay Sherman by selling the beer-brewing equipment, which was brand new and had barely been used.

"Let me get this straight," said Sherman's brother-in-law, Mike Florence, who was one of his money managers. "You are going to use our money to pay us?"

Florence was visibly angry, D'Angelo recalls, but Sherman raised his hand. "If you can pull it off, why not?"

D'Angelo says Sherman was so impressed, he suggested instead that they be partners. "Go ahead, run with it," Sherman said, according to D'Angelo.

The processing plant solved D'Angelo's apple juice problem, and when he took a closer look at the entire production facility he wound up convincing Sherman that they should also become beer barons. The first order of business was travelling to Europe to find the perfect beer recipe, which D'Angelo, a wine drinker, says he did by stopping at the first place he saw on a highway in Belgium. Sherman paid off D'Angelo's $50,000 credit card bill so that Ontario's latest beer maker could afford his plane ticket. Out of the Tiverton plant eventually came Steelback beer and some innovative products: plastic beer bottles, lemon-infused beer, and the first "tall boy" cans. Steelback struggled to find a foothold in the competitive Ontario beer market, though it did win gold, silver, and bronze medals in 2007 in several categories at the Ontario Brewing Awards. At the same time, also with Sherman's financial backing, D'Angelo produced an energy drink called Cheetah Power Surge. He hired as his pitchman disgraced Canadian sprinter Ben Johnson, who in the commercial used the tacky line "I Cheetah all the time." Friends of Honey Sherman recall her pointing to the canned drink in a store and saying, "That's one of ours." One day, D'Angelo had a dozen cases dropped off at Apotex and they sat in the executive hallway for days before they were distributed among staff.

Meanwhile, Sherman and his financial managers at the family holding company noticed that debts were piling up at the brewery and other D'Angelo businesses that Sherman was backing. One problem was that sales revenue was not keeping up with the ever-growing number of events that D'Angelo, with Sherman's support, was sponsoring around the province. D'Angelo's hope was that all Ontario Junior Hockey League arenas would one day be Steelback arenas. One hefty sponsorship that racked up the bills was Toronto's major Grand Prix race car event in July 2007, dubbed the Steelback Grand Prix. During the race, where a big section of Toronto's lakefront road system is shut down for several days, Sherman was spotted by Toronto businessman Paul Godfrey. Godfrey, a former Toronto politician and well-known financier, who is often at such events, recalled how out of place Sherman was among the grease pits and the noise. "Oh, D'Angelo got me involved," Sherman explained to Godfrey over the roar of high-octane-powered cars zipping by on the other side of the safety fence.

Later that year, two things happened that would unsettle D'Angelo's world for a short time. Sherman called him in and told him that he was sorry, but his twenty-five-year-old son, Jonathon, a recent engineering graduate of Columbia University, in New York, was taking over Steelback Brewery after a short stint at Apotex. Not long after, the Shermans put Steelback and some of the other D'Angelo initiatives into creditor protection with a plan to restructure. According to the financial papers filed in court during this time, D'Angelo's companies were $100 million in debt to Sherman, plus $20 million in interest. While D'Angelo maintains to this day that the restructuring papers paint an unnecessarily bleak picture of his finances, he agreed to take a step back. Sherman provided him with a monthly allowance (D'Angelo will not say how much) to keep him afloat.

"I left there destroyed," D'Angelo says of this period of his life. "But the man was so good to me, I trusted him, and he looked after me."

D'Angelo continued to operate the downtown restaurant that Sherman also backed, the Forget About It Supper Club, on King Street, in Toronto's theatre district. Jonathon restructured the brewery, reducing the number of beer brands drastically, won a few awards himself, and then the company closed up in 2010. With the brewery closed, and Jonathon moving on to other ventures, Sherman gave D'Angelo back control of many of the assets, including his juice plant, and the two men continued as if nothing had happened. Jack Kay watched this all unfold. "I didn't agree with Barry as to the amount of money he invested with Frank. I said, 'I don't think we will see any return.' But Barry said Frank is one hard-working guy," Kay tells me.

Today, D'Angelo Brands produces a number of products, including AriZona iced tea and related beverages. At D'Angelo's annual company Christmas lunch at his Mamma D's restaurant (with dishes made according to recipes D'Angelo created), adjacent to the soft drink and juice plant he has in Mississauga, Sherman was always seated beside D'Angelo. Sherman would miss the 2017 lunch, held the day before the Wednesday when the Shermans were most likely killed, because he had a scheduled meeting he could not miss.

Just as Paul Godfrey was surprised to learn that generic drug titan Barry Sherman was backing a beer company which in turn was sponsoring a car race, others would be surprised to learn that the seed money behind movies like *Sicilian Vampire* and *The Neighborhood* came from the Apotex owner. Sherman shared the executive producer role with D'Angelo on all movies, though Sherman's contribution was mainly financial.

"When Frank came up with a new script, I would come in in the morning and Barry would have put it on my desk," Kay says, smiling. "I even had the *Vampire* poster here for a while." The formula for the movies was simple, and they were all shot at breathless speed in a week. Beginning in 2013, D'Angelo's company In Your Ear Productions turned out one or two movies a year. Each featured an actor who was no longer Hollywood A-list but was still a draw, among them Daniel Baldwin, who is in most of them along with Michael Pare, Paul Sorvino, the late Robert Loggia, the late Margot Kidder, and James Caan. Hockey legend Phil Esposito has been in two. D'Angelo said Sherman loved the concept of a movie made quickly and on the cheap though with good production values. As someone who turned out products that had expiration dates, Sherman liked that "our movies had no shelf life," says D'Angelo. In the last few years, the movies (some had theatrical showings but most went straight to DVD) have started to make money through licensing to Fox and Amazon. Sherman also liked the fact that the Canadian government gave him a hefty tax credit because of the movies' high Canadian content. Sherman's only constant criticism was the vulgar language in the scripts. D'Angelo says he patiently told his financial patron, "That's how people on the street talk."

Jonathon Sherman, however, was not a fan. In a 2015 email exchange between father and son, Jonathon expressed dismay that Barry was continuing to fund D'Angelo, and makes the claim (which D'Angelo vigorously disputes) that over the years $250 million had been advanced to D'Angelo with little return. Jonathon writes, "In the past I have been accused of petulance for asking tough questions, and there has been much frustration for both of us. Years ago I did stop asking about Frank because of the strain it caused on our relationship, and left it alone. I am only asking again now because for the past couple of years 'cash is tight.' I have been turning down great investment opportunities, and Frank continues to burn cash at the same rate." Barry responded by defending D'Angelo, pointing out that "major actors in Hollywood take him seriously" and that D'Angelo was producing films with "value in excess of cost." Barry included a link to a movie trailer for *Sicilian Vampire*.

If there is any doubt about the closeness between the streetwise D'Angelo and the nerdy Sherman, their camaraderie is on display in many photos. Dinner parties were held to celebrate each new movie release, and in one photo, a smiling Barry is seated across from such notable actors as Robert Loggia and Tony Rosato. The photo was taken at the dinner celebrating the 2013 premiere of *Real Gangsters*. To the left of Barry is Frank D'Angelo; to Barry's right is Honey. Though Sherman went to D'Angelo's events, D'Angelo was rarely invited to Sherman family events due to the bad blood with Jonathon over the brewery business. D'Angelo was not at the Sherman funeral, at the request of the Sherman children, who asked Jack Kay to deliver the message. Kay did, and promised D'Angelo he would go with him to the gravesite later on, which he did.

In the weeks immediately after Barry and Honey died, family openly floated the idea that D'Angelo was either the killer, or that some financial deal he and Barry were involved in led to the attack. D'Angelo scoffs at this idea. "First, Barry was like a brother to me. I loved him. Second, why would I kill the person who has supported me and given so much?" Insiders have told me that since Barry Sherman died, D'Angelo has had his funding cut off. Over the life of my investigation, D'Angelo was one of several people who frequently touched base, often helping me gain access to good friends of Barry Sherman who otherwise would not have spoken to me. He, like the Sherman children, had his own theories and he was never shy to relate them.

As I did with many people, I asked D'Angelo where he was on the Wednesday night the Shermans died and on the Friday when the bodies were discovered. At the time, D'Angelo and his partner, Gemma, had between them two houses, one in Stouffville, north of Toronto, and one in Kleinburg, northwest of Toronto. Gemma works in the office with D'Angelo at the Mississauga plant. On the morning of Wednesday, December 13, 2017, D'Angelo said he and Gemma were at the Stouffville house and he left early to play his regular hockey game with friends in Toronto. He left the rink, went to work at his Mississauga plant, and at the end of the day, the couple went home to Stouffville. Gemma, who was pregnant at the time (the couple now has twins) said that Wednesday night she and D'Angelo were at home together watching television. The next day, Thursday, Gemma went to work and D'Angelo worked from home in Stouffville, co-hosting a web-based sports radio show. On the Friday, they drove up to Collingwood, two hours northwest of the city, and Gemma, in the passenger seat, got the news of the Sherman deaths on her phone. Gemma, who had met Barry Sherman many times at the annual Christmas party and at meetings with D'Angelo, said the rumpled billionaire reminds her of another well-known tycoon. "There's always a social media post of Bill Gates standing in line for a taco. I will see that and say, 'That's Barry'. You never knew what he had." Both D'Angelo and Gemma were interviewed by Toronto homicide detectives and gave the same account they provided me.

There was only one Frank D'Angelo in Sherman's life, but he backed many others on short-term ventures as diverse as a dating app and a condominium tower. As Jack Kay explains, when one is a billionaire, people will drop by the office with a pitch, a scheme, an idea. Quite often, those people ended up in court being sued by Sherman. And these actions—often involving relatively small sums of money—contributed to the belief that Sherman was overly litigious. "You hit Barry Sherman with a fly swatter, he's coming after you with a fucking sledgehammer," D'Angelo says.

Sometimes Sherman ended up on top; sometimes he lost millions. But he always kept fighting. "Barry's not a quitter," says D'Angelo. "Barry's not a type of guy who would swim halfway across Lake Ontario, get tired, and swim back. He's going to fucking make it all the way."

Sherman's ventures were run out of his family holding company, Sherfam Inc., incorporated in 1991. Headquartered a kilometre from Apotex, on the second floor of an ugly three-storey brown-brick building populated by insurance companies and law firms, Sherfam did not look like a multi-billion-dollar enterprise. While Sherfam's accounting functions were run out of the building, under the watchful eye of South African–born Alex Glasenberg, the Sherfam chief financial officer, Sherman rarely set foot in it. Those who wanted an audience visited him at Apotex.

Pitchmen typically got in to see Sherman because of some previous connection, through social circles, a chance meeting, or, quite often, Toronto's Jewish community. The person would book an appointment and, on a day when Sherman had a few spare minutes, find themselves sitting across the cluttered desk from the billionaire. That's the way it had been with D'Angelo years before. By all accounts, Sherman had a remarkably short attention span unless something interested him. It was not unusual for him simply to get up and walk away during a conversation if he was bored. Kay says that when someone showed up with a "good story" but not one Sherman was captivated by, the easiest way to get the man out of his office was "to write him a cheque."

"Or, if there was more substance, Barry would say, 'Go see Jack,' and I would take it from there," Kay says. Though second in command at Apotex, Kay was often called upon by Sherman to assist with his Sherfam investment plans. Kay and Glasenberg were typically not in agreement with these pitches for get-rich-quick schemes. Sherman was already wealthy, so why take on the headache of a scheme that did not look good on paper? Over the years, Kay would sometimes get very upset with Sherman. He would go home and discuss it with his wife (he remarried after he joined Apotex), suggesting to her that if this kept up he would have to leave Apotex.

"My wife and I had the discussion, and [at dinner with the Shermans] my wife would say, 'Barry, you are going to force Jack to resign,'" Kay recalls. He never did, of course. "Once Barry made the decision, whether I agreed or not, he was the owner and the decision-maker. My job was to operationalize it, whether I agreed or not."

In 1985, ten years after Sherman started Apotex, an investment scheme involving high-end yachts caught his interest. He was a long way from being a billionaire then, but he had made a few million dollars and he hated paying taxes (which his Conservative friends found odd, since Sherman was a lifelong Liberal, a party historically known for funding big government initiatives through increasingly higher taxes). Sherman was always on the lookout for a way to avoid paying taxes. In later years, he had his accountants create a labyrinth of companies, registered in Panama and other tax haven jurisdictions, to shield Apotex profits. But in the 1980s, he was attracted to ready-made schemes, and that led him to the yachts. Einar Bellfield, a Norwegian man a judge would years later describe as suave and intelligent, set up a tax shelter that promised to reduce taxes payable for wealthy businessmen.

Bellfield used tax accountants and lawyers to peddle the concept, and one of them made a successful pitch to Sherman. Fantaseas, also known as Overseas Credit and Guarantee Corp. (OCGC), was raising money to build a fleet of luxury catamarans to sail the Mediterranean and Caribbean. The plan was to build or purchase a fleet of seventy-five boats and lease them to short- and long-term customers. Investors were "loaned" money by OCGC to buy into the scheme and were to make monthly interest payments on the loan. The interest payments and any losses the investors incurred could be deducted from their annual income tax payments to the Canadian government.

In addition to Sherman, more than six hundred others eventually invested in the tax scheme, including Michael Bregman, founder of Marvellous Mmmuffins and the man who purchased and took Canadian coffee chain Second Cup public. This big group of investors, many from the highest echelons of the Canadian business elite, were lured in by lawyers and accountants who received hefty commissions for securing seed money. Some of the glitzy Fantaseas promotional events were held at Toronto's Casa Loma, a Gothic revival style mansion located in midtown. Working out of the den of his condominium, Bellfield, his wife, and a partner created an impressive series of brochures that depicted the fleet of yachts, complete with gleaming state rooms and with glamorous names like *The Great Gatsby*, *Elegance*, *Garbo*, *Gable*, and *Casablanca*. Each year for the next five years, Bellfield and his small team would send out detailed statements to investors describing the growing fleet, with some boats purchased and the majority being built from scratch in shipyards around the world. So specific were the documents that they described the purchase of plush interior supplies right down to linen tablecloths. As to paid charters, many had already been booked, the investors were told.

What no one realized, or apparently did not turn up through the due diligence one would expect of shrewd investors, was that Bellfield was a charming fraud. He had just been discharged from bankruptcy in Canada and was facing fraud charges over some other schemes, and the entire corporate web that attracted Sherman and others was a sham. Only two yachts were ever acquired, and each was sold almost immediately. Fantaseas was a complete fabrication, as investigators and a criminal court eventually found. Bellfield was sentenced to a decade in prison and ordered to pay a $1-million fine, punishments that were unusually harsh compared to other white-collar prosecutions in Canada. In the case files, federal investigators detail how the scheme deprived the Canadian government of several million dollars of tax revenue and deprived investors of much more.

The real pain for investors, including Sherman, came when Canadian tax authorities reassessed years of tax returns and found that the losses the investors had been claiming to reduce their payable income tax were, like the yachts, a mirage. Since there were no yachts, there could be no losses. One of Bellfield's pitches was that since seagoing yachts depreciate quickly in value, the investors would be able to record the depreciation as a loss. No boats, no depreciation, said the taxmen—and they were right.

Caught with their financial pants down, most of the six hundred plus investors made a deal with the Canadian tax authorities and settled. Not Sherman. He kept fighting for several years, though he too eventually cut a deal. He agreed that his deductions should be disallowed, and as part of the settlement agreement the amount he owed was reduced. But Sherman sued Orenstein and Partners, the accountants Bellfield used to prepare financial statements for his scheme. Sherman claimed that the accountants were negligent in not providing a warning in their reviews that Bellfield's company was not a "going concern." Sherman felt that the accountants should have suspected a scam and wanted Orenstein to reimburse him for the $634,996 he had paid in interest during the four years of the swindle. Sherman lost in the lower court, however, and lost again at the Ontario Court of Appeal.

It is quite likely that to do battle with Revenue Canada for several years, and with Orenstein and Partners for more than a decade, Sherman incurred legal expenses greater than the amount he was seeking. In his ruling, writing for a unanimous decision of three appeal court judges, Justice John Laskin wrote that the judge whose ruling they upheld had made a keen observation about the Apotex founder after seeing him testify for two days on the witness stand: "[Justice Maurice Cullity] was left with the impression of a man with too many businesses and other responsibilities and interests to pay much attention to his investments once he had made them."

That Barry Sherman rubbed shoulders with a fraudster was not at all unusual. Around the same time as the yacht scheme, Sherman provided investment funds to Harvey Rubenstein, a shady Toronto stockbroker who would later be convicted of fraud in Canada and the United States. Jailed in Oregon and awaiting trial, Rubenstein telephoned Sherman in Toronto and persuaded the man he had already duped out of more than one million dollars to advance him $100,000 bail money. As Sherman said in a deposition as part of his attempt to recoup some of the money Rubenstein owed him, he saw no point in having the man "languish" in jail. Sherman eventually sued Rubenstein in an unsuccessful attempt to get the bail money back.

Fred Steiner says he was completely unaware of all these private side deals in which his friend was involved. "He never discussed them," says Steiner. "As good and as close a friend as I am, I can't tell you about his outside deals." In retrospect, Steiner, who with Sherman's help built a very stable coffee service business, says he thinks his friend resisted sharing information about his more unusual deals because he was worried that he would meet with disapproval. "I think he felt that I was so legit, he did not want to burden me with anything that was off the wall. I think he did not want to involve me with anything that I might object to. I also think he did not want to be questioned or criticized. And I would have criticized him."

Steiner did become aware of one of Sherman's private deals. Several months before the Shermans' deaths, a mutual acquaintance told Steiner that Barry had made a substantial investment in the development of The One, a retail and condominium tower at 1 Bloor Street West in Toronto, on the southwest corner of Yonge and Bloor Streets, arguably the city's most high-profile intersection. Every city seems to have at least one of these troublesome sites: a choice location for all sorts of reasons, but one where developers struggle to get financed and the project built. Developer Sam Mizrahi had been trying to construct a colossal project for several years but had trouble securing financial backers. In mid-2017, a real estate investment trust that was backing the property had withdrawn financing, and Sherman and other lenders, including an Ontario paving company and a firm based in China, agreed to help out. In late August, Sherman advanced $61 million to Mizrahi in a mortgage at the high rate of 13 percent interest. Other investors, apparently assembled with the help of Sherman, provided hundreds of millions of dollars more, and construction on the eighty-five-floor skyscraper, destined to become the tallest structure in Canada, broke ground. Associates of Sherman told me that the interest rate on his contribution was really only 8 percent, not the 13 percent recorded on the mortgage documents. They said Sherman, to help Mizrahi out, signed documents stating that if the deal went smoothly, he would make adjustments in the money owed so that Mizrahi paid the lower interest rate. For reasons that remain mysterious, Sherman told friends he wanted the public to know he was charging a high rate, yet in fact he was taking much less. No matter the rate, why did Sherman bail out Mizrahi?

"Barry did not want Sam to lose the project," Jack Kay explains.

Born in Iran to Jewish parents, Mizrahi is yet another colourful character in Sherman's life. Mizrahi's previous business was a luxury Toronto dry cleaner named Dove Cleaners, which Mizrahi exited around the time it was having financial difficulties and restructuring. He then got into the real estate development business. In recent years, Mizrahi claimed in a lawsuit that some fellow Iranian businessmen in Toronto had threatened to kill him. As a result, Mizrahi told reporters in Toronto that he had gone into hiding for a time. I interviewed those Iranian businessmen, and they said Mizrahi's claims were "ridiculous." Both sides are locked in a multi-million-dollar dispute over a series of development properties near the 1 Bloor West development. (Mizrahi declined three requests to speak to me about his business association with Barry Sherman and his friendship with both Shermans.)

Sherman continued to deal with the aftermath of investments gone wrong until the day he died. On Wednesday, December 13, his lawyers filed documents in court requesting an early trial date in a case that involved, of all things, a trivia app for smartphones. Steiner and other friends, when asked about this particular side deal, shook their heads and said Sherman never mentioned that one either. The trivia app deal started the way most of them did. Somebody Sherman knew needed assistance. An old friend,

Myron Gottlieb, had approached Sherman in 2015 looking for help. Gottlieb, along with Toronto theatre impresario Garth Drabinsky, had been convicted of two counts of fraud for their role in a scheme to falsify financial statements at their production company, Livent Inc., the firm behind the Toronto production of *The Phantom of the Opera* and so many other big hits. Investors lost an estimated $500 million when Livent went under. Gottlieb was sentenced to four years in prison for his role and released on day parole in 2013 after serving eleven months. While in prison at Ontario's "country club" Beaver Creek Institution (located in cottage country and the usual destination for non-violent white-collar offenders), Gottlieb became friends with convicted fraudster Shaun Rootenberg, a flamboyant and fast-talking con man. Once out of jail, Rootenberg began developing Trivia for Good, a smart phone app. Promotional materials for the company stated that the app would generate revenue by pushing advertisements to the user. Rootenberg needed investors, so he first enlisted Gottlieb, who in 2015 turned to Sherman. The Apotex billionaire agreed to provide $150,000 in return for a share in the trivia company, and he instructed his financial people at Sherfam where to send the money.

Documents Sherman later filed in court as part of a lawsuit allege that his investment was diverted to a separate bank account controlled by Rootenberg and others. There never was a fully functioning app. Sherman said he was the victim of a scam, and he wanted his money back. Had any due diligence been conducted by Sherman and his financial people, they would have uncovered Rootenberg's background and that of others involved in the scheme. As to Gottlieb, Sherman did not go after his old friend. During the same time period, Rootenberg was accused by Toronto Police of "romance fraud," meeting women on the dating site eharmony and convincing them to invest money with him. (At time of writing, those charges were before the court, as was Sherman's lawsuit against Rootenberg and other parties.)

Gottlieb declined a request to be interviewed for this book, instead providing a short statement: "My wife and I were privileged to be friends of Barry and Honey. They were an exceptional couple and their death was both a tragedy and was untimely. Others knew them better and for a longer period of time."

Sherman may not have liked the concept of betting on cards, but he was a risk-taker and a gambler. One of his lawyers told me, "Barry's risk profile was off the charts." Jack Kay says this simply about his friend, "Barry was a schemer." Back in the early 1970s, Joel Ulster had decided to part company with Sherman professionally because he was not comfortable with the risks his friend took. Ulster, Steiner, Kay, and others who knew Sherman very well say they believe Sherman entered into all of these dubious ventures because he believed he was right when he backed someone. In the pharmaceutical world, that was why he backed the researchers on the thalassemia drug. When it came to his many side deals, he believed he had the ability to determine if something was a good bet. As so many of the deals showed, he was not always right. The trial judge in the Fantaseas yacht case quite astutely noted that Sherman's busy life did not allow him the time, nor did he seem to have the inclination, to either dig in and properly vet a new venture or direct one of his staff to do so. As he said in his 2015 email exchange with his son, Sherman did not use "equations for analysis." For him, his judgment was king.

Friends say Sherman was a contrarian. Fellow philanthropist and businessman Ed Sonshine says that if the world seemed to be against someone, Sherman would back the man. "He loved helping financially guys who other people told him were bad guys," Sonshine says. Over the years, Sherman would call Sonshine and ask him for advice. In one instance, where Sherman ultimately advanced $30 million to an individual, Sonshine warned him not to do it. Sherman recouped only a fraction of his investment.

"You want to call it vanity, you want to call it ego, you want to call it an unshakeable belief in his own brain?" says Sonshine. "The more everyone told [Sherman], 'This guy is not going to work out for you,' the more he would be interested in doing something."

On one occasion, Sherman lamented to Sonshine, "Ed, if I only stuck to my own business, I would be a lot richer than I am." Another time, reflecting on some recent losses, he told Sonshine, "If things keep going like this, I will be down to my last billion."

Is there a clue to the murders somewhere in Barry Sherman's business deals? "Follow the money" is something that many people with an interest in the Sherman case have said. Jack Kay says it. Frank D'Angelo says it. The quote comes from the Watergate movie *All the President's Men*, and it is attributed, incorrectly, to the government source Deep Throat, who never actually said it in real life to reporter Bob Woodward. But the concept—follow financial transactions to solve a case—is a good one. But without the search warrant powers of the police, it is difficult to do. Sherman's financial history, holdings, and the estate he left behind are kept secret by court order. Further complicating things is that Sherman's dealings were intensely private and sometimes sealed with a handshake and little or no paperwork.

THIRTEEN

WORKING THEORY

"DETECTIVE CONSTABLE YIM, you have sworn this affidavit and we have gone through a lot of the details. I want to ask you a question that may sound provocative. Is the Toronto Police force on a fishing expedition here?"

It was April 24, 2019, in an Ontario Court of Justice hearing room in the north end of Toronto. The man in the witness box looked at the papers in front of him, which included an affidavit he had sworn stating that should any of the police documents about the Sherman investigation be made public it would jeopardize the probe.

"No."

I looked at the binder on the lectern in front of me, page thirteen of my planned twenty-page cross-examination. I am not a lawyer, but for reasons that include my knowledge of the case and shrinking resources at my newspaper, I was representing the *Toronto Star* in court. The job that day: learn as much as possible about the police probe of the Sherman case with the hope of getting thousands of pages of case information unsealed in the near future.

"What are you doing in this case—that is not a fishing expedition?" I asked.

"We are just following the evidence wherever it leads us," Yim replied.

Dennis Yim had been seconded from his duties as a divisional detective to the high-profile homicide squad the week after the Shermans' bodies were discovered. Now, sixteen months later, he was the only full-time officer on the file, though four other detectives, including Brandon Price, the original officer on the case, were involved part time. Detective Yim was in his mid-thirties, an officer for thirteen years. As I learned during my cross-examinations of him, Yim began each day on the Sherman case at 7 A.M. He clocked out at 3 P.M. He never left the office. His job was to prepare applications for search warrants and production orders, then read, review, and analyze the information that was obtained from those court orders. Those applications, or ITOs, contained synopses of everything the police had learned to date, from the moment the bodies were discovered.

While all court documents are considered "presumptively open" in Canadian law laid down by the Supreme Court of Canada, in practice that is not always the case. Search warrant documents in active murder cases typically remain sealed. But if, after hearing arguments, the court finds either that the case is inactive or that there is no risk to the "administration of justice" if the documents are made public, they can be unsealed. Also, when there is an arrest, courts often unseal at least portions of the warrant files. No arrests had been made in the Sherman case. When I first went down this road four months after the Sherman deaths, I tried the former argument, suggesting that the police investigation was inactive. That failed. Now I was arguing that some of the information could be made public because Yim's affidavit describing the nature of the risk in releasing information was speculative, not well grounded in evidence, which is the Supreme Court test. My problem, or one of my problems, was that I was appearing before Justice Leslie Pringle, the same judge who had issued all the warrants and production orders and then ordered them sealed. Asking her to change her ruling was like a teenager whose parent has said he cannot use the car asking the same parent the same thing five minutes later.

The documents I wanted access to sat near the court clerks, to the right of Justice Pringle, in her black robes and red sash. A mountain of sealed manila envelopes. The thickest of them was 599 pages. That, I learned, was the most recent ITO, reflecting the growing amount of information filed in support of the latest production order. Getting Yim to tell me anything under the watchful eye of Justice Pringle and Crown attorney Peter Scrutton, who represented the interests of Yim and the police in keeping the documents sealed, seemed impossible. It was not that the atmosphere was hostile. Everyone in court was saying all the right things about the importance of the media in bringing scrutiny to the police and courts on behalf of the public. Justice Pringle was patient with me, a non-lawyer, emphasizing that the information would eventually be unsealed, just not at this stage. In the hallway during a break, Scrutton, Yim, and I talked about our kids, mine in university, theirs in elementary school. They even kibitzed about learning that Jonathon Sherman owned a big storage company in the east end of Toronto, which struck me as a non sequitur and about which they provided no more explanation.

After the break, I decided to try a different tactic. Since the original announcement that police were investigating the case as a "targeted double murder," they had said absolutely nothing about the investigation, quite unusual even by close-mouthed Canadian standards.

"Detective Yim, are you making progress in this investigation?"

"Yes," Yim responded.

"And what is the goal of the investigation?" I asked, lobbing a softball at the affable detective.

"To find the truth and to find the perpetrator that committed the crimes."

"And how do you know you are making progress?"

"Additional evidence is coming in."

Something about the way the detective was answering—he was much more at ease than the last time he'd given testimony—made me ask more probing questions. Earlier, Justice Pringle or the Crown had cut me off. Not this time.

"Detective Yim, at this point, sixteen months, does the police force have a theory of the case?"

Yim paused. He was silent for twenty seconds. He looked up once at the Crown and then answered, "Yes."

To say my heart quickened is an understatement. In that moment, I saw the next day's front page. "And what do you mean by theory of the case?"

A second long pause. "An idea of what happened."

I leaned forward on the lectern. "And have you identified any number of persons of interest?"

Scrutton was on his feet. "Your Honour, I am going to object to that question."

Before Justice Pringle could speak, I took a shot. "Your Honour, I appreciate the sensitivity, but now we have just learned the Toronto Police force has a theory of the case. That theory is an idea of what happened, and I would like to explore that. It seems to me pretty revelatory. Theory of the case. An idea of what happened. To me that equals you have a suspect or suspects."

Justice Pringle ruled that I could not continue that line of questioning, on the grounds that for Yim to reveal whether police had a suspect would defeat the sealing order we were arguing about. As the day wore on, Yim did provide more information during another line of questioning. I tried several approaches to get Yim to admit that they had a suspect. The affidavit he had filed in court to oppose my motion to unseal the documents noted that as of April 2019, detectives had interviewed 243 people in their hunt for answers. This was only a handful more than the number they had interviewed by the fall of the previous year, an indication to me that police believed they had most of the information they required—they just needed to build a legal case. Yim did not confirm that. But when I asked him if there were people (police call them witnesses but that does not mean they actually saw something, just that they had pertinent knowledge) police were unable to interview, he paused again, and said that was the case. In fact, Yim said, there were some people who had refused to speak to detectives. I got the strong sense from his answers that it was one or two individuals. In my cross-examination I asked him what reasons the individuals had given. Yim replied: "They don't have to give a reason. They are not obliged to give a statement to police." The detective also said that they were having difficulty with a small number of witnesses because they either could not find them, or they "may have left the country."

Another tantalizing item was that the police were about to receive a significant amount of electronic data from an "entity" in response to a production order obtained two months before. The "entity" had been dragging its feet. What that information was, and whether police detectives knew who the killer or killers were, would have to wait for another day. I speculated that it was someone's cellular telephone records, banking records, or GPS location records. That got me exactly nowhere. Pringle acknowledged the importance of the media attempting to unseal the files. "Open court principles and freedom of the press are extremely important issues, constitutionally grounded in the Charter." She said that one day, she believes these investigative files will be released. But not this time, she ruled. She encouraged me to return to court again on the matter. In her ruling, she stated that the information contained in those manila envelopes was simply too sensitive to release. Her fear was that if it got out, it would damage the police investigation and allow the killer or killers to get away. Rejecting my argument that police were merely speculating about the harm that publicizing at least some parts of the investigation would cause, Pringle said they were real fears. "I disagree that the risks are speculative. In this case of a brutal, targeted, double murder, common sense and logical inference give rise to an obvious risk of violence to witnesses and a real potential for manipulation of evidence by the perpetrator(s)."

The other court challenge I mounted, with the help of the *Toronto Star* and lawyers Iris Fischer and Skye Sepp, related to the estate of Barry and Honey Sherman. My challenge began six months after the Shermans died. Apotex and all of Barry Sherman's holdings were private. Bloomberg data estimated his wealth at Can$4.7 billion. But was he actually that wealthy? Was he worth more? And who were his beneficiaries? Sources had said the money went primarily to his four children, but I wanted to confirm this and learn if there were any terms or strings attached. Hoping to find answers, I frequently checked at the computer terminal on the seventh floor of one of the courthouses in Toronto, which holds records for probate court. One day, I saw Barry and Honey Sherman's names and asked for the files. I was told they were sealed, which is highly unusual; estate files are typically public. In this case, a Superior Court justice (one rung higher than Pringle) had sealed the files out of fear that, by revealing information that identified the heirs or the trustees of the estate, they might be kidnapped or killed. That led to a year-long battle, which at time of writing was still ongoing. As I had done in my search warrant challenge, I argued that the risk was speculative. In fact, as I learned, the Sherman family had not even filed any information from the Toronto Police stating that they were in danger. Besides, it was not a state secret that the four children were the heirs and that their father was a billionaire. A kidnapper would not need a public file to know that, or to find out who the trustees were. I lost my initial argument at Ontario's Superior Court of Justice when justice Sean Dunphy, who had originally sealed the files, ruled that there was simply too much risk in releasing any of the information. I appealed, and six months later, in April 2019, found myself arguing the case in front of a panel of Justice David Doherty and two other judges of the Ontario Court of Appeal. Doherty, writing for the three judge panel, sided with my argument. "The suggestion that the beneficiaries and trustees are somehow at risk because the Shermans were murdered is not an inference, but is speculation." Doherty ordered the entire estate file made public in a week, giving the Sherman family lawyers time to attempt an appeal to the Supreme Court of Canada. At time of writing, both sides await the Supreme Court's decision on whether it will hear the appeal.

While my court challenges have yet to yield official information about the Sherman estate, I have through sources learned bits and pieces of information outside of the court process.

I learned a great deal about Barry Sherman's plans for his wealth, and about the opposition he received from his son over how that money should be spent.

Barry Sherman had a will. Honey did not, a fact never explained by family or friends and something that came as a complete surprise to close friends like Joel Ulster and Fred and Bryna Steiner. Barry's will was a simple document, created in 2013 and described by a lawyer who saw it as being "not too far removed from the boilerplate will you could get from Staples." Should he die before Honey, it set up a "living trust" to look after his wife, under the guidance of four trustees. The names of those trustees were changed in 2015 and again in 2017. When Sherman died, the trustees, which are sometimes also called executors, were Jonathon Sherman, Alex Glasenberg, Jack Kay, and Alex Sherman's husband, Brad Krawczyk—an all-male group of trustees. Jack Kay had been on a mission in 2017 to add a fifth trustee so that if there was ever a contentious issue, there would be a numerical tiebreaker. Sherman was having a hard time finding someone to act as an additional trustee, according to one businessman who said he passed on the offer because he did not want to get tied up in Sherman family politics. As to adding a woman, someone who had in-depth discussions with Sherman about that issue observed that Sherman had chauvinistic tendencies and had commented "I cannot have a woman, they are too emotional." When I heard that, I thought of the senior executive and management team I met at Apotex, both at head office and at the plants I visited. Mostly men. Further, I found it unusual that Barry's will did not turn over his entire estate to his wife should he predecease her. Instead, his will puts control in the hands of the four trustees, who would provide her with living expenses; on her death, the entire estate would transfer to the four Sherman children. I was also told that another section of the will stated that the trustees could, at their discretion, provide for the Sherman nieces and nephews: the children of Barry's sister, Sandi, and of Honey's sister, Mary. The controversy over that section, and a related promise Mary had said her sister had made, was a major factor in the rift between the Sherman children and Mary's side of the family.

The will made no provision for money to go to charity, which surprised many, given how generous the Shermans were in their lifetimes.

The lack of specific instructions regarding charitable donations raises an interesting issue, as people very close to Sherman said he often talked about gifting much of his fortune to philanthropic causes. Joel Ulster told me that Sherman never intended for his children to inherit all the Sherman wealth. "It was just too much," Ulster said, recalling his friend's point of view on the matter. "Over the years, [Barry] certainly told me that he intended to give away the bulk of his wealth to charity, while leaving enough for his kids to be provided for, now and in the future."

Other friends heard similar comments, though it appears Sherman never committed this to paper. Daughter Alex said her father talked with her in the last few months leading up to his death about signing on to the Giving Pledge, created in 2010 by Warren Buffett and Bill and Melinda Gates, where the world's wealthiest individuals commit to donating 50 percent or more of their wealth to charity *in their lifetime*. Alex said she urged her father to do just that, though it appears not to have been done. Jack Kay has no specific recollection of Sherman mentioning the Giving Pledge but says his friend often talked about continuing his practice of making major donations to charity. Barry Sherman clearly said different things to different people. While he mused about giving away the bulk of his fortune in his lifetime, the reality was that most of his money was wrapped up in Apotex, or his Sherfam investments, so to make the kind of charitable donation he was suggesting would require selling Apotex and liquidating his other assets. He did not want to do that, at least not in 2017. Jack Kay said Sherman had a "five-year vision" to expand Apotex facilities in Toronto, to build his new operation in Florida, and to invest millions of dollars in the business company wide. With Sherman alive, most of his wealth was out of reach.

Sherman was also contemplating giving a large amount of money to Honey. His wife lamented to many of her friends, including Bryna Steiner and Leslie Gales, that she had no money of her own. Of course, she had access to cash to go on trips and to shop, but that was not what she wanted. Honey wanted, according to Gales, the same as what her children had received from their father—namely, millions of dollars (though some had received more than others). According to some of Barry and Honey's friends, Barry was planning to give Honey a major financial gift. There was often tension between the couple over Honey's elaborate plans for their new home, and friends of Honey say that if she had her own money, she could proceed on the Forest Hill project without having to go to Barry when costs were escalating. The amount of the gift was to be between $100 million and $500 million, Honey told her friends. The Apotex founder never gave a figure, just that it was to be a "substantial amount of money," according to Jack Kay. Honey's friends say she provided dollar figures, which differed over time. It was generally accepted among Honey's circle of friends that a good chunk of that money would go to support her sister, Mary. "Honey was getting money from Barry, and Mary was going to get some of that," says one source. The planned gift from Barry to Honey apparently did not materialize before their deaths.

It is clear that Barry Sherman had plans for his money, but they were ill-defined. Friends say that though he joked about dying, he never really intended to die. As he often told Jack Kay, he simply had too much to do. How he spent his money was up to him. He wanted, for example, to expand his Toronto operations and purchase and invest in a facility in Florida to manufacture fentanyl and other painkillers for the US market. Cash was tight due to some of his recent court losses, so he decided to focus first on enhancing Apotex's value. But there was one person who pushed back: Jonathon. He reminded his father by email in 2015 that he was a Columbia University–educated man and knew how to analyze deals and determine the best place to spend money. "Mainly it comes down to risk and reward," Jonathon wrote to his father. "How much money do I need to risk in order to return a certain amount of money over a certain period of time and what is the likelihood of failing?" Friends of Barry Sherman say that he tried his best to be patient with his son, but that he did not like to be lectured. It also bothered Barry that his son was suggesting that his business partner might one day play a role in succession in the family business.

Jonathon's business partner, Adam Paulin, was a Toronto man he had met years before at summer camp. Paulin had business degrees from both the Richard Ivey School of Business at London, Ontario's Western University, and the York University Schulich School of Business, where he completed an MBA in 2010. A few years later he and Jonathon started Green Storage, making a series of purchases funded by Barry Sherman's money. They bought small self-storage companies in towns north of Toronto, including Bolton and Aurora. The money that launched Green Storage came from Hour Holdings, which corporate records show is listed in the names of Jonathon Sherman and Adam Paulin. In reality, according to Sherman insiders, it was Barry Sherman's money. Hour Holdings uses Apotex as its mailing address. That financial relationship was alluded to in Jonathon's eulogy at the memorial service for his parents. "When I entered your office about five or six years ago with my good friend Adam, we told you about our plan to start a business together and you were so incredibly supportive and excited. We had the world's shortest shareholder agreement which basically said, 'Anything, anytime.'" At the time of Barry's death, Hour Holdings had registered at least $127 million in loans against either Green Storage properties or a small marina and cottage business Jonathon and Paulin were running. Typically, there is a favourable interest rate and no payment schedule. The information in the public land-title documents provides only the barest detail, and the price paid for two of the purchases is not even listed. Of the cost of the properties purchased that are listed, the total purchase value is $23 million, far less than the $127 million in mortgages attached to the properties. The records do not indicate the cost of renovating the storage warehouses to bring them under the Green Storage banner.

As Sherman was funding his son's Green Storage enterprise, he also continued to pour money into Frank D'Angelo's businesses. Jonathon and Frank had butted heads back in the brewery days. Neither liked the other. Jonathon accused D'Angelo of being a bad businessman. As to what D'Angelo thinks of Jonathon Sherman, he says the word that comes to mind is "entitled."

Matters between Barry and Jonathon came to a head in 2015, a development documented, at least in part, in an email exchange between the two on the last two days of April of that year. The subject line is "Explain it to me," and Jonathon is asking his father why he has poured $250 million into D'Angelo business schemes, a number that Barry does not refute in the email chain, but D'Angelo does.

"Can you explain it to me?" Jonathon asks. "I'm bright and educated. If you explain it to me, I will try and understand."

"Explain exactly what?" Barry shoots back a minute later.

Jonathon: "How you determine that it is worthwhile to invest more money with Frank despite year after year of losses? What are you seeing that everyone else is missing?"

Barry: "It is always a judgment call as to whether it is a better bet to write off what is [already] in, or to invest more to continue to try to increase value, to reduce the loss. Not as simple as you might think."

Jonathon fires back a lengthy email, explaining how he has a knowledge of accounting and finance. "I comprehend most concepts, like sunk cost, investment timelines, NOI, ROI, asset appreciation/depreciation, brand building, etc." He accuses his father of avoiding providing serious answers by making comments such as "I'm in charge so I have to make all the decisions."

Jonathon also describes his approach to dealing with people, which he says is better than what he has witnessed over the years from the acerbic D'Angelo. "I only wish you and I talked more so I could share stories about my interactions with people at the Marina and Storage facilities," he says. "I do everything possible to please my customers and my staff because I value them immensely. I don't work because I want to make money, and I never will. What gives me the greatest pleasure at work is being overly nice to people when they may not expect it, and to see their reactions! I go to work because I have fun providing a great service to people and working with happy staff. Frank, on the other hand, manages to rub everyone the wrong way."

Throughout the exchange with his father, Jonathon refers to the Sherman family investments using the pronoun "we." Criticizing his father's investments over the years, he writes,

"There have been other examples of businesses into which we have invested many millions and eventually determined that conditions would not change for the better. Deerhurst and Steelback are two examples."

Barry's responses, in contrast, are brief. He does not engage with his son on his main points. "It is always a judgment call," Barry says of his decisions. "I have to make the call."

The exchange takes place over two days. On the second day, Jonathon implores his father to meet with him and Adam Paulin so they can make their pitch for an increase in funding to Hour Investments, a company related to Hour Holdings. By this point in 2015, land title records show that Hour Holdings had $71 million registered on title for Jonathon and Adam's businesses. "Adam and I have great ideas for Hour Investments. We have started strong in the storage business and it has been going very well for us," he writes. "We would like to expand Green Storage to become a major player in the storage industry, and that will take about $100 million over 10 years." Jonathon also writes that he and Paulin would like to "buy and manage about 25 percent of the waterfront property on Chandos Lake and it won't cost that much." Chandos Lake, near the small town of Apsley, is the area where Jonathon and business partner Paulin own a cottage and a small marina, purchased with Sherman money. Jonathon estimates that their plan to purchase three hundred cottages will cost "roughly 150 million dollars." With the inflated price of real estate in Ontario's prime cottage country in Muskoka to the west of Chandos, Jonathon's plan does seem a good investment and he writes to Barry that he wants to plead his case for the money to put his "15-year plan" into action. Jonathon vows that if the three agree to meet, "I can promise to remain calm and amicable." He also raises the issue of the future of his father's business holdings. "My genuine goal is to understand this situation and then move on to more important matters (like succession planning and whether Adam and I can play some role in that)."

Barry responds a minute later. "Re more funds for Hour, we cannot discuss that until we evaluate our situation after the Canadian and US import bans are lifted," referring to an issue affecting Apotex. "Will be high priority as soon as we are able to do so."

As to Jonathon's criticisms of D'Angelo, Barry says he cannot debate the matter. "It is simply a judgment call, implicitly based on intuition as to the expectations." He ignores the suggestion that his son and an outsider take up a role in succession planning. Later in the email correspondence, Barry, as earlier noted, sends Jonathon a trailer for D'Angelo's latest movie, telling his son that there is a plan for a fifth movie but there will be strings attached. "I have told [D'Angelo] that we cannot proceed unless and until I am satisfied that the revenues from the first 4 will substantially exceed cost." In what must have further inflamed the relationship between father and son, Barry adds that he likes D'Angelo's business model because he can make a movie for under $1 million and half of that money would come back from the government in grants. "Absurd as it may seem to you, I believe that [D'Angelo] has a talent to produce films with value in excess of cost . . . major actors in Hollywood take him seriously, as you can see." Barry then tells his son that his decisions will likely make Jonathon "a multi-billionaire." As for his association with D'Angelo, Sherman describes it as an issue that he is dealing with. "While you may think that what to do is obvious, I do not." For his part, D'Angelo told me that it "is ridiculous to say [Barry Sherman] gave me $250 million. That is absolutely, unequivocally wrong." D'Angelo adds, "Barry understood exactly what our plan was. The plan was to make one movie that would explode."

Within days, Jonathon wrote an email to his three sisters, according to three people who saw the email at the time and discussed its contents with Barry Sherman. The subject line of the email referred to his sisters as fellow shareholders. In the email, Jonathon suggested that their father's actions were jeopardizing their inheritance. He referred to Barry as the founder, a reference to his founding of generic drug giant Apotex, and argued that there was precedence for removing or overturning a founder. Jonathon, say people who saw the email, was looking for support from his sisters, but the sisters either did not acknowledge the email or refused to go along with the plan. One of them shared the email with their father, who in turn discussed or shared its contents with others, including Joel Ulster and Jack Kay. Both men said that Sherman laughed it off. One person with knowledge of the situation recalled Sherman's remark: "There goes Jonathon, attempting a palace coup." Another who discussed it with Sherman said the Apotex founder said, "Jonathon is talking with his siblings and he wants me declared incompetent and locked up." While this incident was jarring to Barry Sherman's close friends, some have suggested that in the world of the very wealthy, it is not unusual for the younger generation to be vocal about how their inheritances are being handled. In Toronto in recent years, there have been at least two high-profile disputes over how the riches created by a patriarch should be spent, and who is the best person to act as steward of that wealth. In both those cases—the Stronach and the Sorbara families—the disputes eventually spilled over into the courts.

Having someone declared incompetent is not easy, and would involve having an expert conduct a capacity assessment to determine if the person was no longer capable of making financial decisions. The next step would be to take a finding of incompetence to a special provincial board, which would make a determination, which would then be appealable to a court. The attorney general ministry in Ontario, which governs the process, has made it clear that "bad decisions" alone are not sufficient to have a person declared incompetent. Nothing seems to have come of Jonathon's suggestion to his sisters.

It appears no money was advanced to Green Storage or any of Jonathon and Adam Paulin's other ventures following the dustup between Jonathon and his father in 2015. Three people with knowledge of Barry's approach to Jonathon's business during this period say that the elder Sherman told Jonathon that if he wanted to proceed with his expansion plans, he should seek out conventional financing from a bank. It is of interest to note that in the many multi-million dollar deals that Jonathon and other siblings negotiated over the years, conventional financing appears never to have been used. Jonathon, sources told me, did not follow this advice. The battles between father and son had a cycle. A blow up over money would cause an icy standoff, followed by a thaw after some months. That happened in this case. In 2016, $5 million was advanced from the Sherman money at Hour Holdings to purchase a storage company in Orillia. In April 2017, Sherman money funded a $50-million loan for Green Storage to purchase a major storage operation at the east end of Toronto's downtown waterfront. There were no more storage-related loans in 2017, but in September of that year Hour Holdings advanced $1.5 million for the construction of a cottage owned by Jonathon and Adam Paulin, overlooking the small marina on Chandos Lake. In early 2019, Hour Holdings registered a $25-million loan on title following the purchase of a small storage facility in Scarborough, east of Toronto.

FOURTEEN

THE DAY OF

Wednesday, December 13

BARRY SHERMAN WAS LYING ON HIS BACK on his bedroom floor. Stretching.

"I will pay you not to come here," he said, looking up at the
very fit, dark-haired woman standing over him.

"Barry, you have to do your exercises. Let's do the lat pull-
down next," said Denise Gold, the family friend and personal
trainer who visited the Shermans twice a week. The Shermans
had a large master suite on the second floor of their Old Colony
Road house, and at one end was a small home gym.

Sherman got slowly to his feet and walked to an exercise
machine that was thirty years old, purchased when the house
was built. The khaki golf shorts he was wearing were worn and
creased. He checked his watch: 9 A.M. Thirty minutes left in his
personal training session.

"Denise, I'm too old. I am going to die anyway. What's the
point?" Sherman sat on the vinyl-covered bench of the machine,
reached up his arms, and, using as light a weight as he could get

away with under Gold's sharp gaze, began to gently pull the bar down.

"Barry, do this for Honey."

Sherman checked his watch again. Thirty seconds had passed. "How is Bobby?"

Gold had trained Barry and Honey for several years. She also trained Fred and Bryna Steiner, who had referred her to the Shermans. Bobby was her dog, and Barry, who was not usually a pet lover, took an inordinate interest in hearing about the little Morkie, a cross between a Yorkshire terrier and a Maltese. "What did she do today?"

Gold liked that Sherman asked about her dog, but she knew it was just a delaying tactic. She ignored the question and asked her client to start doing some dumbbell curls. Normally, she trained with latex bands that she would hook around Sherman's wrists to provide tension during movements, but today she decided to skip them and just use weights. Gold watched as Barry did his "old man walk" to a rack of dumbbells she had retrieved from the basement the previous week. With the need for the house to be constantly ready for showings, they had been stuffed in a corner of the cavernous furnace room down the hall from the lap pool and garage. Both Barry and Honey had a habit of piling chairs and counters with newspapers, mail, and clothing, and the realtors who had the listing had an ongoing battle to keep the home tidy for prospective buyers. Down on the basement level, which included the six-car garage, the lap pool and sauna, and the spacious furnace room, it had struck the trainer that someone could be in one of these rarely used spaces and the residents of the home would be completely unaware.

"This is really dumb," Barry said, very slowly lifting a light weight. Gold encouraged him to put some muscle into it, and they chuckled when she remarked, "Not many people have the sort of power over you that I do, Barry." Some days, when she trained Sherman, he was completely silent. That day, he was chatty. Looking around the bedroom suite, taking in the place he and Honey had custom built and lived in for three decades, Sherman said, "This place is worth twelve million dollars. It is crazy what it's listed for: six point nine million. That's insane. I don't even know why we have to move."

Gold had arrived just before 8:30 A.M. She entered through the side door on the right of the house. There was a wall that partially obstructed the view of the side entrance from the street. Honey's light gold Lexus SUV was parked near it. The Shermans never used the front door for regular comings and goings. The newspaper was delivered at the front of the house, though, and part of Barry's morning ritual was to open the front door, bring in the paper, and sit in the kitchen and read, sometimes even during the first part of the training session. The arrangement Gold and Honey had worked out was that she trained Barry from 8:30 to 9:30, Monday and Wednesday, unless he had a meeting or a hearing in court. Honey was up next for two hours. That morning, the first fifteen minutes of Gold's time with Barry, as always, involved his breakfast. Frosted Flakes with milk, a few Ritz Crackers with peanut butter, one slice of processed cheese, and he was ready to go. It was all part of Barry's attempt to shorten his workout time. Gold, extremely toned and health-conscious, had long ago given up trying to change the diet of either of the Shermans. On the fitness side, she did the best she could with Barry, a seventy-five-year-old captain of industry who trained only to please his wife. She put the breakfast food away and they headed upstairs. Along with some light weights, Gold had Sherman do walking lunges around a "track" she had designated on the second floor.

At precisely 9:30, Barry looked at Gold. "Is that enough? Is it over?" he asked.

Gold released him, and Sherman headed off to shower and get dressed for work. He kept his clothes in another room upstairs. Honey came into the master suite and began her session. Twenty minutes later, when Honey was doing some active stretching lying on the floor, Barry walked in, ready to head for Apotex. Gold noticed how quickly he walked when he was not trying to get out of exercising. She often felt Sherman was showing off for his wife when he did this. Around his waist was a leather belt Honey had given him, one of two cheap belts she had purchased recently—on sale for $9.99 each—at Canadian Tire. One was a thirty-four-inch belt, the other a thirty-six-inch belt. For weeks, the two identical belts had remained on a padded bench in the room, along with several piles of shirts and sweaters. Today, he had decided to wear one of them.

"Barry, that's too tight for you," Honey said from the floor.

"It's perfect," he replied. The belt was cinched tight at hip level, his ample stomach protruding over the leather.

Honey got up and kissed him on the cheek. As her husband turned to leave, Honey said, "Barry?"

He looked at his wife, nodded, and gave his trainer a peck on the cheek.

"I'll see you at the office at five," Honey said. The couple had a meeting in an Apotex boardroom with the architects designing their new home in Forest Hill.

Sherman went downstairs and drove off in his convertible Mustang GT. It was just after 10 A.M. His day's schedule included an afternoon meeting with Jeremy Desai to deal with a pressing Apotex issue. Since Jack Kay was away in New York with his wife at a concert, he would check in with executive assistant Joanne Mauro to see what else needed his attention.

Kay had bought the concert tickets in June, when he, Sherman, and the thalassemia researchers were being honoured at the Cooley's Anemia Foundation, in New York, for their work developing Ferriprox and bringing it to market. Though the controversial drug had its detractors in the research world, including Nancy Olivieri, the foundation said its members considered it a lifesaver. Foundation board member Maria Hadjidemetriou, a New York City realtor and a thalassemia patient, thanked Sherman and the researchers at the event. "Ferriprox is a miracle drug," she said. "It saved my life. It removed the lethal levels of iron from my heart." After the speeches lauding Sherman for his "leadership" and the researchers for developing the product, there was a charity auction to raise funds. Honey had bid on tickets to see Andrea Bocelli, the Italian tenor. She encouraged Jack Kay to bid too, and when Kay bid a bit higher, she stopped. As a result, Kay and his wife had gone to New York that day to see the production the following night.

Denise Gold had two hours with Honey, who, unlike Barry, was very focused on her session. "I will never give up," Honey said, anytime Gold suggested her client take it a bit easier. When Gold first started coming to the Shermans, she had often told Honey that playing five games of golf a week was not the best exercise for someone who had so many physical ailments. Today, she concentrated on improving Honey's mobility, loosening her joints, helping her rehabilitate the replaced shoulder. Honey was so sore, it was difficult for her even to put both arms behind her back. She was having a hard time holding just a one- or two-pound weight, but she gritted her teeth and powered through. A physiotherapist had given Honey a series of light exercises, and Gold helped her keep on task. Gold had long ago learned to follow Honey's cue: assist her, but do not tell her what to do.

In the same way that Barry Sherman never wilted before a legal battle, Honey Sherman refused to give in to her arthritis and other infirmities. "She challenged herself all the time," Gold says. In 2010, a time when she was having difficulty walking some days, Honey entered a *Dancing with the Stars*-style competition to raise money for the Baycrest Foundation in Toronto. She hired Russian-born Toronto dance instructor Michael Zaslavskiy. A promotional video shows Honey explaining her plan. "I am stepping out of my comfort zone, but I am willing to work hard to try not to fall flat on my face. My husband thinks I am nuts for doing this." The video shows Honey practising dance moves in the months leading up to the competition, including while on a visit to the Great Wall of China. "That which doesn't make you vomit makes you stronger," she says in the video. Zaslavskiy, seen in the video putting Honey through some fairly strenuous dance moves, smiles, wipes his brow, and says, "Was a good workout. She even make me sweat." Honey and her dance-instructor partner took top honours at the gala with a smooth number that was a mixture of swing dancing and jive. In another dance competition she took part in, this one with Toronto businessman David Cynamon as her partner, they dressed up in full costume as "Honey and Cher."

As they often did during the morning workout at 50 Old Colony, the two women chit-chatted throughout the session. One of Honey's pet peeves, which she often brought up with Gold, was how long she had to wait to see the various doctors who treated her. One of the incongruities Gold had noticed about Honey was that she often waited longer than people she spoke up for. When friends—Gold was one of them—needed to get treatment for a family member, Honey or Barry would make a phone call and doors would open. In Gold's case, her sister's husband had been terminally ill some years back, and the family hoped to get him into Baycrest's palliative care ward. The waiting list was long. But once a volunteer and major donor got involved, the man was in a palliative bed thirty-six hours later. When Gold's daughter wanted to go on a special ten-day educational trip called Birthright Israel, which seeks to connect young Jewish adults with Israel and their Jewish identity, no spaces were available. Honey stepped in, and Gold's daughter was given an extra spot. "They were just giving, wonderful people," Gold says.

Like her husband, Honey did not wear workout attire commensurate with her wealth. She wore an old pair of workout shorts she had owned since moving into Old Colony Road in the late 1980s. When there was a hole in the seat of the pants, she took it to a seamstress in the neighbourhood for repairs. "What's wrong, they're perfect!" Honey said when Gold suggested she get a new pair.

They had become good friends over the years, but Gold knew she was not on Honey's "A or B list." Still, they had a real connection and at times they would halt in the middle of a session and head off to rummage through Honey's closets. It boggled Gold's mind that the woman who wore a tattered pair of workout shorts had closets filled with multiple copies of designer jackets worth thousands of dollars, all purchased on sale, many never worn. There was a hoarder mentality about Honey, perhaps stemming from her upbringing.

When the pain became too much for Honey during a session, she paused, went to her night table, and got an unlabelled bottle of pills. Inside was an assortment of pills of different colours, all generic. Honey would shake out two that would help, take them with water, and return to the workout.

Gold suggested they concentrate on improving her balance, and Honey stood up, balancing on one leg, then the other.

During the morning, the talk turned to the house plans. Working in concert with her sister, Mary, Honey had put the Old Colony Road house up for sale along with another house the Shermans had purchased and renovated in Forest Hill. That house and lot had been deemed too small for Honey's grand vision of a mansion, and a second lot, a much larger, pie-shaped parcel just three blocks from daughter Alex and her husband, Brad, had been purchased. Ground had been broken on the new lot, and it would take two to three years to build. Now the Shermans had two houses for sale. "Whichever sells first, we will live in the other one until the new place is built," Honey explained to Gold.

The phone rang and Honey answered. It was a friend of the Shermans from Florida who was hoping to see them the following week. Gold was also expecting to be in Florida over the holidays, and Honey suggested they get together. Perhaps Gold could check out the home gymnasium in the Shermans' condo and make suggestions on how to improve it? The condo had undergone a major renovation, including a $600,000 marble floor, a cost that Barry Sherman strongly objected to but agreed to pay. Once again, it raised the sore point between the couple that Honey did not have her own money.

One of the other topics Gold and Honey Sherman discussed was the upcoming wedding of the Shermans' youngest daughter, Kaelen, the following May. Instead of a local Toronto wedding with hundreds of guests, which Honey wanted, only family and a few of the young couple's closest friends, and their parents' closest friends, would be travelling to Mexico. There was tension over that, too. Honey would have preferred to throw a major Toronto wedding but had to settle for a backyard engagement party the previous summer. Kaelen was marrying an electrician, the son of an elevator repairman and a customer service manager at a home building company. There was concern in the Sherman family as to how Kaelen would handle being married to a man who had a good job but who was not rich. One sign of this was Kaelen's request to her future in-laws that they ensure that all guests attending the wedding in Mexico provide a financial deposit in advance towards their accommodations. The family was taken aback by this, given the Sherman wealth.

The session over, Gold said goodbye and headed downstairs. Wednesdays were almost completely devoted to Honey's ongoing rehabilitation, and coming up the stairs was a woman who provided Honey with regular massage therapy. For the next three hours, the woman would work with Honey. The first two hours of this once-a-week massage session, Honey had told Gold, were extremely painful. Gold, massage therapists, physiotherapists, and doctors were all part of what Honey called her team. The next day Honey had an early-morning committee meeting at one of the charities she was involved with, but today was all about fitness.

The ground floor of the Sherman household was a whirlwind of activity. Gold chatted briefly with Elise Stern, the real estate agent who shared the Sherman house listing with Judi Gottlieb, who was on holidays. Stern was preparing for the return visit that afternoon of prospective buyers, a couple who had toured the house a few days earlier. One worker was repairing a crack in the ceiling, someone else was doing painting touch-ups. Cleaners were vacuuming and wiping down surfaces. Gold walked out the side door, got into her car, and drove off. The sun was shining and she was pleased as she headed to her next client. Later, she would recall that she had rarely seen Honey and Barry so happy.

The executive offices at Apotex were quieter than usual on Wednesday afternoon. Joanne Mauro was busy with several projects. Over the years, her duties had kept expanding. The joke, which was partially true in some respects, was that Mauro ran the company. Barry Sherman arrived in the late morning and worked in his office. Without Sherman and Kay hollering back and forth at each other through the connecting door, the atmosphere was missing its usual spark.

Litigation continued to be a big part of day-to-day business. During the lunch hour that Wednesday, company president Jeremy Desai spoke to their in-house legal counsel about a pressing issue involving one of their many battles with a brand name company. As always, it was a "poker game," as Desai describes it, and the Apotex lawyer wanted to know what hand to play. Desai checked to make sure Sherman was available and then arranged a 2:30 P.M. meeting in a small boardroom across from the executive offices. It was a routine meeting: two in-house lawyers, Desai, and Sherman. After an hour, a decision was made to wait until they received additional information from their regulator, Health Canada, before taking the next step. That would likely not come for a day or so. The meeting adjourned and the four men returned to their respective offices.

Aside from his Apotex business on Wednesday, Sherman had the meeting with Honey and the architects from Brennan Custom Homes later in the day. Brennan was designing the new home in Forest Hill, and Sherman told friends he was not pleased with the estimated costs of the project. Sherman had also likely brought to the office that morning a copy of the home inspection report on Old Colony Road and let his agents know he was going to have a close look at any deficiencies it listed. He was convinced his house was worth much more than the listed price. The meeting with the architects for the new house had originally been scheduled for the day before, Tuesday, but had to be changed to accommodate everyone's schedules. That had prevented Sherman's annual attendance at Frank D'Angelo's Christmas lunch on Tuesday. Sherman had told D'Angelo in advance that he would not make it, and when the Tuesday architects' meeting was shifted to Wednesday, it was too late to get out to the lunch at Mamma D's. He had apologized to D'Angelo Tuesday night by phone, saying he would be there next year for sure. D'Angelo recalls the late-night call from Barry. "He said he was sorry he couldn't make it and I busted his balls for missing. He really liked those lunches."

At 5 P.M. on Wednesday, Honey Sherman pulled into the executive parking spot, taking Kay's space because he was out of town. Another car, carrying two men from Brennan Homes, arrived shortly after, parking beside Desai's Jaguar. Barry Sherman met his wife and the architects in the lobby, and they all retired to the boardroom in the executive suite.

Anyone entering into a home design and building contract with the Shermans would have to know that they had a difficult track record with builders and architects. The first house they built, in the 1970s, resulted in Sherman suing the builder and winning back some of his costs related to what he argued were deficiencies in the project. With Old Colony Road, Sherman took the designers and builders to court, again citing deficiencies. That case took six years to wind through the court system. Sherman testified that the twelve-thousand-square-foot house was a "disaster" when they took possession. The case was settled with all but two of the contractors, and Sherman ended up recouping $2 million of the $2.3 million cost to build the home in the mid 1980s. Sherman continued court actions against the remaining two contractors, claiming they were negligent in the design of the heating and air conditioning. He ultimately lost those relatively small legal battles and had to pay $110,000 in legal costs when a judge determined that, yes, there had been negligence, but there was no proof the Shermans had suffered from the actions of the two contractors.

The new Forest Hill house the Shermans planned to construct was sixteen thousand square feet on a twenty-five-thousand-square-foot lot, purchased in 2016. Friends of the Shermans say that the estimated cost, according to Honey, including purchase of the lot and building the mansion, was at least $30 million and likely more. Where Old Colony Road was big and comfortable, this house would be a true mansion. Work was underway on the foundation in the fall of 2017. As described by the *Toronto Star*'s Victoria Gibson, the planned brick and stone residence had a massive forty-one-foot-long retractable glass roof over an indoor pool, which, weather permitting, would become an outdoor pool at the flick of a switch. The home would have four very large bedrooms, a two-sided fireplace in the living room, extensive patios and gardens, an elevator, and a garage with a car lift so that one vehicle could be raised up and another parked beneath. Other notable features included a sizable home gym and a specially constructed paper shredder in the second-floor office. For the couple that did not like having staff and only had a cleaning lady once a week, there would be staff living quarters in the basement. With an eye to Honey's physical limitations and the couple's advancing age, an elevator was planned and Mary, Honey's sister, had recently asked the father of Kaelen's fiancé if he could install an elevator and "give Honey a good price." Having already spent many unpaid hours fixing the dumb-waiter at Old Colony Road as a favour to his future in-laws, the fiancé's father was surprised that Mary would think he would overcharge. "Of course I will, anything for my future family," the man told Mary.

That Wednesday evening, Jeremy Desai had an Apotex staff Christmas party to attend at a local restaurant. As he was heading out the door shortly after 5 P.M., he received the update from Health Canada that Apotex needed. Normally, he would have popped in to tell his boss, but he noticed Honey's Lexus in Jack Kay's parking spot and decided he would speak to Sherman the next day.

The meeting with the architects ended at 6:30 P.M. Sherman ushered everyone out the door, said goodbye to Honey—who, according to a family member, went to a mall on the way home to pick up Hanukkah presents for her grandchildren—and went back to his office. Magnetic locks at Apotex activate at 5 P.M., so unless someone had a special pass, there was no way back into the building. Apotex security cameras show Honey and the architects, in separate vehicles, pulling onto the main road outside the building and heading south. Joanne Mauro had gone home, and Sherman worked on some of his projects in the quiet of the evening. It had been a busy fall, both for Apotex and some of Sherman's other financial adventures. There was his investment in The One condominium complex to help out friend Sam Mizrahi. He had a small lawsuit in progress with a man he alleged to have scammed him out of $100,000, and examinations for discovery were upcoming. He also owed a $400 million payment to a brand-name firm due to a settlement that had been recently reached. But as Sherman told his business associates, he would live to fight another day. Most notable among his lengthy personal court actions, Sherman had finally emerged victorious from his battle with Kerry Winter and his other cousins. Jack Kay's daughter, Katherine Kay, was his lead lawyer on that case, and Sherman was, as with all his legal cases, closely involved in coordinating tactics. Wanting to exact some form of punishment, they had asked the court to award Sherman $1 million in legal costs, but the judge reduced the amount to $300,000. The cousins were appealing, so that payout was in limbo. Still, a victory for Sherman. And capping that victory, Sherman had been informed that he was to be awarded Canada's highest honour. Though he was a man who never seemed to boast, he wrote to Fred Steiner and Joel Ulster on November 29 that, "I was advised today by the Governor General's office that I have been appointed to the Order of Canada, but it is confidential until announced on Dec. 29."

The upcoming weekend would provide a break from his many battles. Joel Ulster and Michael Hertzman were coming to Toronto for a visit. On Sunday night, a dinner at Riz restaurant in Toronto was planned to celebrate Jeff Ulster's new venture into podcast advertising. Mark Ulster, who Sherman had assisted years before with a job at Apotex and financial support, would also be at the dinner with his wife. Jeff and his wife had extended the invitation to Barry and Honey, but as was often the case, Honey had taken over, booking her favourite restaurant and sending out emails to ensure everyone would be on time. They would be heading to the dinner at Riz immediately after a Hanukkah brunch at Kaelen's fiancé's parents' house. Monday, Sherman would begin the day as usual with a training session with Denise Gold. Honey would be on her way to Florida, where Barry was planning to join her mid-week. She would have a couple of days with her sister, Mary, to catch up and gossip and discuss their various real estate situations. As friends would tell police and the media in the coming days, both Shermans had a great deal to look forward to, and much to be happy about.

The question of happiness was something that Barry Sherman often pondered, his friends say. In his 1996 memoir, he wrote that the root of happiness comes from the instinctual desire to "eat, drink, copulate, protect ourselves and our young, and cooperate with others." Happiness, he wrote, was best defined as the satisfaction of these drives. On two recent occasions, close friends Fred Steiner and Leslie Gales had separately commented to Sherman that he must be happy, given his many successes. To both of them, Sherman replied simply, "What is happiness?"

At 8:13 P.M., Sherman composed an email on his desktop computer at Apotex about some routine drug matter and sent it to Jeremy Desai, copying lawyer Harry Radomski. Around 8:30 P.M., he left the office. Security cameras record him getting into his old Mustang GT, backing out of his spot, driving out onto Signet Drive, and heading south.

Friday, December 14, shortly after 9 A.M.

"Joanne, it's Mary."

Mauro had just arrived at her desk. Honey's sister, Mary Shechtman, was on the phone from Florida. "Have you seen Barry? I need to talk to one of them." Shechtman, who was helping with the sale of the Shermans' house, was trying to reach Honey about some prospective buyers. She had called and sent emails and text messages, but no luck. Honey had been scheduled the day before, Thursday, to attend a regular 8 A.M. committee meeting at the UJA Federation of Greater Toronto. When her chair remained empty, nobody was particularly alarmed. Their busy benefactor likely had a doctor's appointment or a family matter to deal with.

"Okay," Mauro said. "No problem. You keep trying Honey, and I will try Barry."

It was not unusual at all for Barry Sherman to arrive late to the office. In fact, he rarely showed up before 10:30 A.M. His absence the previous day was uncharacteristic but not completely out of the ordinary, particularly since he'd become a grandparent. Once in a while, he spent at least part of the day with daughter Alex, who had just had her second child. Alex had, on the Thursday, wondered why her parents did not respond to texts she sent with photos of their new grandchild, born just a month before. But they had been at her house the previous week, and Alex knew Honey was dropping by that Friday, so she was not overly concerned about the lack of response. In interviews later, though, both Mauro and Desai agreed it was unusual that Barry had not replied to emails sent Thursday night about Apotex business. Since Sherman had first started using a BlackBerry, many years earlier, Mauro had always known him to respond with great speed, sometimes instantly. An insomniac, he often fired off emails in the middle of the night.

After ending her call with Shechtman, Mauro sent Sherman a short email. "Hey. How are you? Are you coming in today?"

No reply.

An hour later, Shechtman called back. Her voice was high-pitched and hard to understand. "Something's happened. Something's happened to them."

FIFTEEN

DUELLING INVESTIGATIONS

DETECTIVE KRISTIN THOMAS TURNED on the tape recorder, gave her name and badge number, and announced for the record that she was beginning an interview with Denise Gold, Sherman family friend and their personal trainer. It was Saturday, December 16, 2017. One day after the bodies of Barry and Honey Sherman were discovered, Toronto Police had set up a temporary investigative office at 32 Division, the closest division to the Old Colony Road home. The official autopsies had been done earlier in the day.

"I was one of the last people to see them alive on Wednesday," Gold told Thomas, a fraud investigator at one of the Toronto Police divisions. Thomas, like fifty other officers from various parts of the force, had been asked to help out with the Sherman investigation in the early days of the probe. Some homicide detectives who likely would have worked the Sherman case were unavailable as the investigation into serial killer Bruce McArthur came to a dramatic head. Another detective canvassing homes on either side of the Shermans' house produced a card from the Toronto Police "Cold Case" squad, according to a neighbour. This, just a few days after the Sherman deaths. Gold was at the police station because earlier on Saturday, she had seen on television that police were asking the public for help in the Sherman investigation. She called the general police number and was asked to come in. Thomas was one of the detectives assigned to conduct interviews. At the time, and for the next six weeks, Toronto Police were actively probing the theory that Barry killed Honey, then killed himself.

Gold had been with both Shermans on Wednesday, first training Barry for an hour, then Honey for two hours. She had heard the news of their deaths on Friday afternoon. The next morning, she had seen in the media a suggestion that the deaths were a murder-suicide.

"It's ridiculous," Gold recalls telling Detective Thomas. "There is just no way."

"What was their relationship like?" the detective asked her, following up with questions about whether the couple were fighting or there were signs of tension.

Gold said everything seemed normal that morning. In fact, she had left their house thinking both Barry and Honey "were in a really good mood." They were chatty with each other, and she noticed that when Barry had got dressed and came to say goodbye to Honey, he strutted into the room, seemingly showing off his strength after the workout. "I can always sense tension in people," Gold told the detective. "Not them. They were free and clear."

The detective asked if Barry Sherman had any marks on his wrists when Gold saw him on Wednesday. That question took her aback. Thomas provided no explanation, which is normal when police conduct an interview; they do not want to give away any information that could be spread as gossip or, in future, hurt their case. Gold told the detective she could not recall seeing any. Often, when training Barry, she used elastic latex bands, looping them on his wrists, and had him do small exercises to strengthen his arms. Wednesday, she had not used them. The detective did not ask her about Honey's wrists. There was nothing more to the interview, no other questions that stood out to Gold. In the days and months after she was interviewed, she wondered why police had not taken her fingerprints or a DNA swab. Gold loved reading mysteries and watching detective shows on TV and had more than a passing knowledge of basic police techniques. After all, she thought, her DNA was all over the Sherman home, on the weights and other items she used to train Barry and Honey, for example. Weren't police supposed to take DNA swabs and fingerprints from people known to have been at a crime scene so as to eliminate those people as suspects? Dahlia Solomon and Anita Franklin, who had recently been on that long golf trip with Honey, wondered the same thing. "I thought, our DNA is all over that Lexus," Franklin recalls. The police would not begin taking *any* DNA or fingerprints until nine months later. In September 2018, a forensic identification officer with the Toronto Police visited Gold at home and took a DNA swab and her fingerprints.

With the questions asked by police of Denise Gold that Saturday, the day after the bodies were discovered, two issues jump into focus. First, the nature of the crime police were initially pursuing. From the outset—although they have never confirmed this publicly—the Toronto Police were actively pursuing only the murder-suicide theory. I was able to prove this when I convinced a judge to release some of the search warrant documents sworn in the first few weeks of the case. When a detective asks a judge to authorize a search warrant, the officer must provide information about the nature of the crime under investigation. It cannot be vague. For the first month of the investigation, police detectives swore affidavits stating that they were investigating the murder of Honey Sherman. Only Honey. That explains why the police initially saw no need to collect basic forensic materials from people known to have been at the scene of the crime. But once it was accepted that this was a double murder, why did the police wait so long to collect this potential evidence? It may have been a matter of a lack of resources in an already stretched homicide department. In 2018, the year that began two weeks after the Shermans died, there were ninety-six homicides in Toronto, a record number. Among those cases were three major investigations: the Bruce McArthur serial killer probe; the April terror attack by a man who killed ten people and injured sixteen with his van on a major street in north Toronto; and a shooting in Toronto's Greektown in July, which killed two and injured thirteen more.

The interview with Denise Gold indicates that the police *were* aware of the telltale markings from restraints of some sort (ropes or plastic zip ties) on Barry Sherman's wrists from the first day of their probe. But it would not be until the expert opinion of a more experienced pathologist was brought to their attention that they gave proper weight to the markings. Why didn't the detective ask Gold whether she'd seen any marks on Honey's wrists? It could be simply that Honey's autopsy was the second one done that Saturday and the information about her injuries was not communicated to the detective before the interview. Still, detectives had certainly seen the bodies, as had the first pathologist, so it's likely that the information would have been passed on. It may be that the detectives were myopically pursuing the murder-suicide theory, though how wrist markings on Barry *alone* would fit into that theory is a mystery.

Toronto Police have repeatedly declined to answer any questions about their strategy. Their belief in the murder-suicide scenario created a deep rift between the police and the Sherman family. It started on the Friday evening, when homicide detective Brandon Price had emerged from behind the yellow police tape at the Old Colony Road home to tell the media two things: there was no forced entry, and they were not looking for suspects. His comments, and what police sources said to the media about it being a murder-suicide, enraged members of the Sherman family. They soon hired Brian Greenspan, who assembled the team of private investigators with the stated purpose of creating a "second lens" through which to view the investigation. Price's comments also prompted the *Toronto Sun*, and later other media, to ask questions of police sources, and that is where the media learned of the suspected murder-suicide theory. To be fair to Price, he also said he was making these comments to "alleviate some concerns in the neighbourhood."

What he did not say, and what was never reported at the time in any of the Sherman coverage, was that there had been a high number of break-and-enters into homes on the streets surrounding Old Colony Road in the previous year. A total of 160 break-ins were logged by police, with millions of dollars' worth of jewellery and other valuables stolen. There had been no violence and no injuries in any of the break-ins, but in some cases burglars entered when the homeowners were in the house. A community meeting had been held on December 4, just over a week before the Sherman deaths, with police and the local city councillor in attendance. Community leaders suggested that people consider installing surveillance cameras and perhaps hire a security company to patrol the neighbourhood. One community leader in attendance told me there was "real pushback" from homeowners. Few wanted to spend the time or money to provide their own deterrents; they wanted the police to solve the problem. When news broke that the couple down the street had been found dead, the neighbours, already on high alert, immediately speculated that it was a burglary turned violent. The Sherman home had been the target of a break-in the year before. Burglars broke through a skylight and dropped from a high ceiling to enter the home. But comments from police were interpreted by neighbours and the media to mean that the killer was Barry Sherman, and he was dead. Police sources speaking to media did the rest.

All of this, along with a call to Sherman daughter Alex from the relative of a couple, Rochelle Wise and David Pichosky, murdered in Florida five years earlier, prompted the Sherman family estate to hire Brian Greenspan.

Greenspan was a natural choice. First, he knew and had worked for Barry Sherman before. More importantly, he was one of the top criminal lawyers in Canada, with a network of contacts and extensive experience dealing with police. For decades, he and his brother Eddie, who died in 2014, were known as the top criminal lawyers in Canada. They were the lawyers you called if you had money and were in serious trouble. Though many of his legal cases involved fraud, Greenspan estimates he has done about thirty murder trials and handled two hundred appeals of murder cases where an individual had been convicted. He is intimately familiar with the justice system. Once he and his team saw the photos of the Sherman death scene, the nature of the crime was clear. "I didn't need one minute of expertise to know this was a double homicide," he says. To this day, Greenspan remains baffled that the police spent so much time on the murder-suicide theory.

Publicly, police claim that murder-suicide was just one of three theories they considered equally, the others being double murder and double suicide. But it appears that it was the murder-suicide theory upon which they initially focused most of their efforts. In Greenspan's own carefully chosen words at an October 2018 press conference where he announced a $10-million reward, this myopic approach "fell well below" the standard the public expects of its police force. "They failed to recognize the suspicious and staged manner in which their bodies were situated: sitting next to each other with ligatures pulled up around their necks and wrapped around a railing, forcing them into an upright position." When the private autopsies were concluded, Greenspan said it became crystal clear "that they were both murdered and that the Toronto Police should not have drawn any conclusion which suggested self-inflicted injuries."

In many hundreds of hours of recorded interviews I conducted with people connected to this case, I heard only one suggestion, from Kerry Winter, that murder-suicide was a possibility. I did hear from many people very close to the Shermans why it was *not* a possibility. Some of the reasons were personal, some were business related. These same people provided this same information to the police in the early days of the investigation. Joel Ulster, for example, had arranged to have a family dinner with Barry and Honey on Sunday, December 17. It was something both Shermans were looking forward to, particularly Barry, who had played such a strong role in assisting Joel's children in business and in life. Daughter Kaelen's wedding was being organized, and both Shermans were excited that their youngest was taking that step. As Sherman told Jack Kay on more than one occasion, he wanted twenty-five grandchildren and was hopeful that all his children would have children. Lauren had one son, Alex had a son and daughter, and Jonathon and his husband, Fred, were looking into surrogacy with the aim of having two boys, something that eventually happened in June 2019.

On the business side, Barry had several cases that were important to him to resolve, personal ones where he felt he had been wronged. He had depositions lined up for the new year. He was also making plans to expand Apotex and to invest in a Florida facility to produce fentanyl. One day, according to Jack Kay, they would sell the business, but that was not anytime soon. Sherman had talked to Kay about a five-year plan to grow Apotex. To his family he said he had a fifteen-year plan and wanted to ensure that the business he had built would be in good hands when he finally retired. One reason he stuck with Jeremy Desai through the corporate espionage allegations was that he saw Desai as a key part of his succession plan. Of great importance to Sherman was making sure that the Apotex employees, many of whom called him by his first name, were well looked after, and he wanted to ensure that whoever took over maintained the integrity of the company.

As to Honey, friends, including Bryna Steiner, shared their emails planning their Florida vacation. In a few cases, Honey had even double-booked dinners: different couples on the same night later in December. She was planning to leave for Florida on the Monday after the dinner with the Ulsters. Barry would follow later in the week.

Perhaps the most significant indication that this was not a murder-suicide was the Shermans' bond with Alex and Brad's children. Barry and Honey's new Forest Hill house was supposed to include a giant playroom, and it would be just up the street from the grandchildren's home. Finally, there is the intangible of faith, or lack of faith, more appropriately. Sherman did not believe in God or any kind of afterlife. "For people to have said that he killed himself is impossible," says Jack Kay. If someone believed there was an afterlife for their immortal soul, then it might be understandable, he says, but that was not his friend's belief. Kay firmly believed that, in his friend's case, "You would never take your life if you believed this was it."

It is, of course, impossible to assess a person's inner thoughts. Sometimes, outwardly happy people do kill themselves. Around the same time the Sherman case was being probed as a murder-suicide, a couple in Oakville, west of Toronto, died. The husband shot his wife, then himself, police concluded. Neighbours said the couple seemed happy, though there had been recent business troubles. Forensic officers and detectives at the scene quickly determined the manner of deaths and an official announcement was made. It was not the case with the Sherman file, in which police took six weeks to make a determination. The conventional wisdom was that if Barry Sherman was going to commit suicide, the pharmaceutical genius would have used pills. That he would somehow hang himself, leaving their bodies in such a macabre position, made no sense to people who knew him.

It seems, based on all information available at time of writing, that the police simply got it wrong. Officers at the death scene appear to have made a hurried assessment that a husband had killed his wife, then himself. The case moved from division officers on the first day to the homicide unit on the weekend. Homicide detectives concurred, for a time, with the murder-suicide theory. Dr. Michael Pickup, a relatively junior pathologist, took a great deal of time to make a determination over the manner of death, but behind the scenes his transparency over his findings, including providing scene photographs, helped the more experienced private pathologist make that case. The two separate investigations, police and private, proceeded at a different pace and, by their nature, with different abilities and access. During the first six weeks, the Toronto Police detectives and forensic technicians controlled the Old Colony Road scene. Police, whether speaking on the record or on background, were reluctant to give away too much information about what they had done or were doing, or about what they had found. By filing three separate court challenges to unseal search warrant materials, I learned that police had, as of spring 2019, executed thirty-five search warrants and production orders. In the first challenge, police revealed that they were requesting health records for the Shermans, banking records, and airline loyalty plan data, but the courts refused to say whose banking and loyalty plan records police obtained. In my second and third challenges, police and the courts refused to release even generic information, stating that the new warrants were "too specific" and, if released, could alert the murderer or murderers.

Police submitted hundreds of pages of interview and case synopses to a judge to get judicial authorization to seize records. That material remains sealed. When I last cross-examined the detective who has prepared all of this information, Dennis Yim, I did learn that the police had amassed a great deal of information that they were still assessing, including 3,700 pages of documents and 1,390 electronic files. That content remains sealed too, at least for now. I also learned that cell phone records were seized but not who the phones belonged to. Cell phones, which "ping" off new cell towers with each location change, would allow police to follow the movements of the Shermans or any other person whose cell phone was at issue. The police also seized both Sherman vehicles. Honey's, which was more modern, had an onboard GPS system, and the police would have been able to determine her vehicle's movements by accessing the data.

What was most surprising to me was that, after an initial flurry of interviews and forensic work by fifty officers, by mid-2018 the Sherman investigation had only one permanent officer assigned to the case, Detective Dennis Yim. Detective Brandon Price, who had made the original statement about no suspects being sought, was still on the case but was working on other files as well. He was promoted to detective sergeant and would remain in the homicide unit. Detective Sergeant Susan Gomes, who had led the investigation, was promoted to inspector by the end of 2018 and moved to a uniform job in the police force's operations division. Yim, a junior officer whose job was to prepare search warrant applications on the Sherman case and analyze the "return"—the information that comes back from a search—told me in court that as of April 2019 the case was very much still ongoing. No information about what had been discovered or what theories were being pursued could be released, because, he said, it would tip the hand of the murderer or murderers. Toronto Police Chief Mark Saunders, himself a former homicide detective, said much the same at a press conference in late 2018, where he was critical of some of the information the Greenspan team had made public. "I have to be cognizant," he said, "that the suspect or suspects no doubt are watching this now. I know that for a fact." Saunders said he had to be careful not to provide any information that would help the killers. Whether Saunders's bold statement was from actual knowledge or the hunch of a veteran cop, he did not say. Arguably the most significant comment police have made on the case since Detective Sergeant Gomes pronounced it a "targeted" double homicide came from Detective Yim, who said in court in April 2019 that police had a "theory" of the case and "an idea of what happened."

The lack of police information that so frustrated the media and the public, and close friends of the Shermans, must also have been frustrating to the detectives on the case, but for a completely different reason. Media coverage of the Sherman investigation focused on mistakes the police made. To detectives on the case who, presumably, have since made progress, it must be difficult to have to keep silent.

On the topic of apparent missteps, one that baffled people was the time it took police to interview key individuals. Jeremy Desai, who was on the final email chain with Sherman on the Wednesday evening and was an extremely close colleague, was not interviewed until February 1, seven weeks after the deaths. Kerry Winter, who made astounding claims to the media about how he fantasized about killing Sherman, was not interviewed until the beginning of February. The same delay occurred with Frank D'Angelo, who was, according to Jack Kay, someone who spoke to Sherman almost every day. Others, like Jack Kay and Fred and Bryna Steiner, were interviewed more promptly. The Shermans' four children, according to Brian Greenspan, were interviewed by police in the first few days of the investigation and "some" (he would not say which ones) were re-interviewed in early 2019. Greenspan said that the Toronto homicide officers had three meetings in summer 2018 with Jonathon, Alex, and Alex's husband, Brad, to update them on the progress of the investigation. Those meetings were short, as there was nothing to report. In my discussions with Greenspan I was baffled by his response—or lack of response—to a question he said at first he would answer, and ultimately never did. It was a question I tried to ask everyone. In the case of the Sherman children, Greenspan had asked that I pose questions to him, as their representative. Where were each of the children on the evening of Wednesday, December 13, 2017? By not responding, Greenspan said that he was honouring a police request not to interfere with their investigation. I had also asked Greenspan if he would tell me specifically when and where the

Sherman children were interviewed. He would not answer that question either.

As part of my interviewing process, I often asked people what police detectives had asked them. Generally, I found that when police detectives did talk to people, they typically said they could relate little that was positive about the investigation. One detective reportedly said to one person, nine months into the case, "We are at loose ends." To another person, "We do not know if we will ever solve this one." It's possible that the police were deliberately spreading misinformation in the hope that the killers would hear it, relax, and make a mistake. Possible, but unlikely. The fact that police did not begin taking DNA and fingerprints from people like Denise Gold until nine months after the murders indicates yet another misstep in the investigation. At other times, it seemed that police had not done even the most basic research before asking questions. When a police detective contacted Joel Ulster, weeks into the case, the officer did not know whether Kerry Winter was a "man or a woman," Ulster recalled. Katherine Kay was interviewed by police at one point and the detective asked if she had ever been in the Sherman home. Kay said she had, once, at a party that was a fundraiser for Liberal leader Justin Trudeau. "Oh," the detective asked, perking up, "who else was there?" Kay thought the detective was joking, given how widely reported on that particular fundraiser was due to allegations of improper lobbying. The officer relented when Kay said there were literally hundreds of people at the event.

The private investigation began the day after the bodies were discovered. Greenspan assembled his team and arranged the private autopsies. His detectives canvassed the neighbourhood and began interviewing friends of the Shermans, but six weeks had elapsed since the murders before they were allowed inside the house to conduct their own probe. Control of the Sherman house was turned over to the family at the same time that police held a press conference to announce that the case was being treated as a double murder. The private team wore white forensic suits, gloves, and cloth boots over their shoes. Moving through the house, they were surprised to find it in disarray. In the bedrooms, police had removed clothing from closets and then piled the clothing on the beds or other furniture. The same in the kitchen, where items were taken out of cupboards and left sitting on tables and counters. The walls showed numerous markings where finger and palm prints were dusted and lifted.

According to Greenspan, his group of retired detectives and forensic specialists discovered that the police had not performed what they believed were basic crime scene functions. They had not used a special fine-particle vacuum on the pool deck where the bodies were discovered. "The intruders might have left behind a small sample of hair or fabric," Greenspan later told reporters at a press conference. He said his specialists determined that although the police team had lifted some fingerprints from the scene, they had "missed" twenty-five finger and palm prints. His team lifted those prints. Greenspan and his team hung on to everything they collected for many months—including two small vacuum cleaner bags used when they vacuumed the floor in the pool room—while he and Scott Hutchison, a lawyer hired by the police department, tried to sort through a way to maintain a legal chain of custody and hand over this new "evidence." It was eventually turned over to police in stages throughout 2018 and the early part of 2019. Whether it amounted to anything, police will not comment. Going forward, Greenspan has said he wanted a "private/public partnership" between his investigation and the police probe. The Toronto Police have been dismissive of this suggestion, and columnists, including the *Toronto Star*'s Rosie DiManno, derided the Sherman family and Greenspan for trying to institute a "two-tier" police system in which the rich used their wealth to get justice more quickly than those who lacked financial resources.

At the tail end of his press conference—ten months after the Shermans were murdered—Greenspan announced a $10-million reward from the family for information leading to the capture and prosecution of the killer or killers. It was unprecedented in Canadian crime history. Police occasionally issue rewards, but it is rare that a family would post its own reward. The idea of announcing a reward came from Alex Sherman. She suggested a $1-million reward and had been pushing for this almost since the case began. Shortly before the press conference, Jonathon suggested that if they were going to do a reward offering, it should be $10 million. He was initially going to speak at the press conference, but it was decided it would be better for Greenspan to handle the announcement. The amount far exceeded the normal $10,000 to $50,000 offered in a murder case. But what made it more astounding is that anyone with information was told to call the representatives of the Sherman family. All tips were then to be vetted by the private investigation team and "any meaningful information" would be passed on to police. A panel made up of a former police chief, a criminal lawyer, and a forensic psychiatrist was created to oversee matters related to the tip line. Greenspan invited Chief Mark Saunders to appoint an officer to join the panel, but Saunders did not take up Greenspan's offer. In fact, at time of writing, the members of the panel had never met. Greenspan says they decided to convene the panel only if they had a particularly serious matter to discuss, including whether or not the reward should be paid out. As to calls and emails received by the tip line, Greenspan says he worked out a protocol with a Toronto Police lawyer to simply hand the information over to police on a monthly basis. Nothing substantive has appeared on the horizon. Often, the people who contacted the tip line were psychics or people unrelated to the case who had a notion they wanted to pass along. Police have said in court that they have received 279 tips from Greenspan's team but will not say if any of them were helpful. When I spoke to Greenspan about the tips, he said some people were uncomfortable with calling a tip line and reached out to him directly instead. At time of writing, Tom Klatt and the other private investigators, and Greenspan, were still working the case. One lead that real estate agent Judi Gottlieb had been excited about—the "odd ducks" that came through 50 Old Colony Road a few days before the murder—turned out to be a dead end, according to Greenspan.

Well over a year after the initial flurry of work by his private team, Greenspan said he was disappointed that the Toronto Police would not agree to share information with him. "What if we want to re-interview Frank D'Angelo or Kerry Winter?" he mused. "I would like to know from the police if that would interfere with anything they are doing. We are concerned that we might step on police toes and screw things up."

When Greenspan mentioned the names of Winter and D'Angelo, I saw an opportunity to raise questions regarding his own clients, the children of Barry and Honey Sherman. Technically, his client is the estate of Barry and Honey Sherman, but that is controlled by four trustees on behalf of the children. After all, I pointed out, as sole heirs they appear to be the only people who stood to gain a vast fortune upon the death of their parents. I made it clear to Greenspan that I was simply asking questions. By this time in my investigation, I had heard that among family and friends, fingers had been pointing in all directions during the preceding months: at Kerry Winter, at Frank D'Angelo, even at Jack Kay. Sources, including those within the Sherman family, had informed me that in fall 2018 Jonathon Sherman had told people, including his sister Alex, that he thought Jack Kay may have had something to do with the murders. When I asked Kay and D'Angelo whether they were involved, both said that they loved and respected Barry Sherman and that it was ridiculous to suggest they were implicated. Winter, who had made the outlandish comments to the media about his fantasy of killing his cousin, said he simply did not do it.

Now, sitting in Greenspan's office, I told him that I had no evidence or information implicating the Sherman children, but that as a matter of journalistic procedure, I wanted to ask each one if he or she had anything to do with the deaths. I also wanted to know whether Greenspan thought police had done the legwork to eliminate the heirs as suspects. I reminded him that he was the one who told me that a good homicide investigation begins at the centre and moves outward, eliminating suspects as the probe progresses.

There's a floor-to-ceiling plate glass window in Greenspan's second-floor office in Toronto. As he digested my line of questioning during the March 2019 interview, I mused aloud that while he might be angry enough to have me tossed out the window, I would survive the fall. Greenspan responded that anybody making such an allegation against his clients would be in serious trouble.

"To suggest that any of the Sherman children were involved is shameful, reckless, and libelous. It is an attempt by people to cast suspicions, and let me tell you, those people who make those claims would be our suspects."

Two months later, still awaiting answers from my interview with Greenspan, I wrote a letter directly to Jonathon Sherman. Months before he had tentatively agreed to meet me, but only if I agreed in writing to allow him editorial control over any portions of a book or newspaper story that concerned him, an offer I declined. I now had many more questions for him: about Green Storage; about the email discussions he had with his father in 2015; about the email he sent his sisters suggesting their father was incompetent. I wanted to ask him about Frank D'Angelo, Jack Kay, his aunt Mary, and his whereabouts on both the Wednesday evening his parents were last seen alive and the Friday when their bodies were discovered—the latter a question I'd asked everyone. I also wanted to ask him directly if he had anything to do with the murders, just as I had asked others. I had no knowledge of any police theories— it was simply a question I felt had to be asked. I sent a list of thirty-one queries to Jonathon. It took a couple of weeks but I received responses in late May from both Jonathon Sherman and Brian Greenspan. Sherman's response was addressed both to me and the *Toronto Star* publisher, and he described how my "bullying tactics" had placed him in a dilemma. "He has attempted to force me to choose between not honouring our family's commitment not to discuss our parents' murder publicly or suffering the consequence of making 'no comment' to what I can only term are his insane accusations that I am implicated in the murder of my parents." Sherman said that he believes that the people I have spoken to and who provided me with the information on which I based my questions are "people who we believe to be persons of interest in the murder of my parents."

While Sherman maintained that he could not publicly answer any of the questions I asked, he suggested that what I should have done was send my questions to the Toronto Police and "let them ask me." Sherman then made an interesting revelation. He said that after receiving my thirty-one questions, he had prepared "comprehensive written responses to each and every question" I had posed. And he said in his letter, which he copied to one of the Toronto Police detectives on the case, that he had sent those answers to the Toronto Police along with an offer. "I will also arrange an interview with Detective Price at his earliest convenience to further elaborate on, and if necessary explain, the details which I have provided to him in response to the queries made on behalf of the *Toronto Star*."

SIXTEEN

THE MOST LIKELY SCENARIO

HONEY SHERMAN LEFT APOTEX ON Wednesday, December 13, at 6:30 P.M. as soon as the meeting with the architects concluded. She drove off alone in her gold-coloured Lexus SUV. Her daughter Alex says a credit card statement her husband has seen indicates that Honey stopped at Bayview Village Shopping Centre and went to a children's store to purchase gifts for Hanukkah. Barry Sherman stayed in his office until 8:30 P.M., when he too left Apotex, also on his own. The police have not shared any information regarding whether the billionaire couple stopped anywhere on their routes home. Lawyer Brian Greenspan says he has heard the theory that Honey stopped at Bayview Village before coming home but that it is unconfirmed by his investigators. There are also reports circulating among the Sherman friends that Honey stopped at Bayview Village and someone got into the car with her. But there is no evidence of this. I asked questions at Bayview Village but did not find anyone who saw Honey that day. Security cameras were not installed at the upscale mall until 2018, long after the murders. Speculation among Sherman friends ranges from a scenario where Honey was carjacked to a story that she was at a local plaza, picked up someone she knew, and drove that person to her home. Traffic cameras may have recorded their movements on the roadway. It is likely that Honey was home by 8 P.M or 8:30 P.M.

Honey's Lexus was later found parked in its normal spot on the right side of the house, near the entrance to the underground garage. It was Honey's habit to enter through the side door immediately to the left of this parking spot. Whether she went into the house on her own or with someone else, it is likely that she went in through that door. The partial wall that obscures the side entrance would also obscure from passersby the view of any struggle that may have taken place while leaving the SUV.

Earlier in the day, Honey had been at home for her personal training session with her good friend Denise Gold, followed by a three-hour massage given by a woman who provided regular massage therapy to Honey. While Honey was receiving training and massage upstairs that Wednesday, the house was buzzing with activity. One of the couple's real estate agents, Elise Stern, was present, overseeing workers with the goal of polishing the house for upcoming showings. No viewings were booked by the time Honey left on Wednesday for the architects' meeting. By the evening, when she arrived home, the workers and the agent were gone. Honey would have used a key to open the side door. Once inside, if she followed her normal routine, she would have left the door unlocked. Barry, if he parked in the driveway and not underground, would then come in the side door when he arrived home. The Sherman couple did not believe in having a security system. There was no alarm on the entrances and windows, and there were no security cameras. The previous weekend, Barry and Honey had had a Sunday dinner prior to attending a Toronto Maple Leafs hockey game with their good friends Leslie Gales and Keith Ray. Over their meal, at the Hot Stove Club at the Air Canada Centre (as it was then named), Gales recalls making what had become a frequent suggestion, telling Barry it would be wise for a man of his wealth to have a security system and perhaps even a driver or bodyguard. "We don't believe in that stuff," Barry said in reply. "If they are going to get you, they are going to get you."

It was not unusual for Honey to be alone in the house for several hours in the evening. Unless she had a social or charity event, she would head home and wait for Barry to arrive after his lengthy workday. Years before, in a conversation with Aubrey Dan, Honey had expressed surprise that Aubrey and his wife and their children, if they were not away, would eat dinner together each night. "That is not the case in our house," Honey had told him. "Barry works too late for that."

Whether Honey entered their house on her own or with someone else that Wednesday evening, she was violently attacked inside the house at some point. It was most likely before Barry came home. One clue is that her iPhone was found on the floor in a main floor powder room that she rarely used. That has fuelled speculation that she ran into the room to get away from her attacker and in the ensuing struggle the phone was dropped. Based on her facial injuries, she may have been struck on the face to subdue her, dying by strangulation almost immediately after. At some point, most likely while she was still alive, a thin rope or plastic tie was used to fasten her hands. One story the Sherman friends have been told is that Honey was hit with a laptop. Other friends have said they were told Honey's facial injuries were caused by her being dragged down a stairway to the basement level. With the police not providing any information, friends looking for answers have latched onto these pieces of information or speculation. To get downstairs, either the main staircase or a smaller spiral staircase would have been used. Honey weighed about 170 pounds, and it is most likely that two people were present, given the difficulty of moving a heavy person who was unconscious or dead. Why she was taken to the pool room is a question that's also been the subject of much speculation. The lap pool does not appear to have had any particular significance in their lives and was rarely used now that the children were grown and out of the house.

Barry Sherman walked out of Apotex at about 8:30 P.M., after sending a routine work email from his office desktop computer at 8:13 P.M. The email went to several people, including Apotex outside counsel Harry Radomski and company president Desai. He left the building and drove south. With him, he likely had a copy of the home inspection report their realtors had arranged, detailing the state of 50 Old Colony Road. With no security cameras at the home, it is impossible to know if he was alone in his car. The house across the street does have security cameras that pick up, in the background, the Sherman home. The family handed the security footage over to police and the private detectives but never checked it themselves to look for activity on the Wednesday, and neither the police nor the private team will say what they saw on the video. Presumably, it shows when the Shermans arrived home that evening, though it was after dark and the street is not particularly well lit. And while Sherman often parked overnight in the circular driveway near the front door, his car was found in the basement parking garage, giving rise to speculation that he decided, for some reason, to park there that evening. Snow was predicted for the following day, and that may have contributed to his decision. Or perhaps he had a passenger in the car who suggested, or insisted on, parking underground. The ramp to the garage and the driveway of the Sherman home are heated, so no footprints or tire tracks would be recorded in the snow. Once he drove down the ramp, Sherman would have parked his car and left the garage through a door that opens onto a long hallway that leads to the two staircases, one at either end of the hallway. It seems likely that Barry was carrying the home inspection report in his hand. The report was found lying in the hallway near the garage door two days later by real estate agent Elise Stern when she was showing the prospective buyers and their agent through the house. It is reasonable to conclude that Barry was grabbed as he exited the garage and entered the hallway, dropping the report. However he was grabbed, the assailant or assailants did not damage his face or his eyeglasses. At some point, his wrists were bound together as Honey's were, using either a thin rope or a plastic tie. He was taken to the pool room. To get into the pool room, a button at shoulder height has to be pressed to release a magnetic lock. No security code is needed.

That morning, when Barry got dressed after his training session, he had donned one of the two belts Honey had purchased for him on sale at Canadian Tire. The other belt he had apparently left somewhere in the master bedroom. The autopsies indicate that both Barry and Honey were strangled with something soft, cutting off their wind but not crushing the hyoid bone in the neck. It appears likely that the recently purchased belts were used. This is an indication that at some point one of the attackers went upstairs and got the second belt. Once dead, Barry and Honey were pulled or pushed up against the metre-high stainless steel railing that surrounds one end of the basement lap pool. The belts were looped around their necks and tied to the railing, holding them up in a seated position. Their legs were straight out front, away from the pool. Of note is that more thought appears to have been given to Barry's positioning. His right leg was crossed over his left, and his glasses, which presumably were knocked askew or off during the attack, were positioned perfectly on his nose. Whatever ties had bound their wrists were removed. Their jackets were pulled back off the shoulders and down, which would have had the effect of pinning their arms back. How that related to the binding of the wrists is not clear. It is most likely that the wrists were bound when they were alive, then unbound when they were unconscious or dead, and the jackets pulled down after they were killed, possibly as part of an attempt—a weak attempt, it seemed to many—to make it look like double suicide or murder-suicide. Barry was wearing his bomber-style winter coat when he was found. Honey was wearing a short outdoor coat of a weight more suited to fall weather.

That Honey had damage to her face and Barry did not, and that more care was taken to position Barry, invites speculation that the killer or killers felt differently towards husband and wife. A theory discussed among close friends of the Shermans is this: perhaps the killer or killers regarded Barry more positively than Honey and wanted him to appear serene in death. Or it was simply happenstance, or an attempt to make the crime scene confusing. Or, even more simply, to give the indication that Barry had attacked his wife, killed her, then killed himself.

Upstairs, the bed in the master bedroom was made up as it had been earlier in the day and had not since been disturbed, a strong indication that the attack happened Wednesday evening, not overnight or Thursday morning, as some have speculated. The clothes the Shermans were wearing were the clothes they wore that day at the Apotex meeting. Barry and Honey Sherman were most likely dead long before midnight. It was impossible to pinpoint the exact time of death, forensic sources say, because of the environment where the bodies were found. Human tissue decomposes faster in warm temperatures and humid conditions. Being in the pool room meant that the bodies would degrade faster than if they were in a cool, dry environment. Was that why they were left there, to make it harder to determine when they died? Or was the pool room, with its tiled floor, chosen as the best place to clean up any stray bits of evidence the killers dropped? Also, it is possible the pool room was chosen because it is out of the way and rarely used, meaning it would take longer for the bodies to be discovered.

As to what happened during the attack, two scenarios seem most likely. First, that the attackers wanted something from Barry and showed him his injured wife and threatened to kill her if he did not do what was asked. Second, that the couple was killed outright to get them out of the way for financial or other reasons. In the first scenario, it was an attempt at extortion. In the second, either hatred or revenge were in play or it was a cold-blooded attempt to obtain something with the death of both of the Shermans. A third and unlikely scenario, that the attack was a home invasion gone wrong, does not seem to fit the crime scene, as the house was not left in disarray and nothing appears to have been missing. A fourth scenario, that this was payback specifically to Barry Sherman for some business deal, also seems unlikely, as it would have been much easier to kill him as he left his office at his usual late hour. Barry Sherman had said that to friends many times over the years, which was his primary reason for not bothering with a security protocol at home. If it was payback for a business deal, why kill Honey? And why try to make it look like a murder-suicide?

What has also struck people close to the Shermans is the perfect storm of circumstances that kept anyone from discovering the bodies for nearly thirty-six hours. Several Apotex officials emailed Barry Sherman Thursday morning about routine matters, but there was no response. His absence did not alarm anyone enough to visit Old Colony Road looking for the boss. When Honey did not show up at her committee meeting at the UJA Thursday morning at 8 A.M., nobody checked on her. Alex Sherman had texted photos of her newborn to her parents on the Thursday. Jack Kay, who would have noticed his friend's absence, was out of town in New York. No real estate viewings of the home were scheduled. There was the arrival on Thursday morning, caught on the neighbours' video camera, of an unknown man who parked on Old Colony Road and, over the space of roughly an hour, appeared to either enter the Sherman home three times or stand at the front door, for a total of twenty-nine minutes on the Sherman property. Police say they know who the person was, but they will not say what if any significance his actions and identity have to the investigation. Then there is the still unexplained 911 call police investigated roughly ten doors east down Old Colony Road at the same time as the visitor was at the Sherman door. Was it a crossed wire? Was there a police officer at the Sherman door while their bodies lay dead in the basement?

And later on Thursday, Sherman realtor Elise Stern, trying to organize a Friday morning showing, called Honey to get her permission. Honey's phone, lying on the floor in the downstairs powder room, rang in the silent house. Stern would continue trying to reach her and eventually got in touch with Mary Shechtman.

Outside, on Thursday evening, a light snow began to fall. Snowflakes landing on the driveway melted immediately. In New York, Jack Kay and his wife attended the Andrea Bocelli concert at Madison Square Garden. Joanne Mauro was busy at home with family activities and preparing for the holidays. Others, close friends and family, were busy with the normal routines of daily life. For many, once they learned what had happened at Old Colony Road, there were sleepless nights thinking of the possible scenarios that played out. Was it a quick death? Jonathon Sherman said in an eyebrow-raising moment in his eulogy that he and his siblings were glad "neither of you had to suffer like we are suffering now." Friends like Frank D'Angelo have a different feeling. D'Angelo says he has nightmares, and at spare moments in the day he is visited by horrible thoughts of what it must have been like in the basement pool room at Old Colony Road that night. "I just feel sick about what they must have been going through. I am supposed to be this tough guy, and Barry should have been able to count on me to keep him safe. But I let him down and now he is dead." Joel Ulster, Sherman's oldest and best friend, is easily moved to tears well over a year later. "It is the brutality of it. I am seventy-five. You expect people to die at that age. But not in such a brutal way." Lawyer Harry Radomski says he has imagined that if Barry had any time to attempt to reason with his killers, he would have looked at them and said, "It is not logical. What you are doing is simply not logical."

Did Barry and Honey Sherman know their killers? I believe so. After spending a year and a half delving into this case, I believe that the killer or killers had an intimate knowledge of the Shermans, including their routines. I also believe that the killer or killers were not trained professionals and that the attempt to make it look like a murder-suicide was a poor one, though it obviously worked for a while. As to having an understanding of their movements, consider this: the Shermans were killed soon after they both attended a meeting at Apotex to discuss their house-building plans. That meeting was originally scheduled a day earlier and was rescheduled with little notice. Also, they were killed in their home on a night when neither had a scheduled event that would keep them out of the home. Another timing issue is that the Shermans were killed the night before a day on which Barry had no important work meetings planned and his office mate for most of his working life was away. True, Honey did have a morning meeting on Thursday. Perhaps the person knew Barry's schedule but not Honey's? All these pieces of the puzzle suggest that the killer or killers had more than a passing knowledge of the Shermans.

The location of the murders is also noteworthy. I think the killer or killers knew the layout of the house, including where the pool is. In addition, while the pool had a security camera visible to anyone walking through the room, the cables to power it and connect it to a monitor had never been hooked up. Only someone with insider knowledge would know that. It is also quite likely that the killer or killers arrived at the Sherman house from the rear, accessing it from the street immediately to the north of Old Colony Road, hopping two low fences and entering the north side of the property. The basement rooms can be entered through a door from the backyard. Police say there was no sign of forced entry, but it is possible the door had been left open, or the killer or killers had a key, picked the lock, or had the access code to the lockbox. Greenspan, at the press conference where the $10-million reward was announced, said that his investigators believed police failed to thoroughly check all entry points to the home. As to the lack of outdoor cameras on the Sherman property, a casual casing of the house by the killer or killers might have been all that was needed to determine if there was visible evidence of video surveillance. But modern video cameras can be easily hidden, so it seems that the killer or killers must have known enough about Barry Sherman to know that he did not believe in having any security measures installed at his residence.

Shortly after the bodies were discovered, a series of increasingly far-fetched rumours began circulating about who the killers were. In the "honey pot" theory, Barry Sherman had a liaison with a prostitute, her pimp was extorting him, and in a fit of anger the pimp killed both Shermans. In another theory, Mossad agents had been sent from Israel on behalf of an Israeli generic firm that had a grudge against Sherman. In another, Hells Angels bikers had committed the murders as part of a turf war over who controlled fentanyl distribution. In another, it was fraudsters being sued by Sherman, who were seeking a quick end to a lengthy litigation. Alternatively, it was arranged by the Clinton Foundation, in relation to a dispute over Apotex's supply of drugs to relief efforts in Puerto Rico, Haiti, and Rwanda. At social events, I have been dragged into a quiet corner by a seemingly sane person who has told me he has heard from "a reliable source" that "Bill and Hillary ordered this hit." Here is just one of dozens of emails I received after my first story on the Sherman case appeared in January 2018:

> The Sherman case will only be solved if Donald Trump exposes the Clinton Foundation and invokes the executive order he issued December 20, 2017. People in our government are involved in the cover-up. Sherman and Apotex were part of a criminal pharmaceutical ring perpetrating genocide in third world countries with the use of sub-standard drugs.

I have never believed this was a case of international intrigue, spies, or a business deal gone bad. Big Pharma and some government regulators did not like Barry Sherman, that is true. But they sue; they do not kill. This story has always seemed to follow the same pattern as most murders: a pattern that suggests it involved someone they knew.

SEVENTEEN

AFTERMATH

CANADA'S GENERIC GIANT APOTEX, Barry Sherman's child, is up for sale. The directive, say sources close to the business, came from the four Sherman children within two months of the murders: sell Apotex at the highest price available. The Florida property, intended for opioid production, purchased for US$50 million in the months before Barry was killed, was sold for $30 million in early 2019. The European operations had been sold off six months after the murders. Though the four children technically own Apotex equally (with a few minor shareholders, including Jack Kay), Jonathon has asserted himself as the controlling force. Sisters Lauren and Kaelen have sat back and watched. Sister Alex has not. She has pushed back in certain areas, particularly in the area of philanthropy, where she has assumed the title of president of the Sherman Foundation. Mark Gryfe, a well-known figure in Canadian philanthropy circles (former president of Baycrest Foundation and campaign director of the UJA for years), said he is impressed with how the Sherman children are continuing their parents' tradition of giving. "They have taken up the mantle in ways that I am beyond impressed. I see so many families where kids are inheriting millions and, in some cases, billions, where there is very little interest in philanthropy." He said the four Sherman children are being approached "left and right" and there are "million-dollar gifts and multi-million dollar gifts being distributed with incredible generosity. I think Barry and Honey would be very proud." There is tension, though, over where the charitable dollars should go. Alex and Jonathon have sparred over ideas. He and some of his business partners asked in 2019 for "$40-$50 million" from the Sherman Foundation to build what he has described to others as a "premium" hockey arena for youth and adult programs that would be affiliated with the UJA. Alex has resisted this, concerned that it does not fit her parents' charitable vision.

With Barry and Honey gone, the four children and the extended family have settled into an uneasy relationship. At various times, one group is not speaking to the other. Kaelen has moved to Israel; Lauren spends most of her time at her west coast retreat teaching yoga and providing therapy to clients with depression and anxiety. Jonathon and Fred, through surrogacy, now have two baby boys, and Jonathon is busy with Green Storage and a new business (Harlo Capital, a secondary market mortgage provider) he started in the fall of 2017. Meanwhile Alex has daily strategy meetings regarding the family's goal of continuing Barry and Honey's giving legacy. Mary, Honey's sister, was not invited to Kaelen's wedding in April 2018 at the McMichael Canadian Art Gallery in Kleinburg. Her marriage to the electrician did not last long. Within three months, the couple separated and by summer 2019 were divorced. People close to the Shermans use the word "collateral damage," a military term, to refer to what happened in the aftermath of the murders. Friends like Bryna Steiner wake up from nightmares, their sleeping selves conjuring images of what happened to her friends. Joel Ulster will find himself walking along a street or watching a play and something will trigger a memory and "then the tears come." Kerry Winter, who caused a great deal of upset to the Shermans with his comments immediately after the murders, has had his own issues to deal with. His young children have been bullied at school, harassed by fellow students who say Kerry is a "murderer." At Apotex, veteran employees say they miss seeing Barry Sherman walking the halls in his white labcoat, at ease both with the science of the laboratory and the business of the boardroom.

The biggest sign that there was a changing of the guard came on December 14, 2018, at the Apotex offices. It was one year after the murders. Jack Kay was sitting in his office, which used to belong to Barry Sherman. He was CEO of the organization, called in by the trustees to take over that role after Jeremy Desai left. Kay's plan, as he had told colleagues at Apotex, was to retire on March 31, 2019. There would likely be a party—not that he liked parties—but he expected there would be some sort of event. It would be bittersweet, of course, but still a recognition of his many years of service. There had been tension between Kay and Jonathon Sherman in the past few months. Kay was balking at how fast the plans for selling Apotex were moving. He wanted to honour Barry Sherman's legacy and ensure that the employees were protected. At one point, according to Sherman family sources, Jonathon had suggested that Kay was somehow involved in the murders, and tried unsuccessfully to convince his sister Alex that this was the case. At 5 P.M. on the dot, Jonathon Sherman and Jeff Watson walked into his office. Watson, a longtime Apotex executive and protégé of Kay's, and a former Canadian Football League offensive lineman, was next in line in the corporate structure. Jonathon held no formal role in the company. As a source with knowledge of what transpired that December day describes, Jonathon told Kay that "the beneficiaries believe it is time for you to leave." Jonathon gave Kay a paper to sign. Kay did not sign it. He asked about his files and the items on his desk. Jonathon told him they would be sent to him. Both Sherman and Watson walked Kay out of the building. A week later, while Kay was out, Jonathon delivered several boxes that held files and personal items from his time at Apotex to Kay's home. Watson was appointed president and CEO, under direction of the estate trustees. The next day, in Apotex's executive parking lot, Watson's nameplate was affixed where Kay's had been. Beside it, still adorned with a cluster of flowers, old and new, was Barry Sherman's space and nameplate.

At time of writing, the police investigation continues, as does the Sherman family's private investigation. My sources tell me that the two family members who have been most active in pushing the police to stay focused on the now almost two-year-old investigation are Alex and Mary, frequently passing on information they think might be pertinent.

The deaths of Barry and Honey Sherman left a gaping hole in the Jewish community in Toronto and far beyond. But for some who had a close connection to the couple, there is a sense that their impact will be long-lasting. Joanne Mauro, Sherman's steadfast assistant, has remained at Apotex. She says she misses Sherman every day.

"Barry had such an impact on so many people. Since his passing, I feel I am a different person. I don't let anything bother me anymore."

Barry and Honey Sherman were buried in a Jewish cemetery in the north end of Toronto. Their headstone is identical in size and shape to the other headstones in the cemetery, but where others refer simply to "loving parents," or "much-beloved mother and father," the Barry and Honey stone highlights their legacy of service. "Mom and Dad were beloved leaders and members of our community, and they are dearly missed by all who knew and loved them." The home where the Shermans lived and died, at 50 Old Colony Rd., was the subject of an application to the city in early 2019. The Sherman family had asked for and obtained permission to demolish the house due to the "bad memories and a stigma attached due to the incident that took place." The Toronto Police were aware of this development but took no position on the plan, as they had returned the home to the family long before. Construction hoarding went up around the home and in May 2019, excavators tore the house down, filling in the outdoor pool and the basement lap pool where their bodies were found. The property was graded flat and the family plans to sell it as a building lot. Whatever clues to the murder the home might hold are now buried forever.

AUTHOR'S NOTE

A word about the sources in this book. While I have tried to name the source of information in each case, there are some instances where, to protect a confidential source, I have not named the individual. In an ideal world, all of the more than two hundred people I spoke to would have provided information on the record. But in a case that deals with murder, money, and often great acrimony, that, unsurprisingly, did not happen. Where conversations are presented, typically conversations people had with the late Barry and Honey Sherman, the most accurate recollection of the dialogue has been provided by the other party or parties to the conversation. In an effort to be as responsible as possible in providing an accurate account of the Sherman story, I have put contentious issues to individuals and given them weeks and sometimes months to respond. In most cases, people provided their side of the story. In others, including the Toronto Police and several individuals, I either received no comment or was told that to speak about any part of the case would hurt the ongoing investigation. While I did communicate with various members of the Sherman extended family, both directly and in some cases through intermediaries, some simply refused to give interviews. For example, lawyer Brian Greenspan wrote to me in July 2019 saying that both Lauren and Kaelen Sherman had elected not to provide an interview. Like their brother, their responses to my numerous questions would instead be sent to the Toronto Police.

ACKNOWLEDGMENTS

I had only heard the names Barry and Honey Sherman in passing prior to their murders on December 13, 2017. In the almost two years that I have been immersed in this project, I have had the privilege of getting to know them through a large cast of characters that included friends and family members who generously shared their stories, both happy and sad, about the couple. I cannot publicly acknowledge everyone because they are too numerous and because some gave assistance behind the scenes. But I do want to give a heartfelt thanks to some key people who risked speaking about topics that were both painful and secret.

In the early days, Aubrey Dan, Linda Frum, and Frank D'Angelo provided background information and went out of their way to help me understand the complexities of the Sherman family. They also connected me to others who otherwise might not have spoken to a journalist. Jack Kay, Harry Radomski, Jeremy Desai, among others, taught me about generic drugs and the passion Barry Sherman brought to all of his ventures. Bryna and Fred Steiner, lifelong friends of Barry and Honey, were gracious about my many queries. Joel Ulster and Ulster family members were open and honest, and I thank them for sharing their memories, painful though it almost always was. Joel's recollections of his and Barry's high school days and early business ventures seemed to help him deal with the shock of losing his best friend.

Many of the executives and staff at Apotex, including Jordan Berman, were helpful. So too were Dr. Jim Cairns, Brian King, Celia Pasternak, and many others—in more ways than I can describe. I would also like to acknowledge people in the justice system who patiently allowed a non-lawyer to enter their world. Among them, crown attorney Peter Scrutton, Justices David Doherty, Leslie Pringle, and Sean Dunphy, and lawyers Tim Youdan and Chantelle Cseh.

Thanks to my wonderful agents, Samantha Haywood and Jesse Finkelstein of Transatlantic Agency, who helped negotiate this commissioned project with Penguin Random House Canada and were enthusiastic supporters from the beginning.

The Penguin Canada team, led by Publishing Director Diane Turbide, was truly terrific, providing encouragement and a steady hand throughout. Assistant Editor Justin Stoller put up with many changes and additions with subject matter that was ever changing. Copy editor Alex Schultz was, to use the title of the Tina Turner song, "simply the best." Thanks to Managing Editor David Ross and to proofreader Karen Alliston whose sharp eyes and attention to detail ensured accuracy and consistency.

There would be no book without the support of the *Toronto Star* and its many talented leaders, chief among them Editor-in-Chief Irene Gentle and our former boss Michael Cooke.

A big shout-out to librarians Astrid Lange and Rick Sznajder for help in piecing together the labyrinth of corporate and property records. My mentor and long-time lawyer Bert Bruser offered advice, encouragement, and toughness at every step. To Iris Fischer, my lawyer on this book and many of my investigations: thank you for making them right and sharp.

And a big thank you to the person I discuss life and crime with more than anyone else—my wife, Kelly Smith.

INDEX

NOTE: Barry Sherman is referred to as Sherman; other family members are referred to by first initial and surname.